So Said the Wise

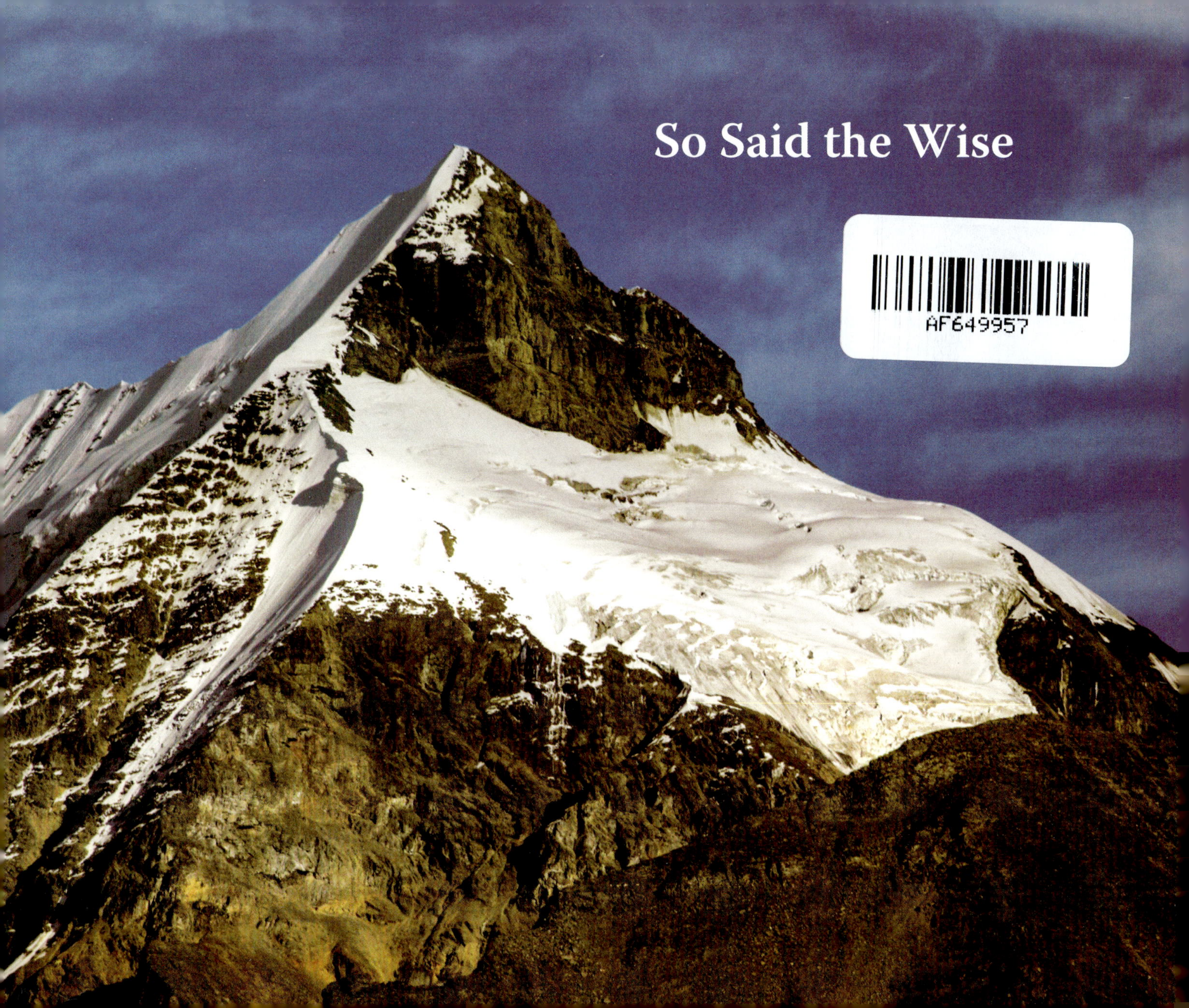

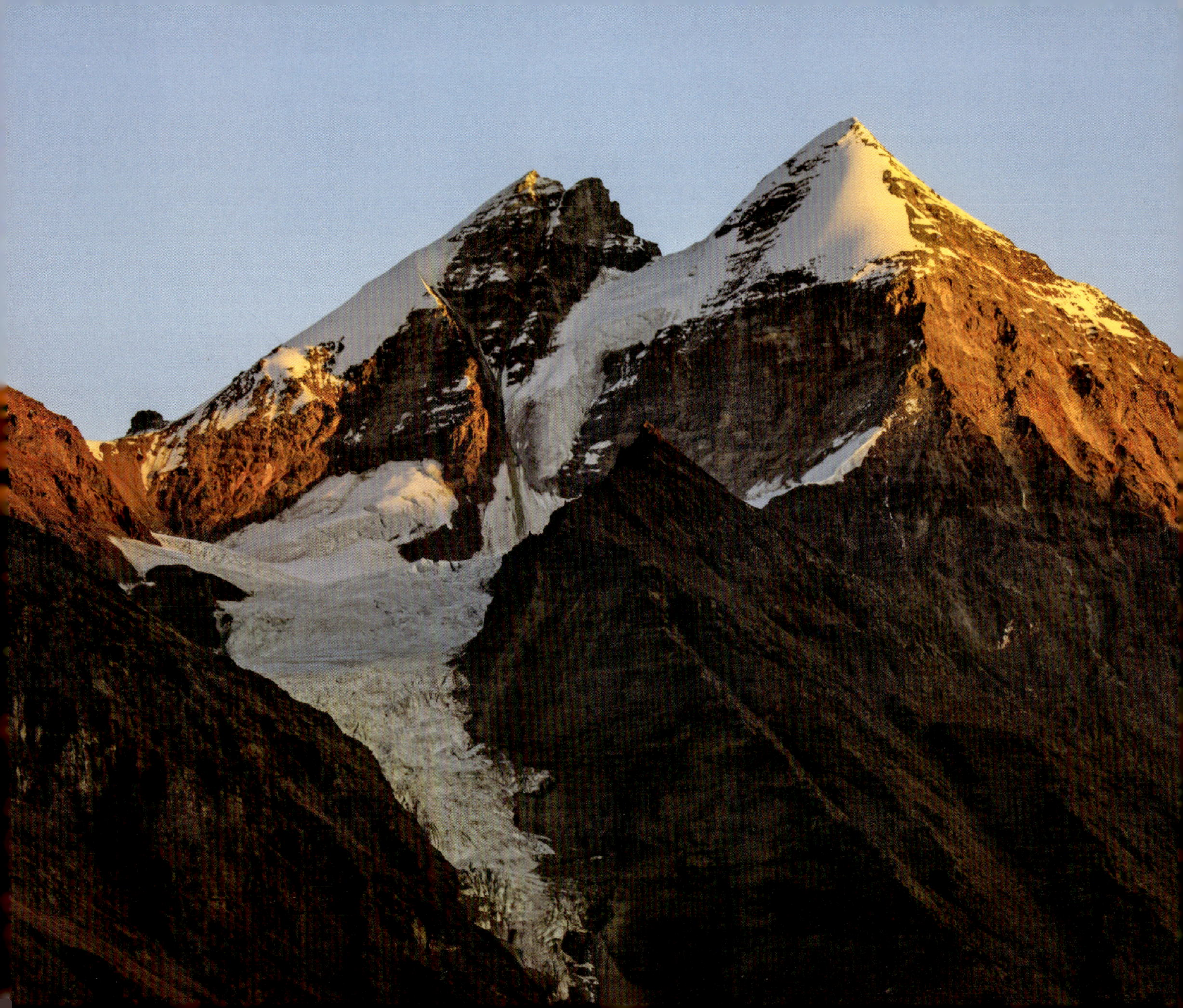

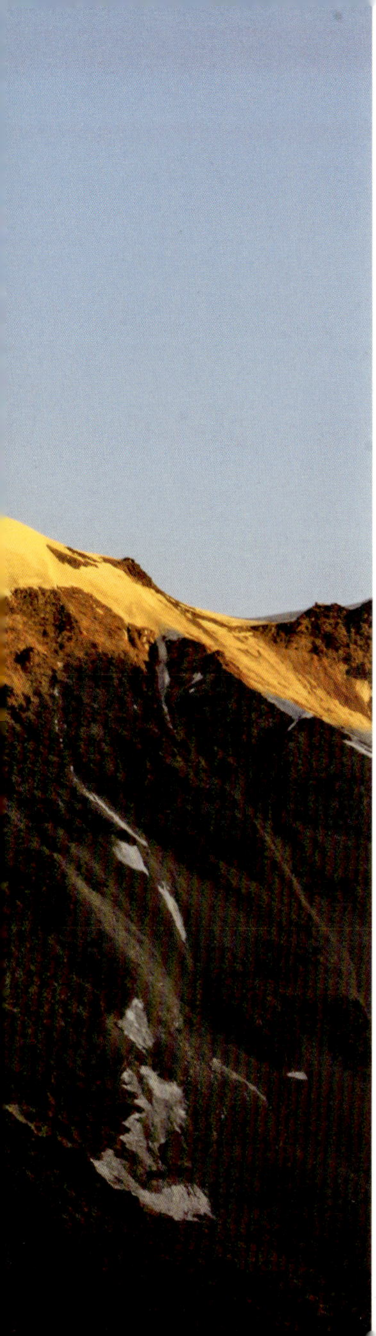

So Said the Wise

Ashok Dilwali

NIYOGI
BOOKS

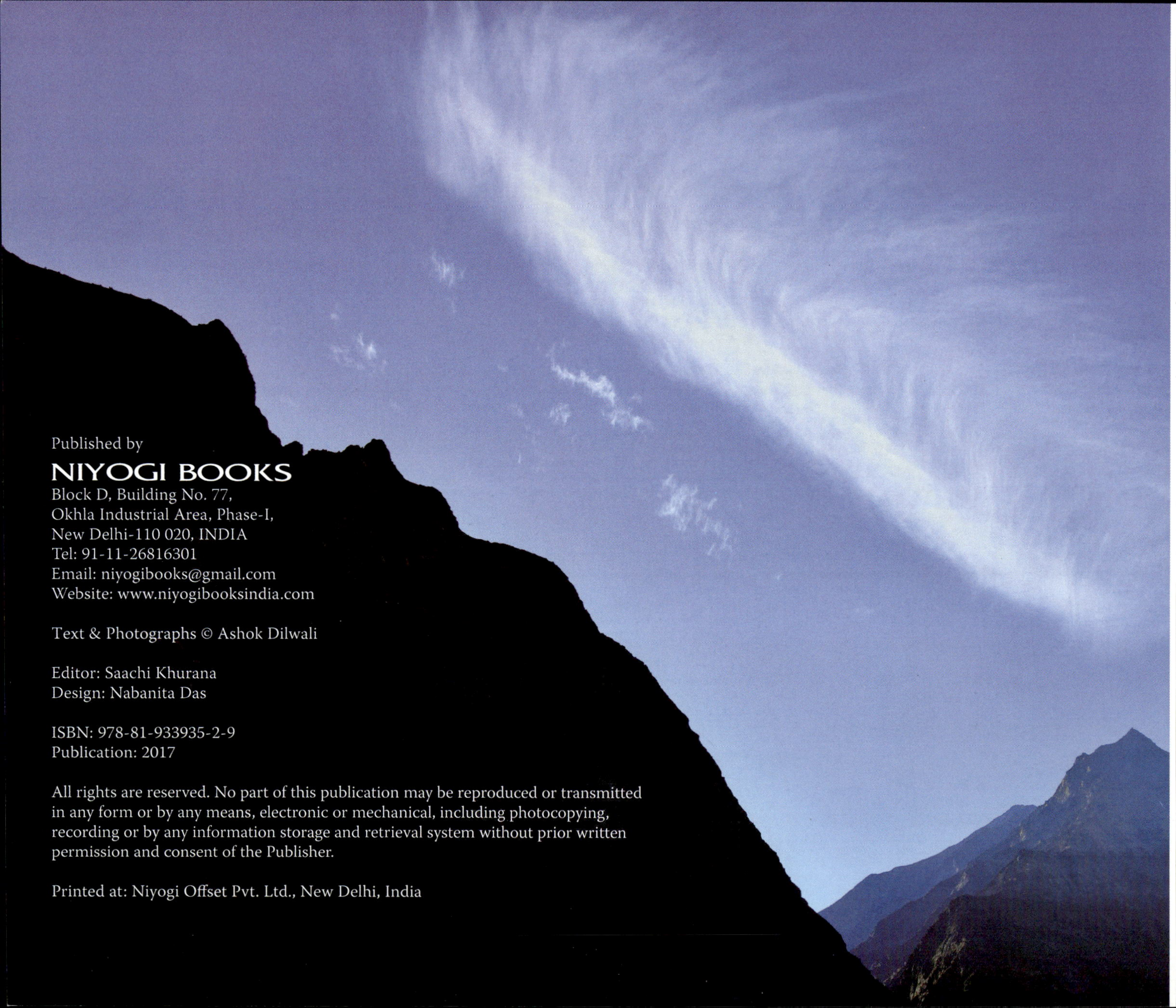

Published by

NIYOGI BOOKS

Block D, Building No. 77,
Okhla Industrial Area, Phase-I,
New Delhi-110 020, INDIA
Tel: 91-11-26816301
Email: niyogibooks@gmail.com
Website: www.niyogibooksindia.com

Editor: Saachi Khurana
Design: Nabanita Das

ISBN: 978-81-933935-2-9
Publication: 2017

Printed at: Niyogi Offset Pvt. Ltd., New Delhi, India

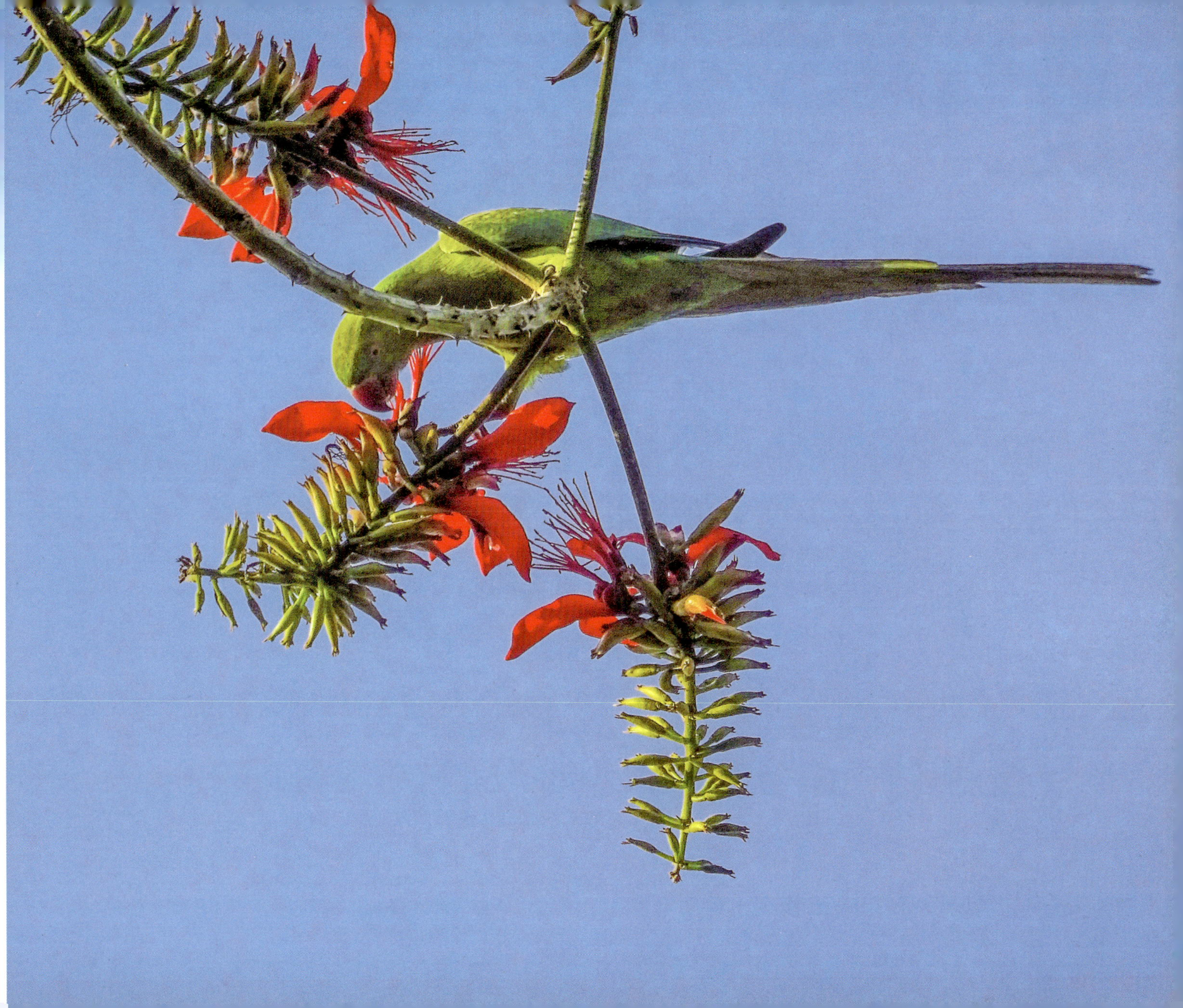

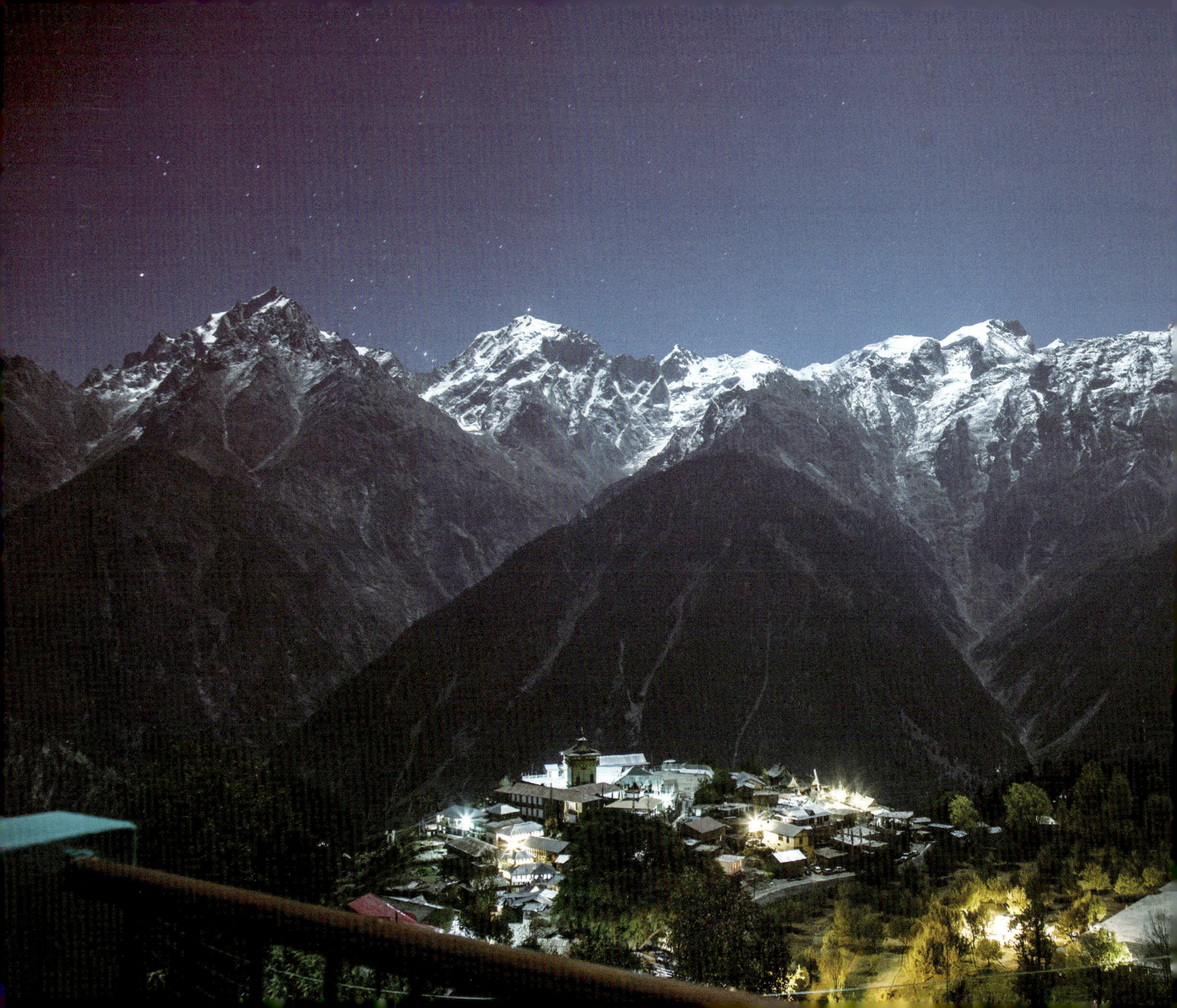

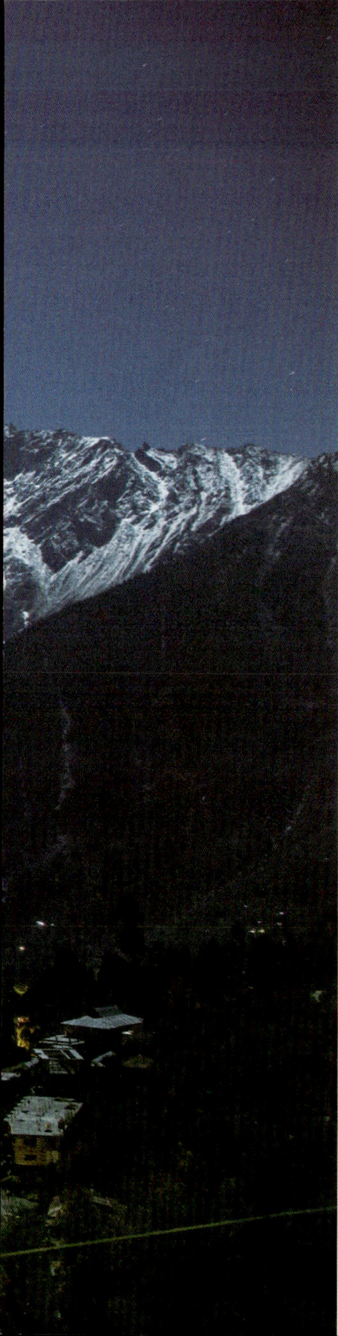

INTRODUCTION

For over 50 years—from my college days, to be precise, which go back to the beginning of the sixties—I have been fond of reading lines of wisdom and often of jotting them down in a diary. This has continued for a long time, and indeed even today, when I come across something that touches my heart, I reach for a diary and make a note of it.

Much to my wonder and amusement, I read that the legendary writer, the late Khushwant Singh, also did the same thing. He called it a "Khichri Diary"; it was a collection of miscellaneous nuggets of humour, wisdom, *shayari* (poetry), and so on.

As a professional photographer for over four decades, I travelled to many nooks and crannies of the Himalayas in search of works of the Almighty, and as a result I ended up with thousands of images of nature in its pristine glory.

Then an idea dawned: why not combine a visual with an elevating thought? India has a great number of minds whose quotes and writings have been hailed as many of the most profound of humankind.

This book is a collaboration of these two ingredients, a good visual and an inspirational thought. Visuals often brighten up a page, and it is my desire that this experiment should succeed. The reader, I hope, will be happy to read what such enlightened souls have said and also enjoy the accompanying photograph.

The visionaries included come from different walks of life, and by virtue of their scholarship and erudition left indelible impressions on our country and indeed on the world.

I would like apologise, right at the beginning, for some other significant personalities have been left out. This is so merely because all such people cannot be assembled in one book.

I dare imagine that this volume will be cherished for many times to come, because wisdom is eternal and cannot be dated.

With this hope I offer this potpourri of photographs and memorable quotes that go beyond all societal boundaries.

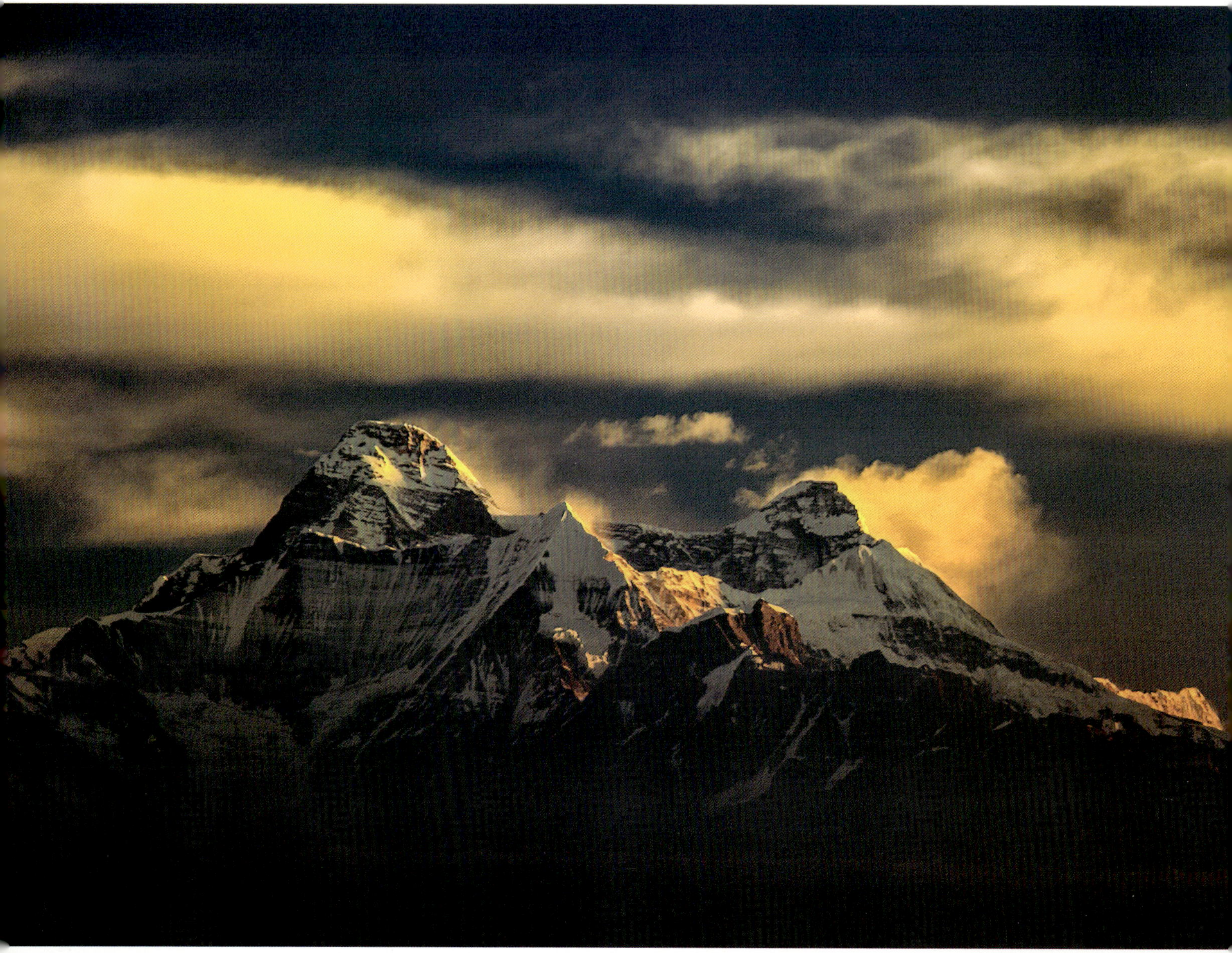

"

Let us sacrifice our today so that our children can have a better tomorrow.

~

Look at the sky. We are not alone. The whole universe is friendly to us and conspires only to give the best to those who dream and work.

~

You have to dream before your dreams can come true.

~

Excellence is a continuous process and not an accident.

~

If a country is to be corruption-free and become a nation of beautiful minds, I strongly feel there are three key societal members who can make a difference. They are the father, the mother and the teacher.

~

We should not give up and we should not allow the problem to defeat us.

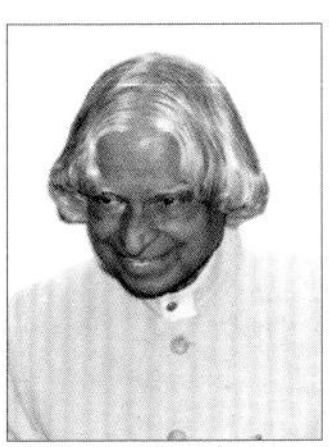

A.P.J. Abdul Kalam (1931–2015) was the 11th president of India. He was a scientist who took to politics later on. He studied physics and aerospace engineering in Tamil Nadu. He was the unanimous choice of all political parties for his amiability, humility and scholarship. He proved his mettle both as a scientist and an administrator. Because of his involvement with rocket technology and ballistic missile technology he came to be known as "The Missile Man of India". He was highly respected for his work and gave lectures on his subject at various prize institutions. His interaction with the student community and his motivational speeches made him quite popular among the youth. He was recognised for his meritorious services and was awarded the Bharat Ratna, the highest civilian award of the country.

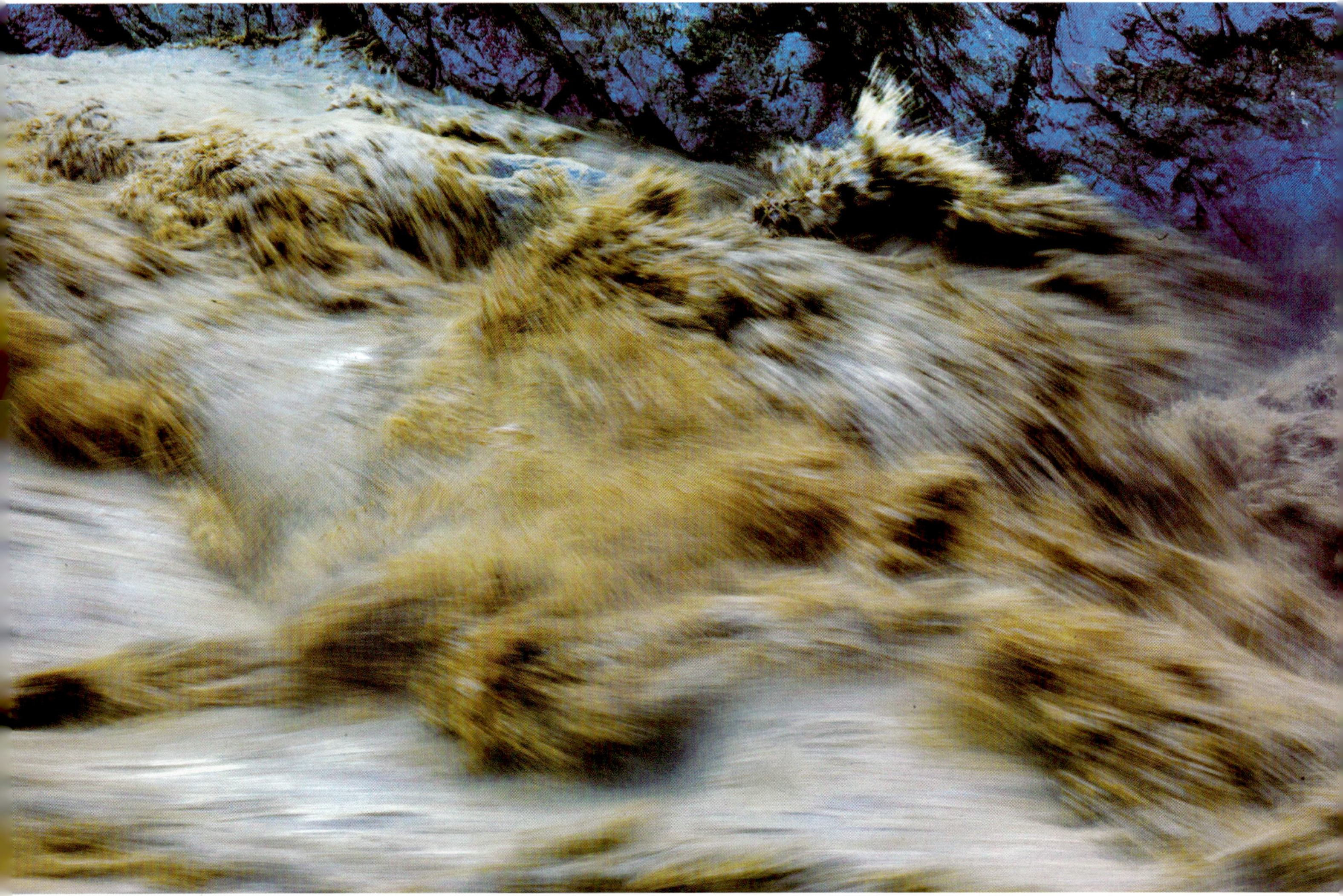

"

Do not be proud of wealth, people, relations and friends, or youth. All these are snatched by time in the blink of an eye. Giving up this illusory world, know and attain the Supreme.

~

Do not look at anybody in terms of friend or foe, brother or cousin;
do not fritter away your mental energies in thoughts of friendship or enmity.
Seek the Self everywhere, be amiable and equal-minded towards all, treating all alike.

~

The world, like a dream full of attachments and aversions, seems real until the awakening.

~

Curb your senses and your mind and see the Lord within your heart.

~

As gold purified in a furnace loses its impurities and achieves its own true nature,
the mind gets rid of the impurities of the attributes of delusion,
attachment and purity through meditation and attains Reality.

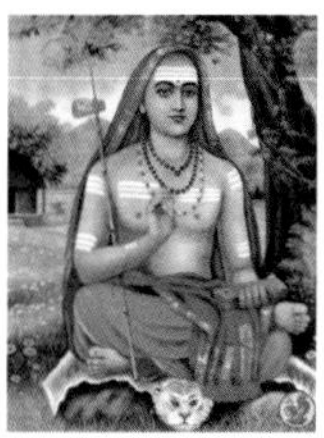

Adi Shankara (788–820) was a Hindu philosopher who was born into a poor family in south India in the 8th century. His teachings had a large influence on the growth of Hinduism. He is remembered mostly for his noteworthy interpretations of Hindu scriptures and his discourse on Vedic literature. He was inclined towards spirituality and religion from a young age. He mastered all the Vedas and the six *Vedangas* and travelled broadly, spreading spiritual knowledge along with the views of Advaita Vedanta. He is believed to have died at the early age of 32, at Kedarnath, a Hindu pilgrimage site in the Himalayas. However, some texts assert that the location of his death is Tamil Nadu or Kerala.

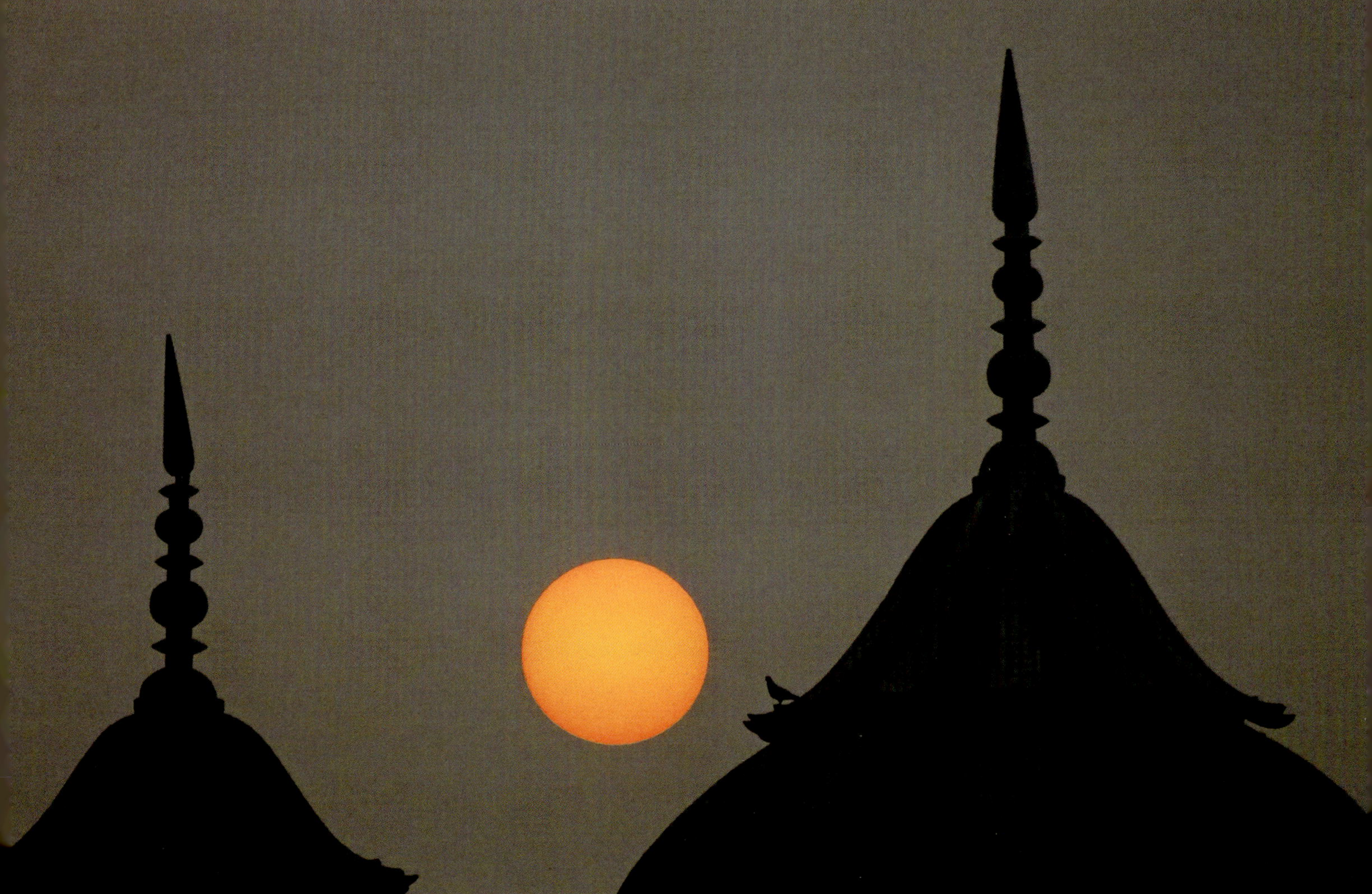

“

Utter a word of truth that goes against the king,
and behead yourself with the sword of your own tongue.
~
There are those who consume naans and kebabs even in their dreams;
and there are those who don't even dream, Since they can't sleep due to starvation.
~
If you ask me the road to hell,
I would say a night in a lonely bedroom.
Man can never be satisfied, even if he gets to the heaven; How can he?
Adam himself couldn't.
One who laughs at the plight of lovers, himself needs being cried at.
~
A needle is better than a sword;
The latter cuts, while the former sews.

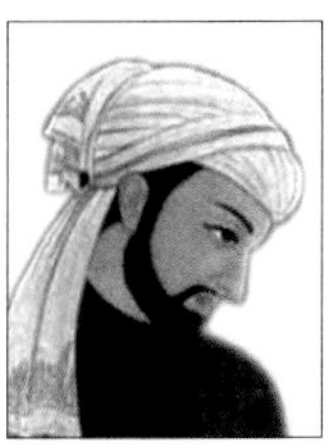

Amir Khusro (1253–1325) was a champion Sufi poet, scholar and musician. He is an icon of Indian culture. Amir Khusrao had a deep and profound knowledge of music. The Indian musical instruments, the tabla and sitar, are the gifts he blessed the world with. He wrote poems mainly in Persian, the court language of those days. Furthermore, he is the father of *qawwali*, a form of Sufi devotional music, and he also introduced the *ghazal* style of song to India. He is also the originator of the *khayal* and *tarana* styles of music. In a nutshell, it would be hard to imagine what music would have been in the subcontinent without Amir Khusrao's great contributions.

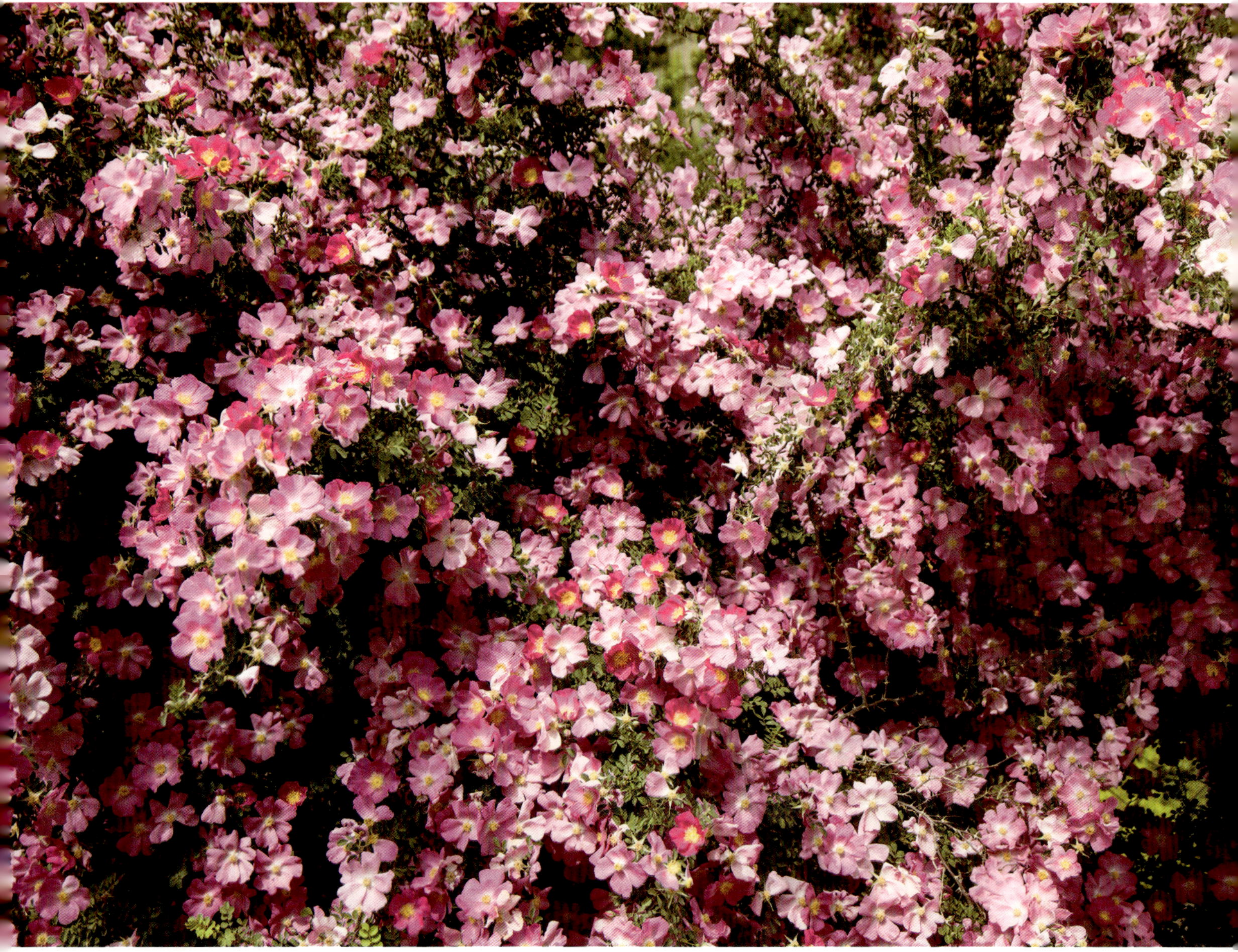

“

Better remain silent, better not even think, if you are not prepared to act.

~

India is a country in which every great religion finds
a home.

~

The destruction of India’s village system was the greatest of England’s blunders.

~

After death we live for some time in the astral world in the astral body used during our life on Earth, and the more we learn to control and use it wisely now the better for us after death.

~

A common religion is not possible for India, but a recognition of a common basis for all religions, and the growth of a liberal, tolerant spirit in religious matters, are possible.

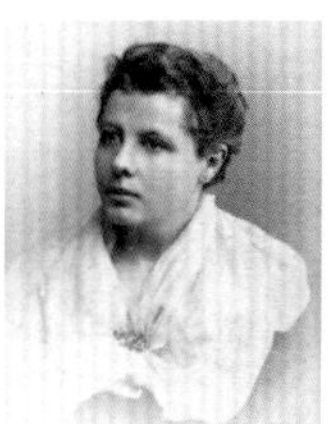

Annie Besant (1847–1933). She was born in Clapham, London. A distinguished women’s rights activist and orator, she strongly supported the freedom of India from the foreign rule of Great Britain. A meeting with Helena Blavatsky changed her life and she became interested in theosophy. She visited India because of this interest. In 1898 she helped establish Central Hindu College and in 1922 she aided in establishing the Hyderabad National Collegiate Board in Mumbai. She became the president of the Theosophical Society in India. Gradually she entered Indian politics and joined the Indian National Congress. When World War I broke out, she launched the Home Rule League and campaigned for democracy in India. For her activity and sympathetic attitude towards India, in 1917 she was elected the president of Indian National Congress.

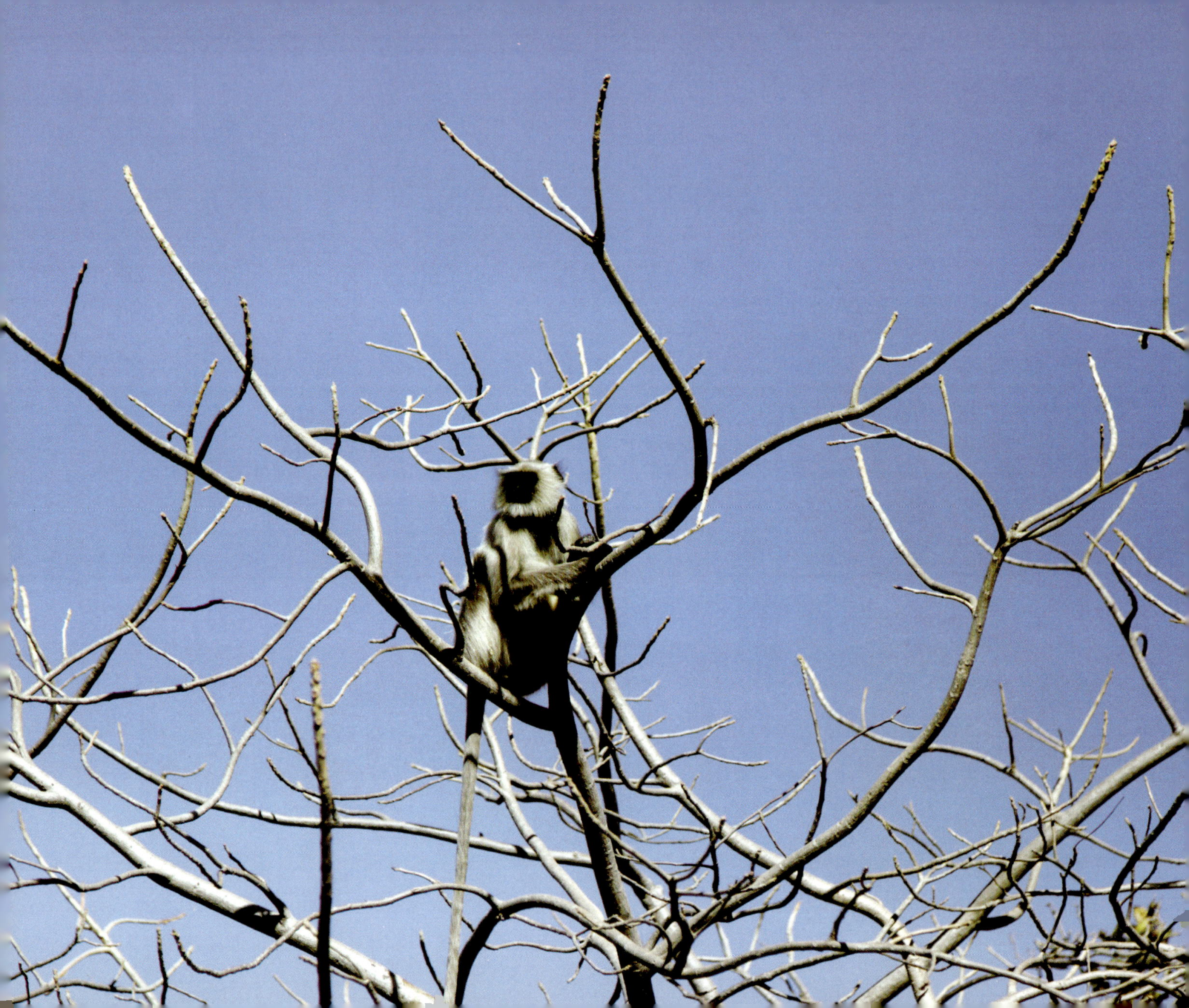

"

I sought my soul, but my soul I could not see; I sought my god, but my god eluded me; and then I sought my sisters and my brothers, and in them I found all three.

~

The future belongs to the common man with uncommon determination.

~

I don't want to be a great leader; I want to be a man who goes around with a little oil can and when he sees a breakdown, offers his help. To me, the man who does that is greater than any holy man in saffron-coloured robes. The mechanic with the oil can: that is my ideal in life.

~

Happiness is a continuous creative activity of imaginatively comparing your experiences to things that aren't as good and thereby feeling happy and grateful.

~

I took up leprosy work not to help anyone, but to overcome that fear in my life. That it worked out good for others was a by-product. But the fact is I did it to overcome fear.

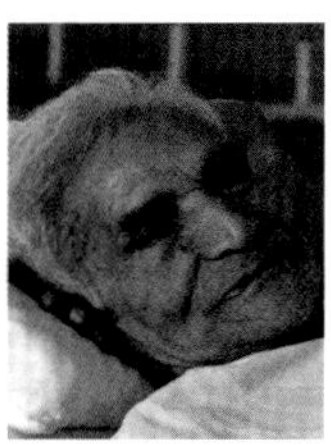

Baba Amte (1914–2008). Known affectionately as Baba Amte, his full name was Murlidhar Devidas Amte. He was a social worker and was devoted to social service, particularly to make life better for people with leprosy. He was disturbed when he first saw the misery of those suffering from this terrible disease, and he decided to try to empower them, because they were ostracised by society. He founded many ashrams and hospitals for them. He participated in the Indian Independence Movement under the mentorship of Gandhi, and was sent to prison in 1942 for partaking in the Quit India Movement. He won the hearts of many people through his selfless service and received the Ramon Magsayay Award, the Padma Vibhushan, and the Gandhi Peace Prize.

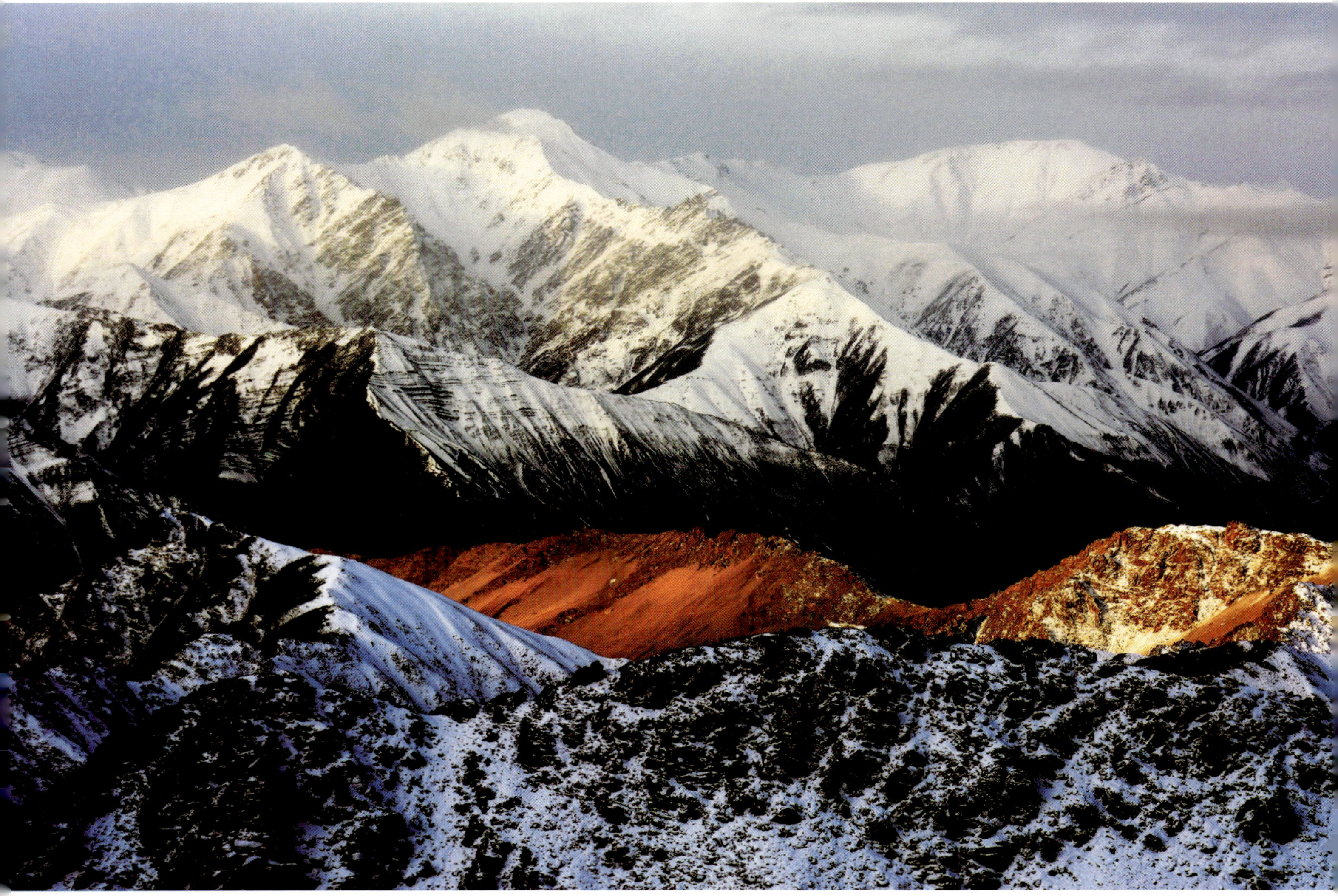

"

I had requested for a long life a life of four days. Two passed by in pining, and two in waiting. How unlucky is Zafar! For burial even two yards of land were not to be had, in the land of the beloved.

~

My life gives no ray of light, I bring no solace to heart or eye Out of dust to dust again, of no use to anyone am I barred the door of fate for me, bereft of my dear ones am I. The spring of a flower garden ruined alas, my autumn wing am I.

~

I came into the world and what did I see? Whatever I saw was just like a dream. Man is moulded from clay but I saw him as a bubble of water.

~

That heart alone is dear which delights in you,
That life is dearly prized which is pledged to you, albeit I'm the wayside dust, but, Zafar, I fear,
Lest this dust too heavily lies on that delicate shrew.

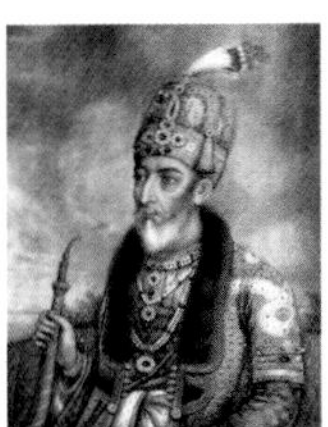

Bahadur Shah Zafar (1775–1862) was the last Mughal Emperor of India. He succeeded his father Akbar II when the latter died in 1837. His influence extended only over Delhi, as the British government had taken over the whole of India and Zafar was just a puppet with no real authority. He was a poet of great repute and is remembered even today for his skills. During his reign the Revolt of 1857 happened and he, being the head of India, was held responsible for it. As it ended in a fiasco, Zafar was exiled from India and sent to Rangoon, the capital of Burma, a British-controlled country.

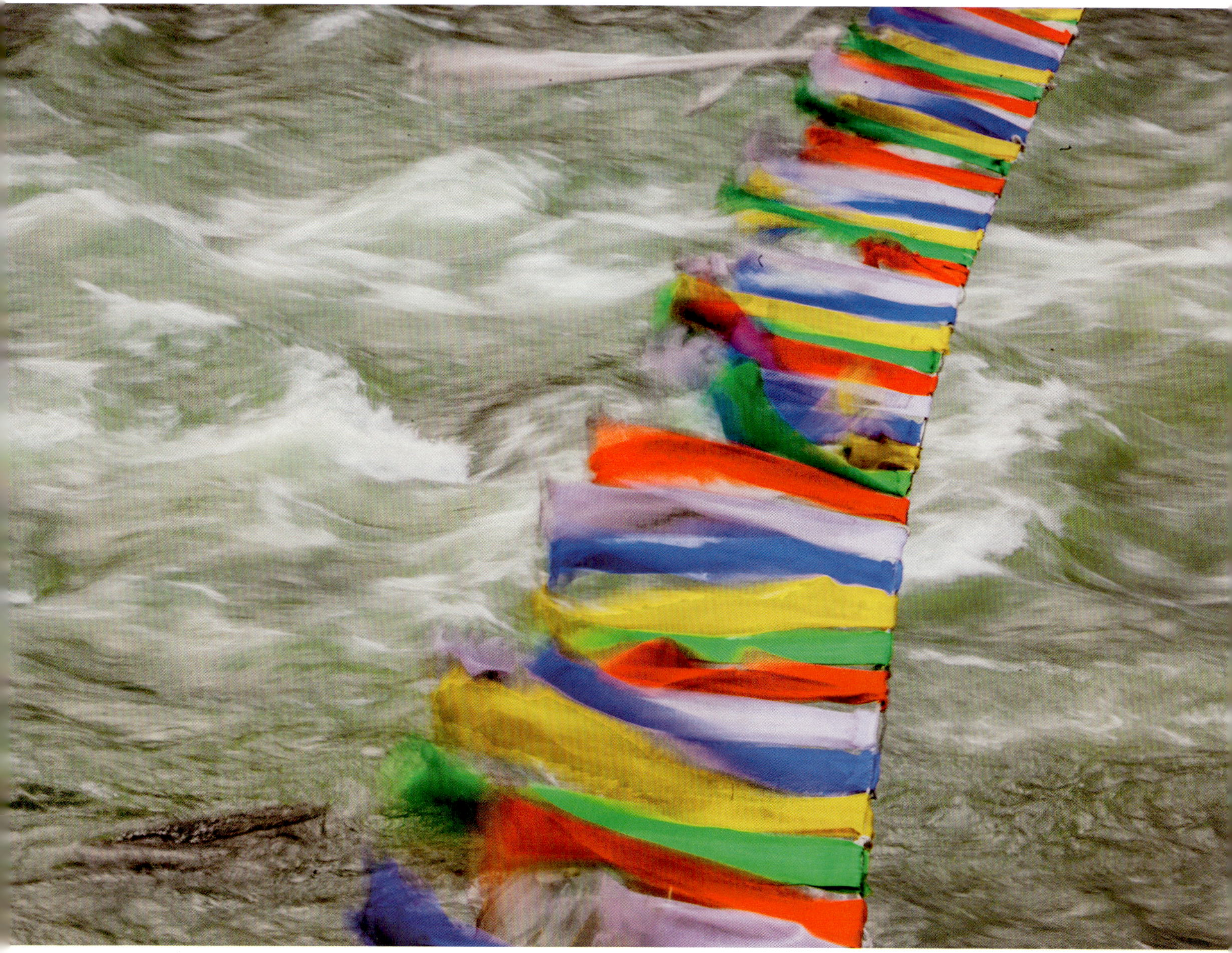

"

Freedom is my birthright. I shall have it.

~

Progress is implied in independence. Without self-government,
neither industrial progress is possible nor the educational scheme will be useful to the nation.

~

If God is put up with untouchability, I will not call him God.

~

It may be providence's will that the cause I represent may prosper more by
my suffering than by my remaining free.

~

It is true that lack of rain causes famine but it is also true that the people of India
have not the strength to fight the evil. The poverty of India is wholly due to the present rule.
India is being bled till only the skeleton remains...all the vitality of the people is being sapped and
we are left in an emaciated state of slavery.

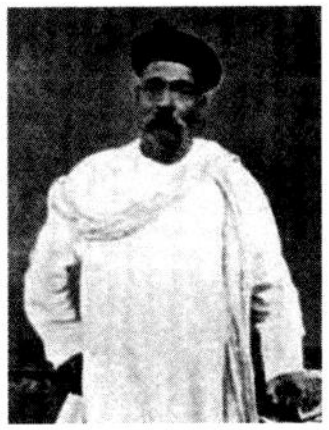

Bal Gangadhar Tilak (1856–1920). His role in promoting Home Rule for India was hugely significant. "Swaraj is my birthright and I shall have it" was the statement that caused India to take action. He desired from the British government favourable conditions in India to enable Indians to govern their own land. He stood for national education, self-government, self-reliance, and the boycott of foreign goods. The British called him the "Father of Indian Unrest". He was given the title of "Lokmanya", which means "accepted by the people (as their leader)". He disagreed with Gandhi on the means to attain freedom and did not believe in non-violence or satyagraha, and supported the use of force if necessary.

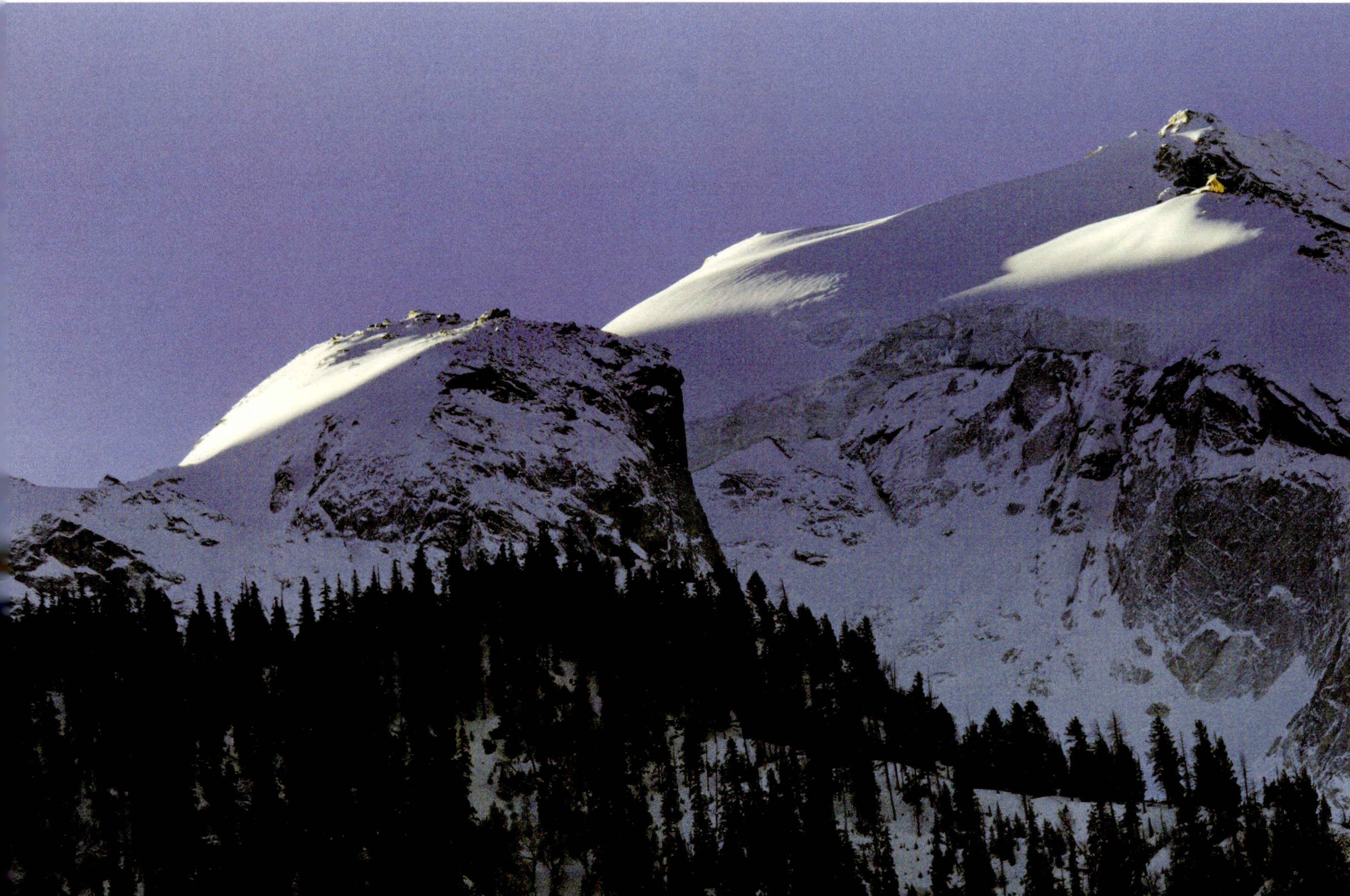

"

The relationship between husband and wife should be one of closest friends.

~

I measure the progress of a community by the degree of progress which women have achieved.

~

Law and order are the medicine of the body politic and when the body politic gets sick, medicine must be administered.

~

Cultivation of mind should be the ultimate aim of human existence.

~

So long as you do not achieve social liberty,
whatever freedom is provided by the law is of no avail to you.

~

We are Indians, firstly and lastly.

~

I like the religion that teaches liberty, equality and fraternity.

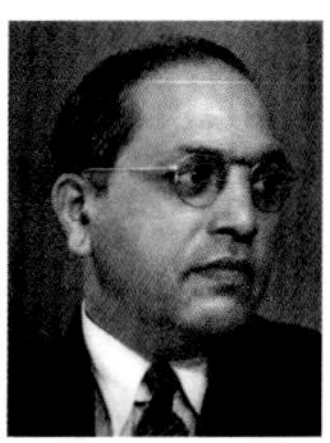

Bhimrao Ambedkar (1891–1956). He was one of the creators of the Indian Constitution. He was a well-known politician and a respected jurist. He made noteworthy attempts to eliminate social evils like caste restrictions and untouchability. Throughout his life, he advocated for the rights of Dalits and other socially backward classes. He was appointed as India's first Law Minister in the cabinet of Jawaharlal Nehru. Posthumously, in 1990 he was awarded the Bharat Ratna, India's highest civilian award. He also doggedly fought for the cause of women's emancipation and labour empowerment. He converted to Buddhism and this was followed by a mass conversion of Dalits. At the end of his life he suffered from severe health problems and passed away 1956.

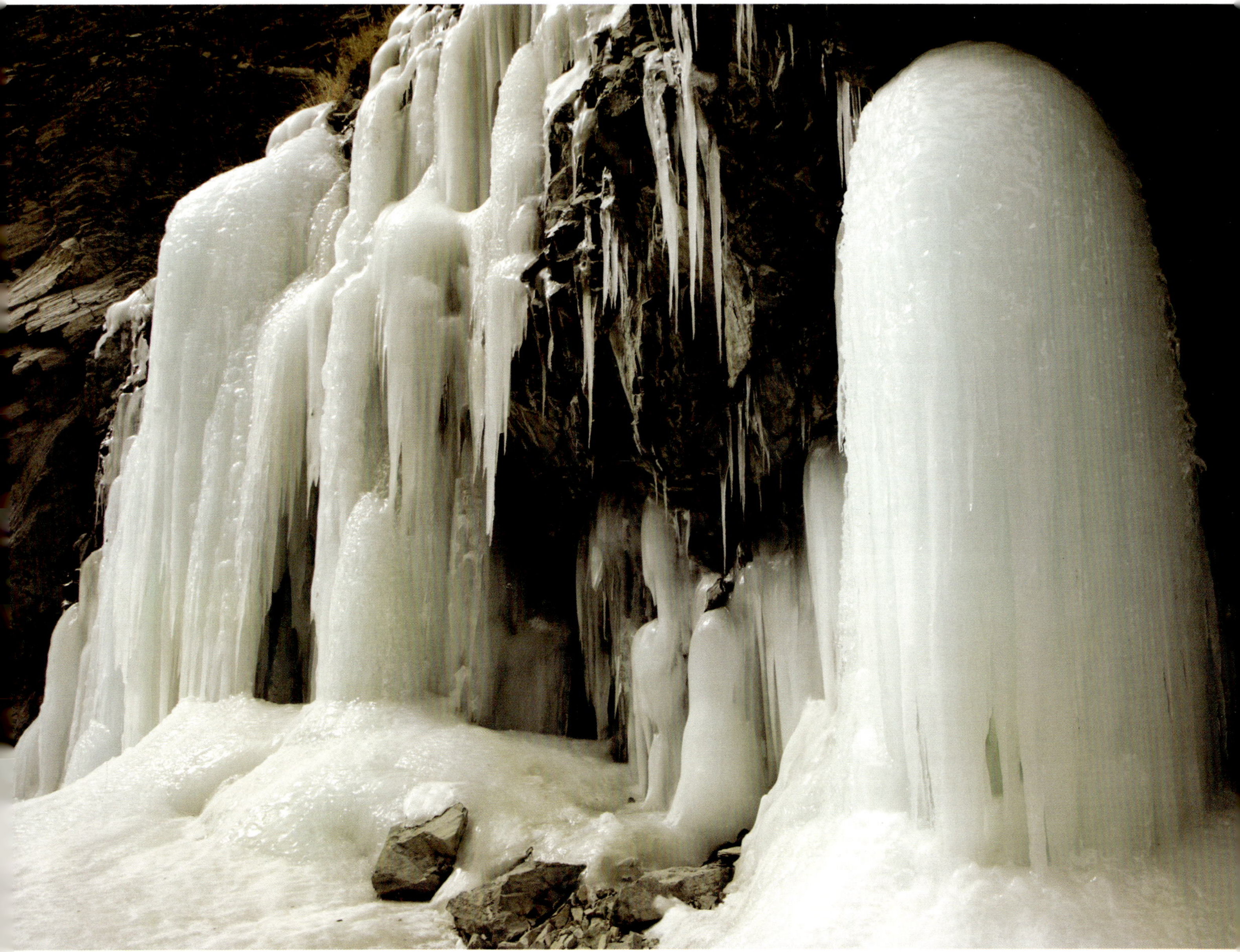

"

Going to Makkah is not the ultimate
Even if hundreds of prayers are offered.
Going to River Ganges is not the ultimate
Even if hundreds of cleansings are done.
Going to Gaya is not the ultimate
Even if hundreds of worships are done.
Bulleh Shah, the ultimate is
When the "I" is removed from the heart!

~

You have learnt so much and read a thousand books. Have you ever read your Self?
You have gone to mosque and temple. Have you ever visited your soul?
You are busy fighting Satan. Have you ever fought your ill intentions?
You have reached into the skies, but you have failed to reach what's in your heart!
You alone exist, I do not, O Beloved!
You alone exist, I do not!
Like the shadow of a house in ruins,
I revolve in my own mind.

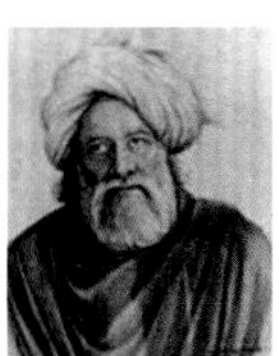

Bulleh Shah (1680–1757) is believed to have been born in Bahawalpur. There is much disagreement among historians regarding his exact date of birth, and a sizeable amount of his life is known only through legends. He was a Punjabi Sufi poet, a humanist with much piety, and a philosopher. He was the pupil of Inayat Qadri of Lahore, a renowned Sufi teacher of his times. Bulleh Shah was also known for his *karamat*, his miraculous powers.

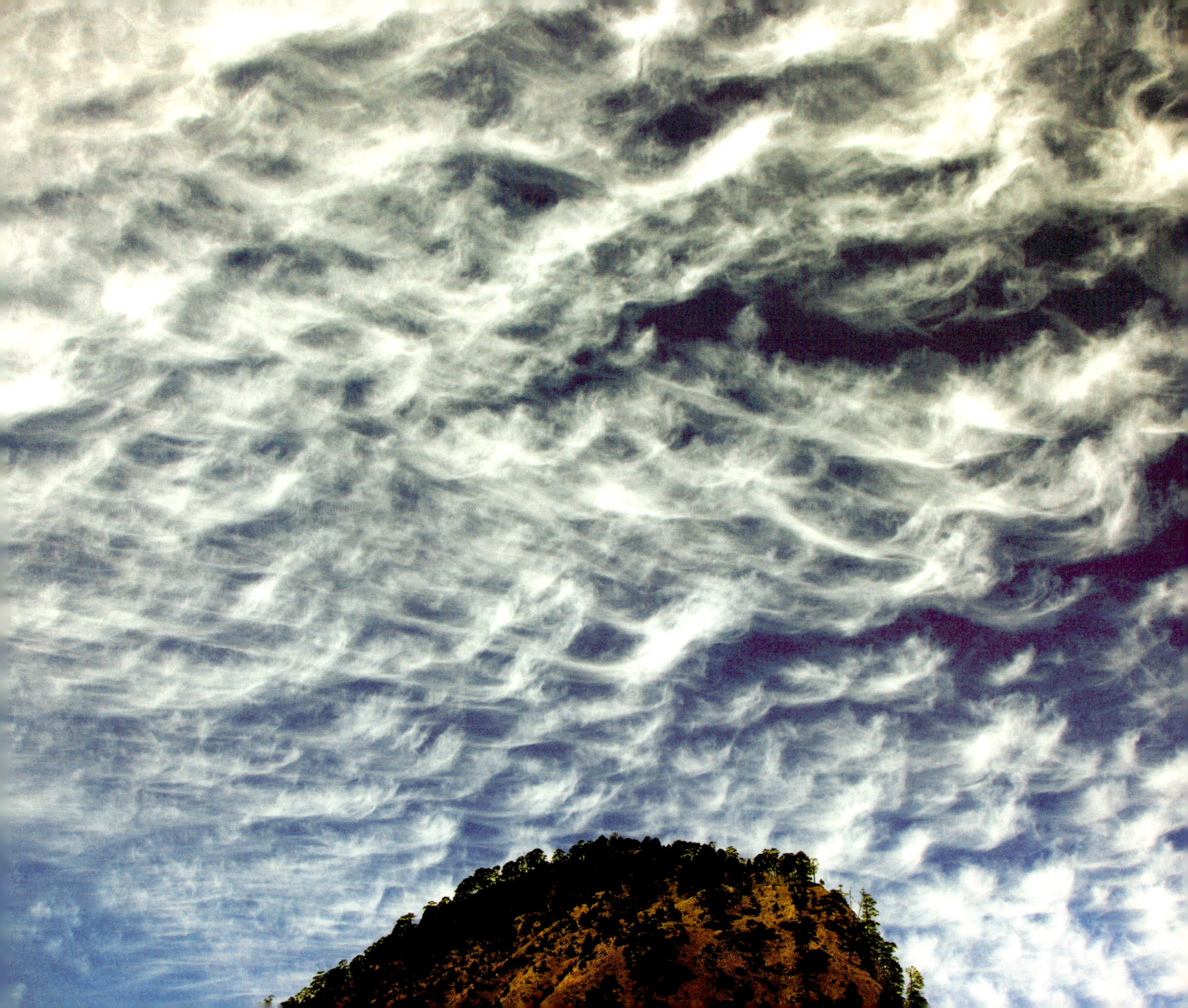

"

Do not demand love. Begin to love. You will be loved. It is the law and no statute can alter it. If we do not follow the law, and let the law die with the teacher, we shall become accomplices to the murderer. But if we follow the law with our hearts, [Bapu] will live with us and through us.

~

If India's government is to be an institution integrated with her people's lives, if it is to be a true democracy and not a superimposed Western institution staged in Indian dress, religion must have an important and recognised place in it with impartiality and reverence for all the creeds and denominations prevailing in India.

~

If civilisation is to be bound up with material advancement, we must accept its inevitable consequence, loss of freedom in exact proportion to the forward march.

~

What is wanted to save parliamentary democracy is an opposition that will operate not privately and behind the closed doors of the party meeting, but openly and periodically through the electorate.

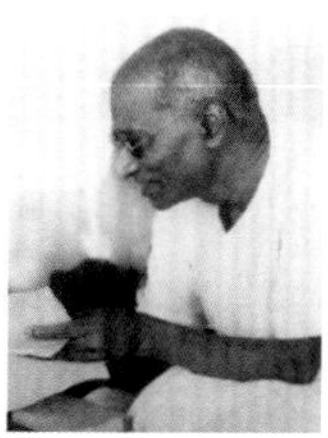

C. Rajagopalachari (1878–1972). Affectionately called Rajaji and C.R., he was a lawyer, politician, and statesman. He was the last governor general of India and held a major position in the Indian National Congress. After some years he left the Congress and founded his own political party, the Swatantra Party. He also served in prime offices as premier of Madras Presidency, governor of Bengal, minister of Home Affairs of the Indian Union, and chief minister of Madras State (Tamil Nadu). He was given the Bharat Ratna, the highest civilian award of the country. He protested firmly against nuclear weapons, which he felt would inevitably lead to disaster, and was a great proponent of world peace.

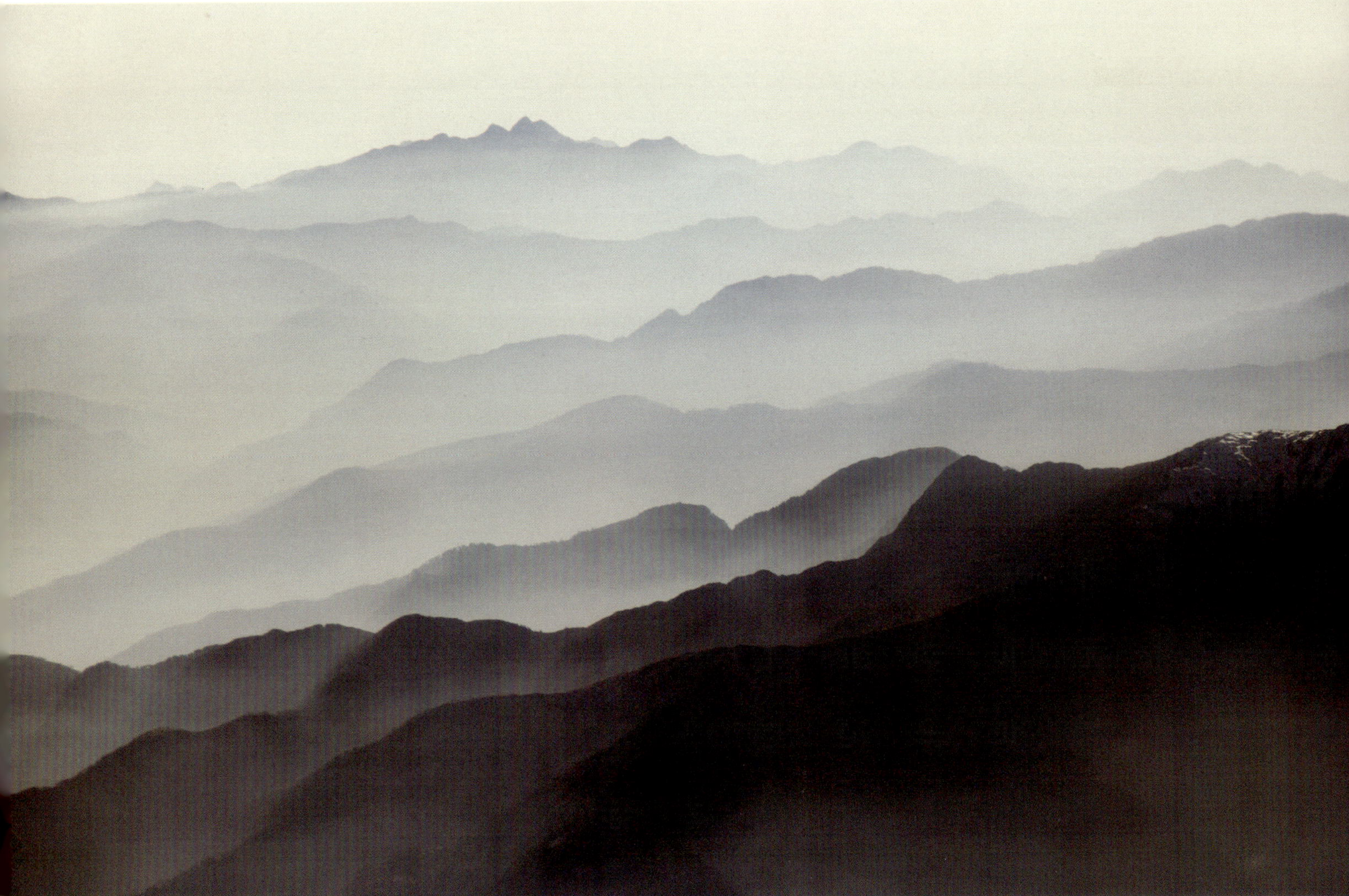

“

The Vedic literatures composed by the MahamuniVyasadeva are evidence of all spiritual existence. Only through these revealed scriptures can all conditioned souls attain knowledge.

~

The essence of all religious principles in the age of Kali is chanting of the holy names of the lord. One cannot be delivered by following any other religious principles.

~

The word Brahman indicates the complete Supreme Personality of Godhead, who is Sri Krishna. That is the verdict of all Vedic literatures.

~

In Vedic literature Krishna is the central point of attraction and His service is our activity. To attain the platform of love of Krishna is life's ultimate goal. Therefore Krishna, Krishna's service and love of Krishna are the three great riches of life.

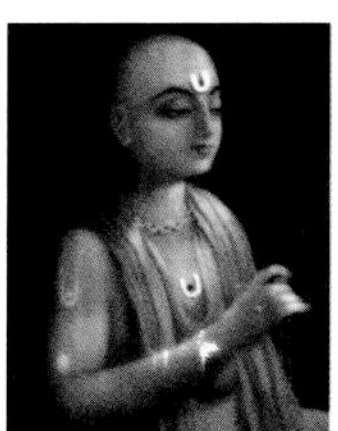

Chaitanya Mahaprabhu (1486–1534). He was a Bengali spiritual teacher and the founder of Gaudiya Vaishnavism. He was a devotee of Lord Krishna and was so deeply revered by his followers that they considered him an avatar of Krishna himself. His bhakti (devotion) to Krishna was very deep and many people took this as a message of how to attain perfection in life. His bhakti was based on the *Bhagavata Purana* and the Bhagavad Gita. Chaitanya Mahaprabhu popularised the chanting of the Hare Krishna mantra and created eight devotional prayers in Sanskrit.

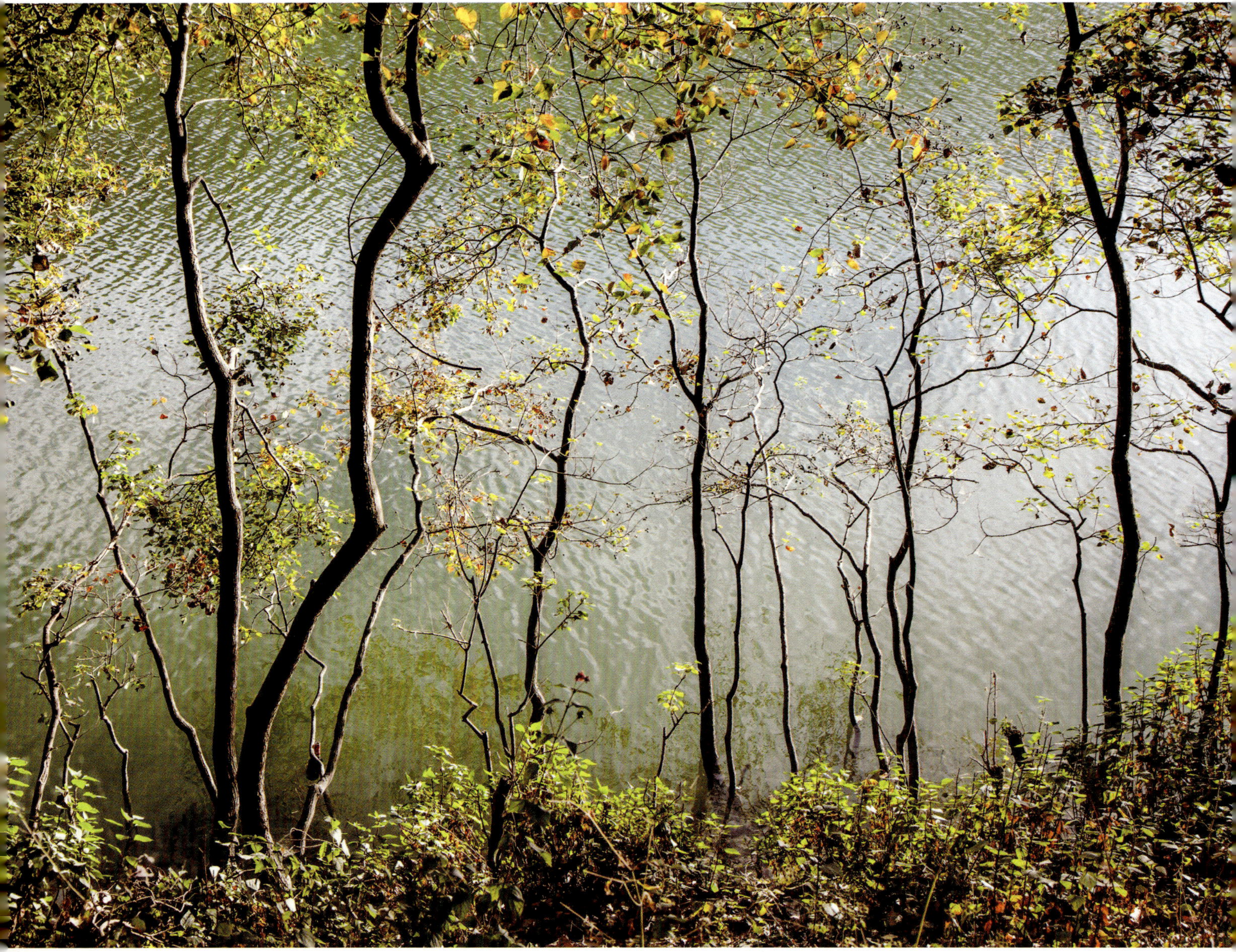

"

Learn from the mistakes of others; you can't live long enough to make them all yourselves.

~

A person should not be too honest. Straight trees are cut first,
and honest people are victimised first.

~

He who is overly attached to his family members experiences sorrow and fear,
for the root of all grief is attachment. Thus one should discard attachment to be happy.

~

The fragrance of flowers spreads only in the direction of the wind.
But the goodness of a person spreads in all directions.

~

Once you start working on something, don't be afraid of failure and don't abandon it.
People who work sincerely are the happiest.

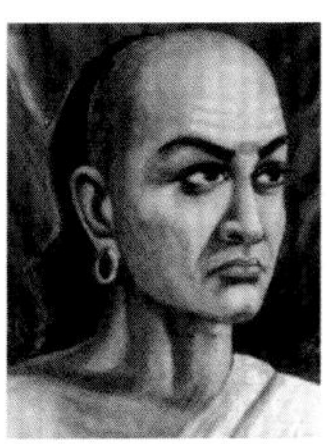

Chanakya (371 BC–283 BC)was a renowned teacher, philosopher, economist and advisor in the 4th century BC. He is also known by other names, like Kautilya and Vishnugupta, and is believed to have written *Arthashastra*, a political treatise. Rightly for this, in India he is known as the "Father of Political Science and Economics". Due to constant turmoil in the country because of foreign invasions and other disturbances, his work was lost until 1915. He advised both Chandragupta and his son Bindusara. Hence, the Maurya Empire owes part of its establishment to this man.

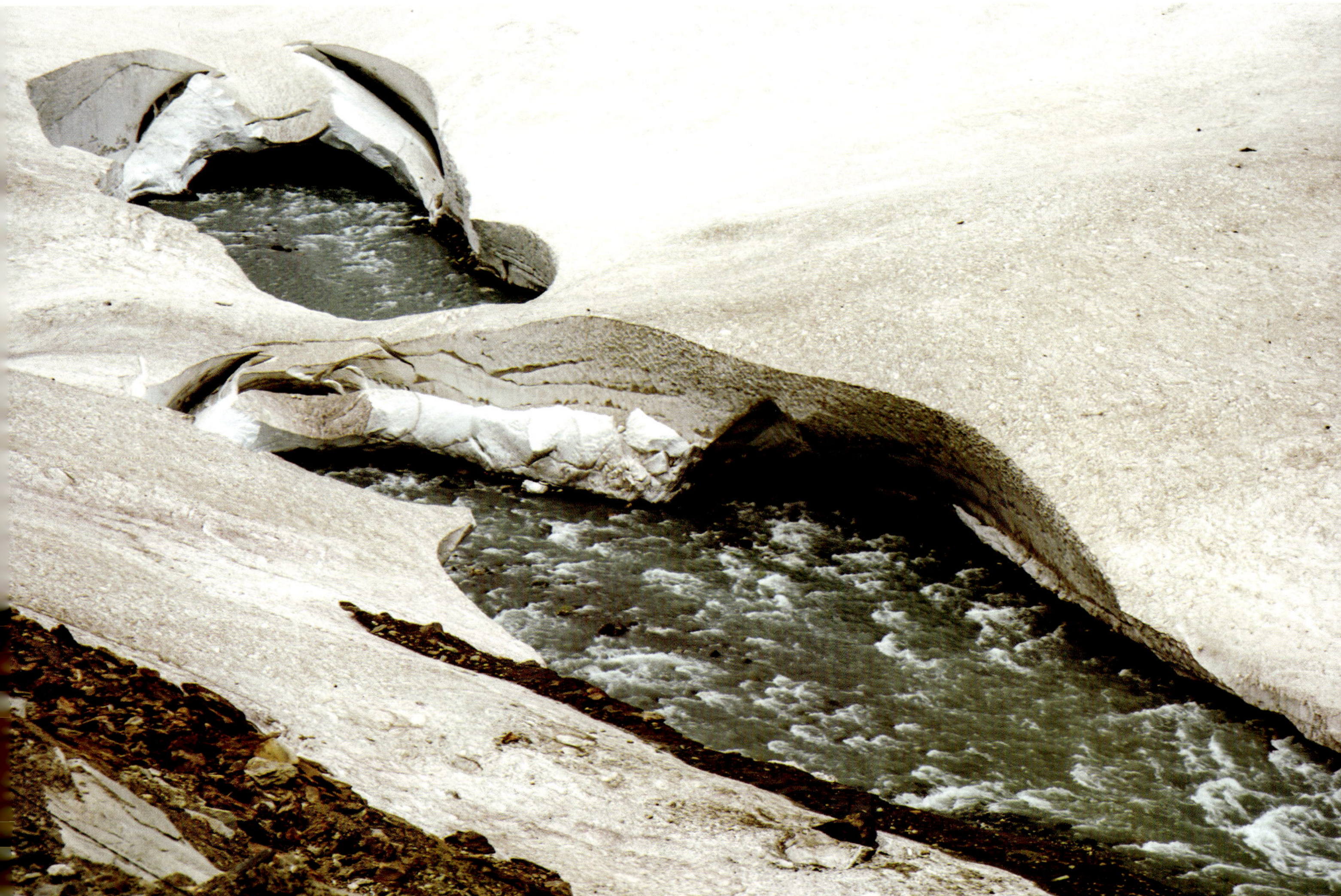

"

Our lack of compassion stems from our inability to see deeply into the nature of things.

~

Don't let someone who is no longer in your life continue to run your life.

~

Don't play with someone's feelings just because you're unsure of your own.

~

All the treasure in the world is worthless, unless you have someone to share it with.

~

I never belonged to you. I was never yours. We were never us. You confused a great friendship for something more than it was, and I'm sorry.

~

People forgive you when lies are told and hate you when the truth is told.

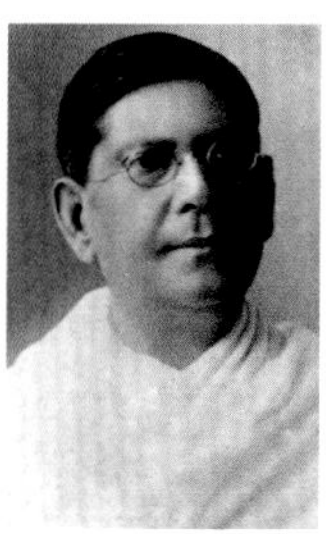

Chittaranjan Das (1869–1925). Lovingly called Deshbandhu ("Friend of the Country") and also C.R., he was an Indian politician and the founder of the Swaraj (Independence) Party in Bengal during the Non-Cooperation Movement, which was launched in 1919. It was his idea to stop exploitation by the British government by boycotting imported goods, which crippled the Indian economy and led to widespread unemployment. He became the mayor of Calcutta Corporation and supervised the Gaya round of the Indian National Congress. Fuelled by patriotism, he left his profession as a lawyer to participate in the Indian struggle for independence.

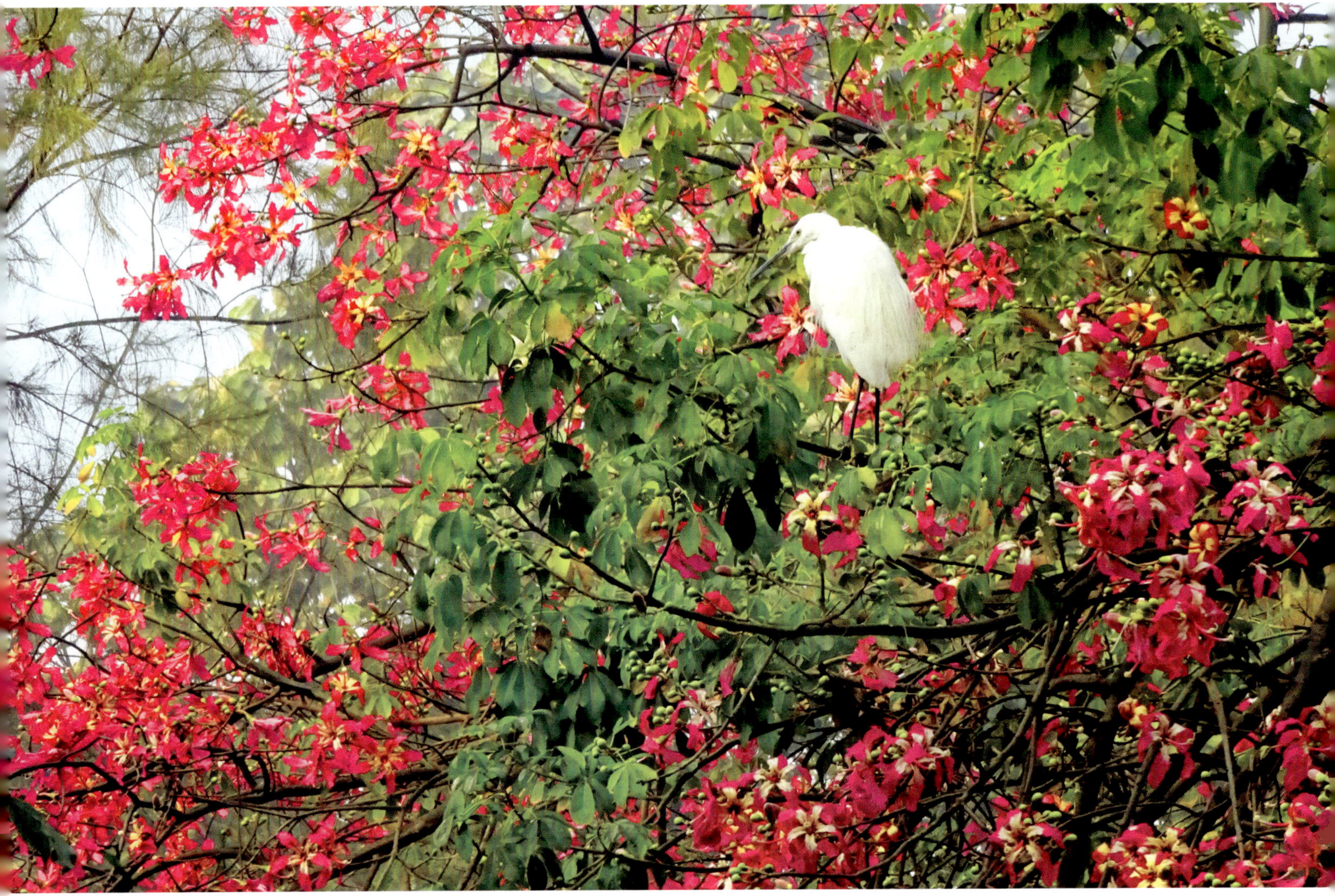

"

Indians have every right to claim an honourable fulfillment of our British pledged rights... It is futile to tell me that we must wait till all the people are ready. The British people did not wait for their parliament. Self-government is the only and chief remedy. In self-government is our hope, strength and greatness. I am a Hindu, a Muslim, a Parsi, but above all an Indian first.

~

Be united, persevere, and achieve self-government, so that the millions now perishing by poverty, famine, and plague may be saved, and India may once more occupy her proud position of yore among the greatest and civilised nations of the world.

~

Financially: All attention is engrossed in devising new modes of taxation, without any adequate effort to increase the means of the people to pay; and the consequent vexation and oppressiveness of the taxes imposed, imperial and local.

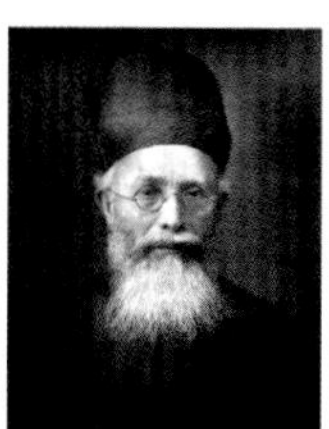

Dadabhai Naoroji (1825–1917). Affectionately called the Grand Old Man of India, he was an educator, intellectual, and political leader. For some years he was a Member of Parliament in the UK House of Commons, and the first Asian to hold such a post. He studied in depth the exploitation of the Indian economy by the foreign rulers, and after exhaustive work wrote the book *Poverty and Un-British Rule in India*. His book details how the British were systematically draining the wealth of our country.

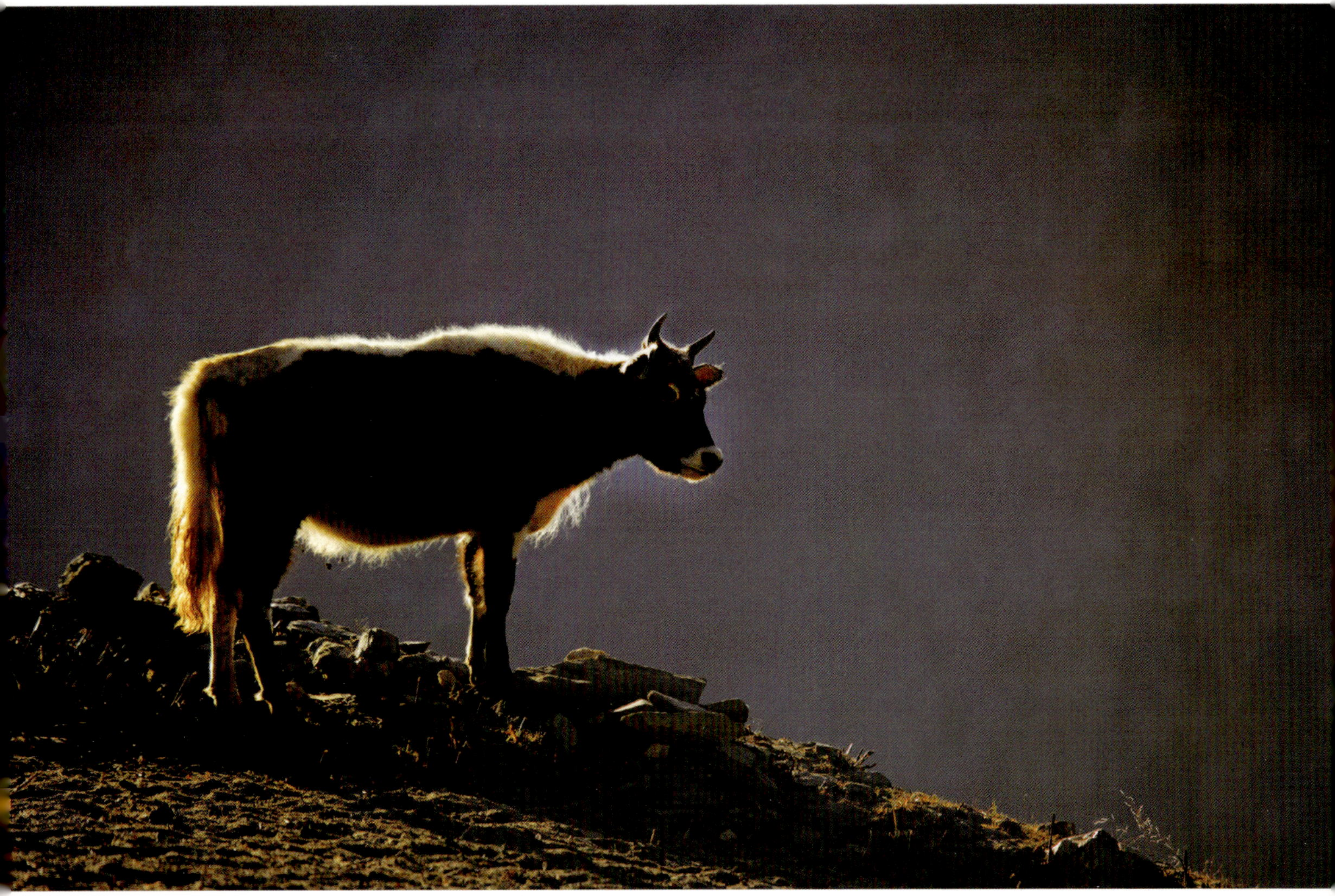

"

Prayer in any form is efficacious because it is an action. It will, therefore, have a result. That is the law of this universe in which we find ourselves.

~

The greatest musical instrument given to a human being is the voice.

~

Because a human being is endowed with empathy, he violates the natural order if he does not reach out to those who need care. Responding to this empathy, one is in harmony with the order of things, with dharma; otherwise, one is not.

~

In life, loss is inevitable. Everyone knows this, yet in the core of most people it remains deeply denied: 'This should not happen to me'. It is for this reason that loss is the most difficult challenge one has to face as a human being.

~

The earth should not be taken for granted. You have no right to abuse it and you can't disuse it. Make sure that you are a contributor, not merely a consumer.

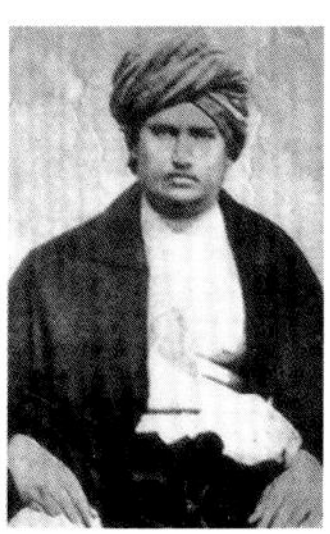

Dayanand Saraswati (1824–1883). Born into a wealthy Gujarati Brahmin family, he was earlier known as Mool Shankar Tiwari. He was an important socio-religious reformer. He promoted an egalitarian approach to the Vedas at a time when casteism was widespread. He founded Arya Samaj in 1875 in Mumbai to advocate for his idea of social service, which believes in gender equality and denounces the caste system. He gave new ideas to reform what he felt was stagnant Hindu thought through his book *Satyaprakash* ("the Light of Truth"). Because of his radical thought, Swami Dayanand made many enemies.

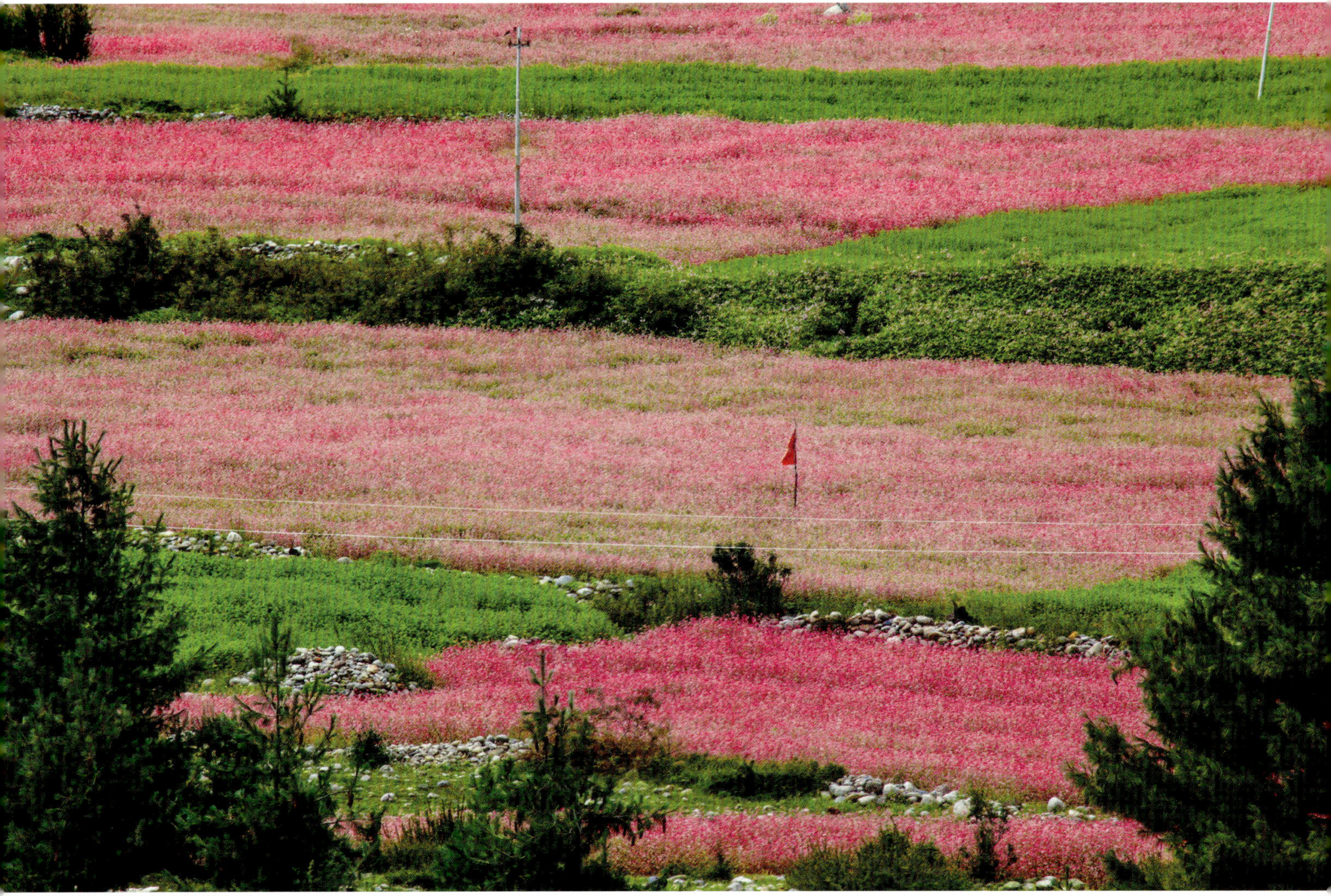

“

You will not be punished for your anger; you will be punished by your anger.

~

Thousands of candles can be lighted from a single candle,
and the life of the candle will not be shortened. Happiness never decreases by being shared.

~

No one saves us but ourselves. No one can and no one may. We ourselves must walk the path.

~

Do not dwell in the past, do not dream of the future; concentrate the mind on the present moment.

~

The mind is everything. What you think, you become.

~

Peace comes from within. Do not seek it without. We are shaped by our thoughts;
we become what we think. When the mind is pure, joy follows like a shadow that never leaves.

~

Better than a thousand hollow words is one word that brings peace.

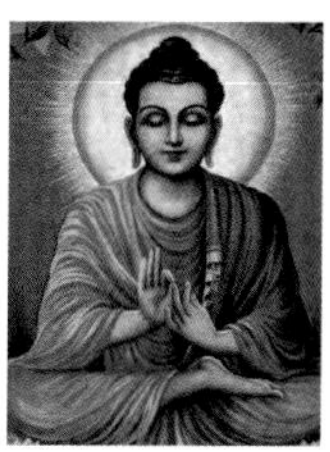

Gautam Buddha, born as Siddhartha, was the founder of Buddhism, and was born in eastern India/Nepal between the 6th and 4th centuries BC. When he was a young child, some scholars predicted that he would become either a successful king or an acclaimed spiritual leader. His father desired that he would become a king. Hence, Siddhartha was shielded from all religious knowledge and was unaware of the concepts of sickness, death, and old age. Once on a trip through the city he witnessed a diseased person, a corpse, and an old man. This knowledge about the sufferings in the world gave rise to several questions and the prince soon renounced all his worldly affairs to begin a journey of self-discovery. After years of contemplation and meditation, he attained enlightenment, and became the Buddha, meaning “the enlightened one”.

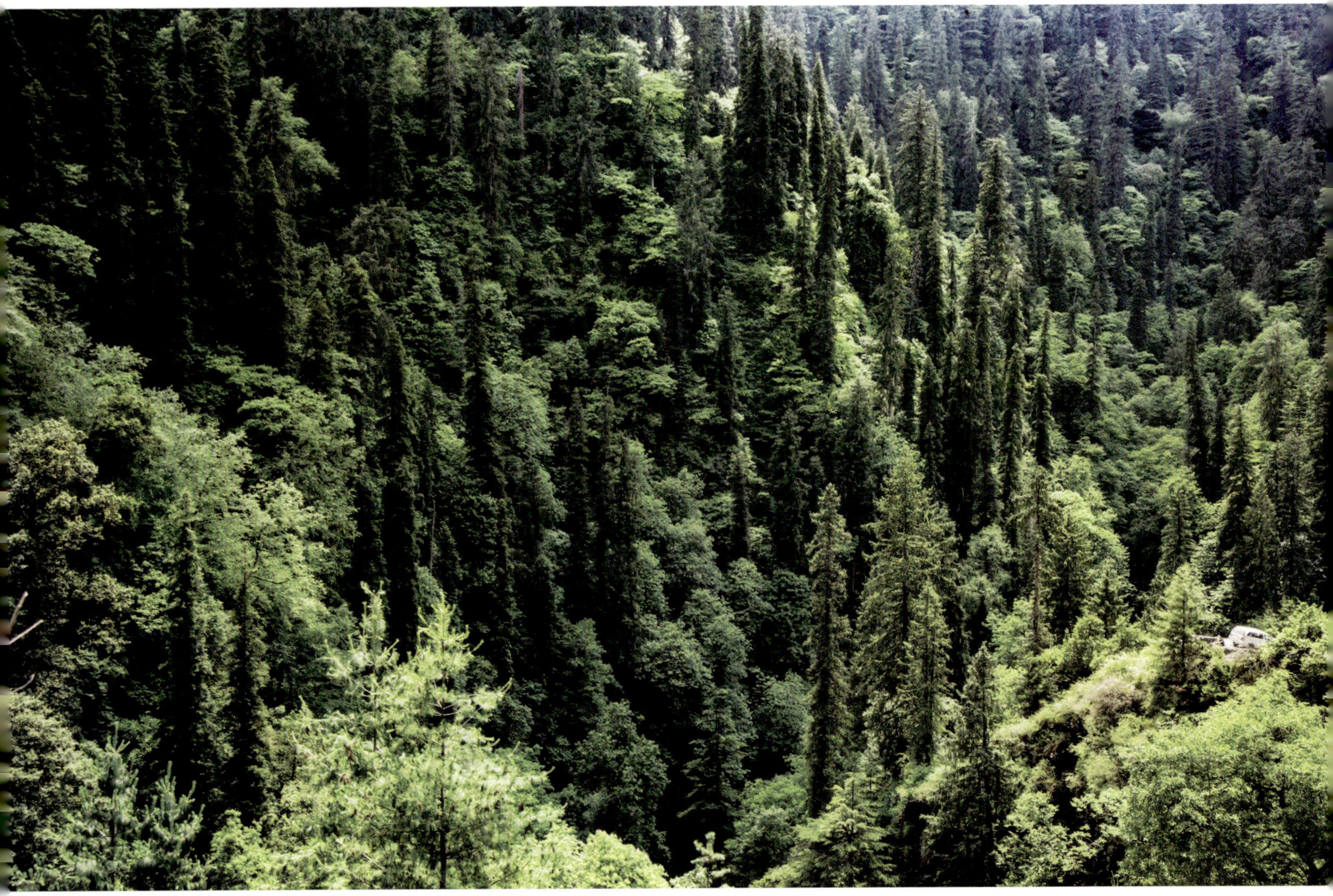

"

Those who have conquered themselves...live in peace, alike in cold and heat, pleasure and pain, praise and blame...To such people a clod of dirt, a stone, and gold are the same...Because they are Impartial, they rise to great heights.

~

A taxation so forced as not only to maintain a budgetary equilibrium but to yield as well large, continuous, progressive surpluses—even in years of trials and suffering—is, I submit, against all accepted canons of finance.

~

I think all fair-minded persons will have to admit that it is absolutely monstrous that a class of human beings, with bodies similar to our own, with brains that can think and with hearts that can feel, should be perpetually condemned to a low life of utter wretchedness, servitude, and mental and moral degradation, and that permanent barriers should be placed in their way so that it should be impossible for them ever to overcome them and improve their lot.

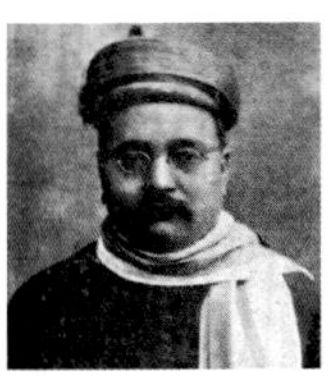

Gopal Krishna Gokhale (1866–1915) was one of the earliest freedom fighters of India. He was born in Maharashtra. He was one of the first political leaders to struggle for independence. He was a leader of the Indian National Congress. His views were mostly moderate. He also founded the Servants of India Society, which advocated expanding Indian education. His approach was two-points oriented: non-violence and reforms within existing government institutions.

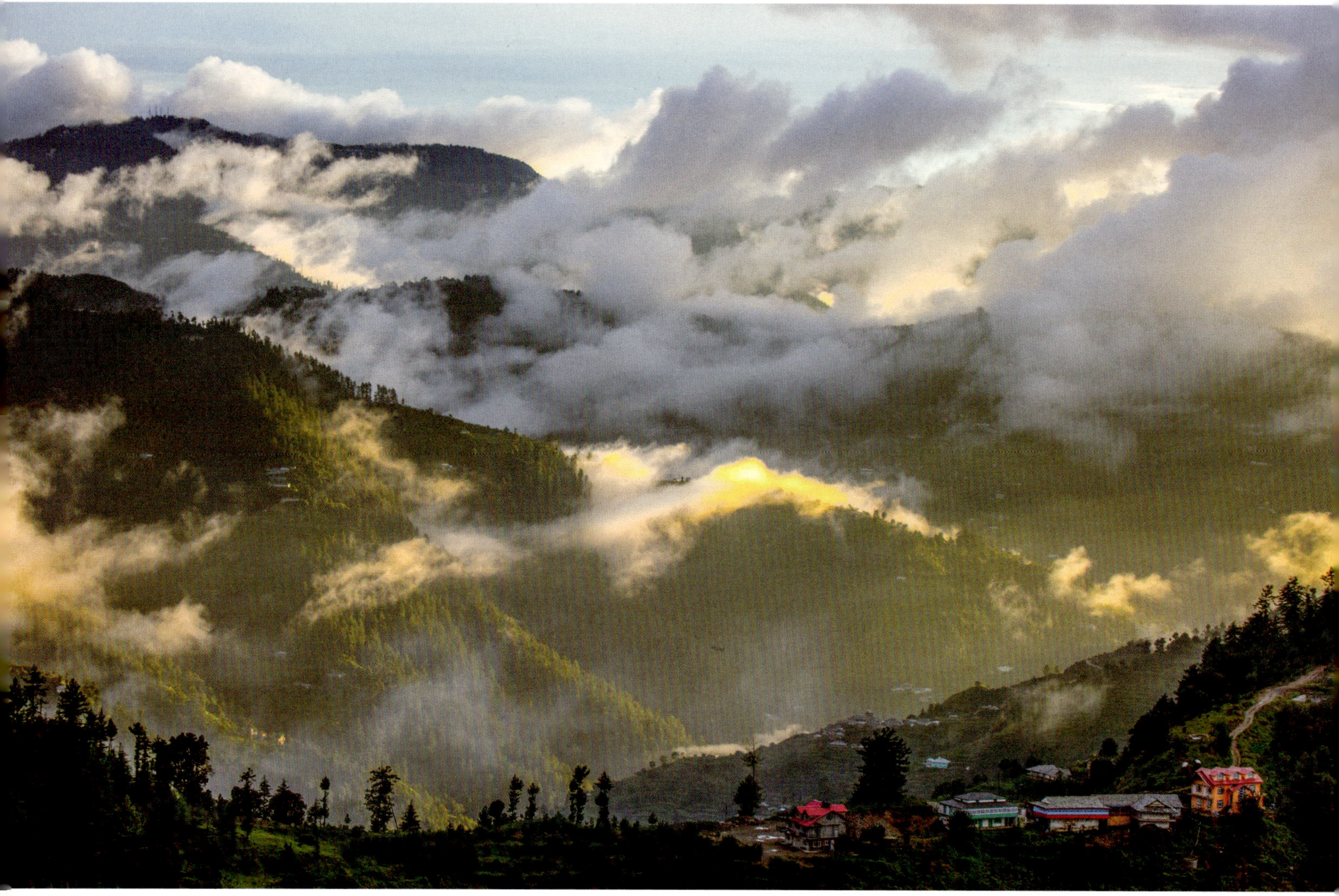

GURU GOBIND SINGH

Those who call me God will fall into the deep pit of hell.
Regard me as one of his slaves and have no doubt whatever about it.
I am a servant of the Supreme Being, and have come to behold the wonderful drama of life.

~

The greatest comforts and lasting peace are obtained when one eradicates selfishness from within.

~

Let no man in his error wrangle over differences in names.

~

Worship the one God who is the Lord of all.
Know that His form is one and He is the one light diffused in all.

~

I came into the world charged with the duty to uphold the right in every place,
to destroy sin and evil...the only reason I took birth was to see that r
ighteousness may flourish, that good may live, and tyrants be torn out by their roots.

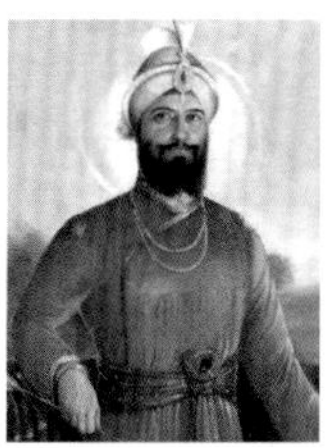

Guru Gobind Singh (1666–1708) was a spiritual figure and great thinker. He was the sole child of Tegh Bahadur, the 9th Sikh Guru, and was the last of the 10 Sikh Gurus. After his father's death, he became the head of the Sikhs at the early age of nine. He is believed to have introduced the concept of the Five Ks. Additionally, he created the Khalsa, the Sikhs responsible for all military, executive, and civil authority in the Sikh community. He completed the composition of the Guru Granth Sahib, a collection of hymns that describe the traits of God. Guru Gobind Singh affirmed the sacred text as his successor and passed on spiritual leadership to it.

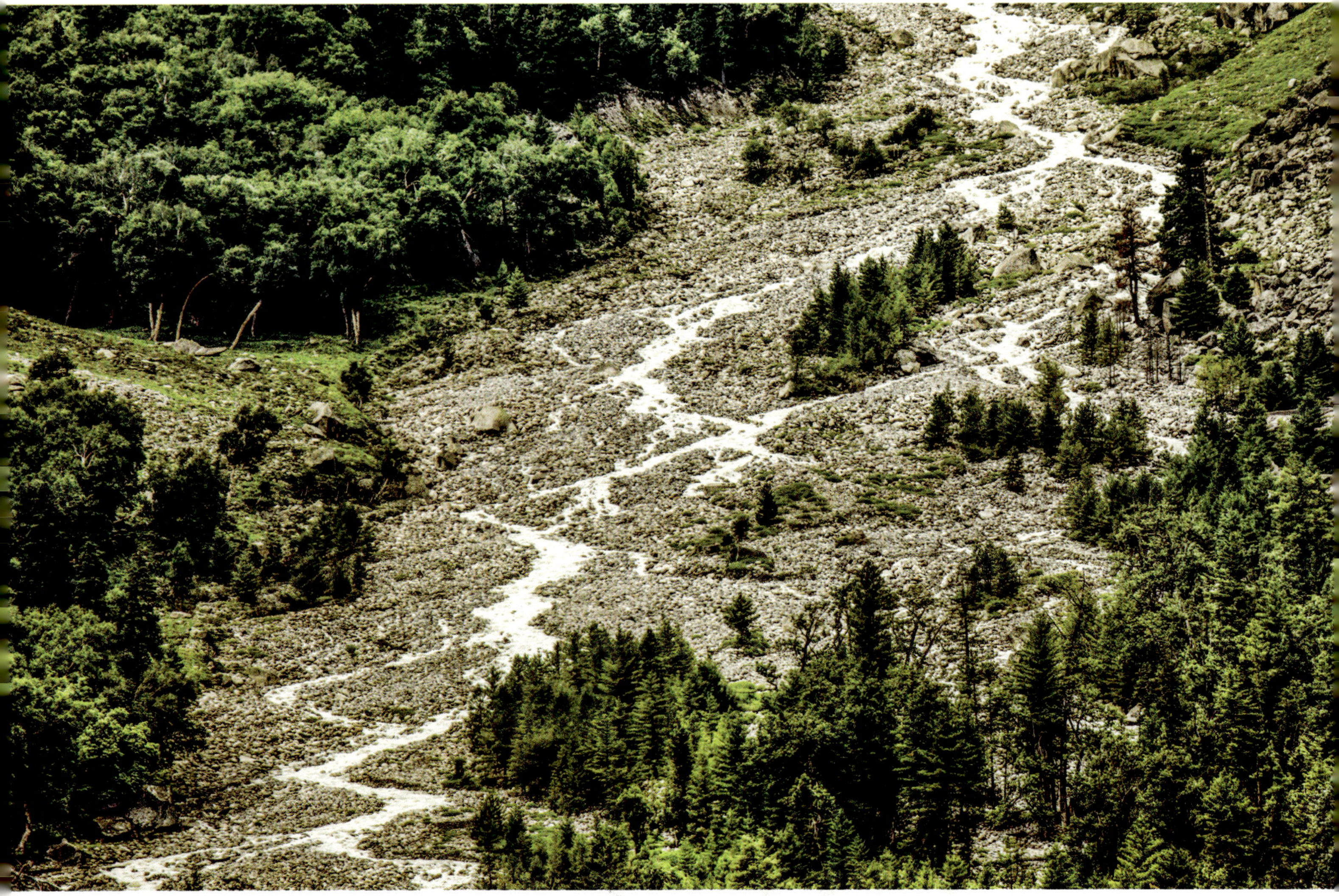

"

Even kings and emperors with heaps of wealth and vast dominion cannot
compare with an ant filled with the love of God.

~

Let no man in the world live in delusion. Without a Guru none can cross over to the other shore.

~

One cannot comprehend Him through reason, even if one reasoned for ages.

~

Whatever kind of seed is sown in a field, prepared in due season, a plant of that same kind,
marked with the peculiar qualities of the seed, springs up in it.

~

Sing the songs of joy to the Lord, serve the Name of the Lord, and become the servant of His servants.
I bow at His feet constantly, and pray to Him, the Guru, the True Guru, has shown me the Way.
Thou hast a thousand eyes and yet not one eye; thou host a thousand forms and
yet not one form. The world is a drama, staged in a dream.

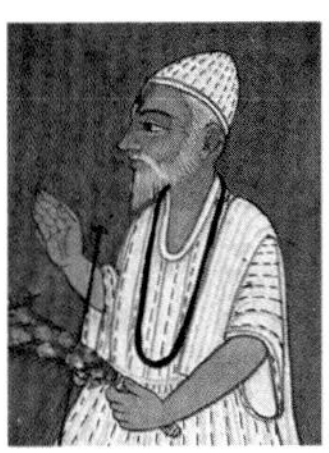

Guru Nanak (1469–1539). Guru Nanak was a saint who founded Sikhism, which emphasises the idea of the oneness of God, and was the first of the Sikh Gurus. His ideologies draw on both Hindu and Islamic thought, but are also unique. His strong spirituality surprised his family and they attempted to involve him in worldly affairs. Yet even an arranged marriage at a young age did not prevent Nanak from taking the spiritual path. Sikhism is the fifth-largest religion in the world, with approximately 30 million followers. He also established the system of the langar, or communal kitchen, to demonstrate the need to share and to encourage equality among all people.

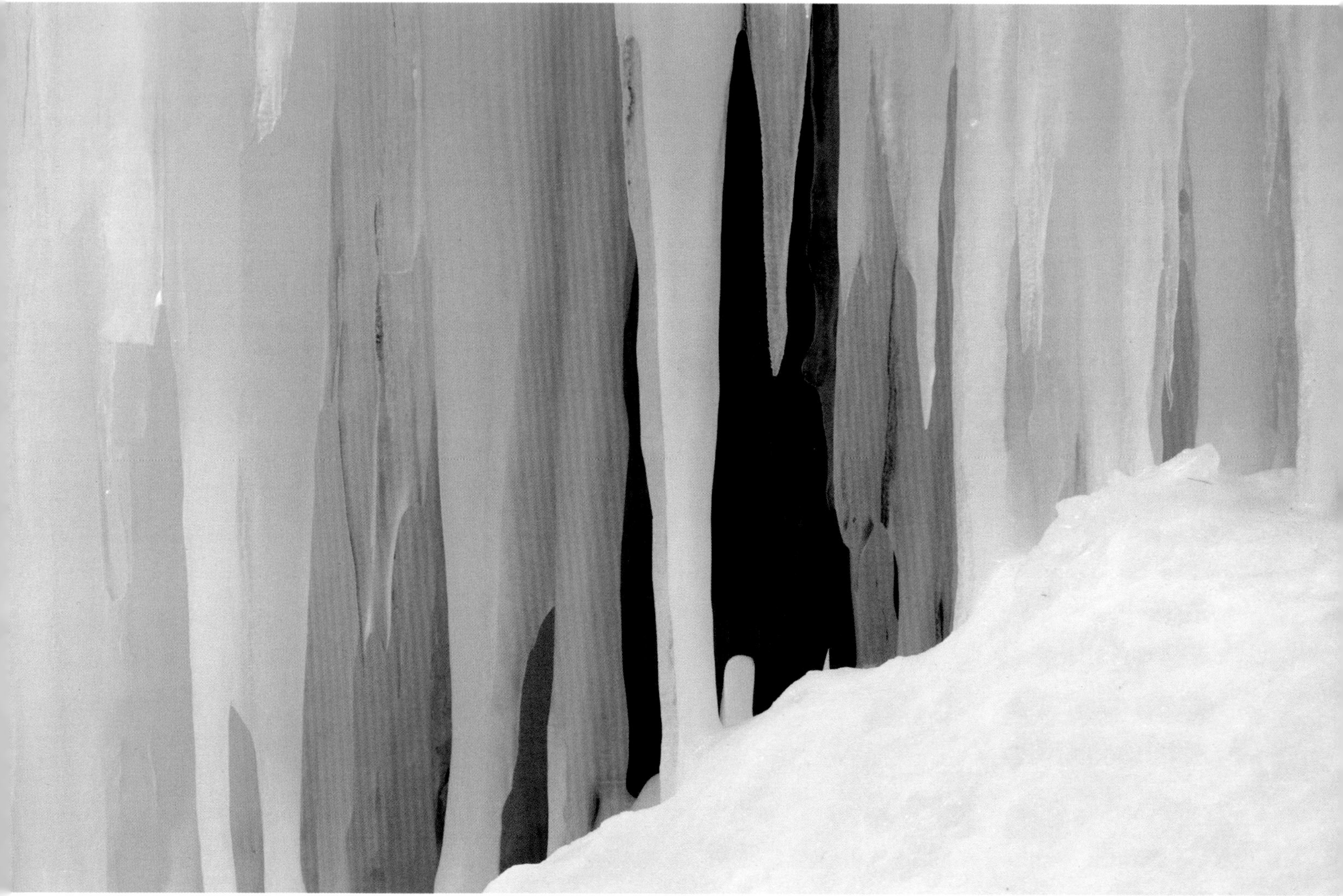

HARIVANSH RAI BACHCHAN

“

Look at the sky’s vastness, so many stars have broken away, so many loved ones,
it has lost the lost ones, were they ever found? But tell me, for the broken stars,
does the sky ever grieve? That which is past is gone.

~

There was a cup of wine in life, which you gave your heart and soul for when it broke, it did break.
Look at the wine house’s courtyard shaken, where many cups are fall,
and merge with the ground that which fall, do they ever rise?
But tell me, for broken cups does the winehouse ever regret?
That which is past is gone.

~

There may be huge, warm and shady trees all around,
don’t even as the shade of a single leaf,
walk on the Path of Fire, walk on the Path of Fire.
You will not stop, you will not turn, you will not halt, take this oath,
take this oath, take this oath, walk on the Path of Fire, walk on the Path of Fire.

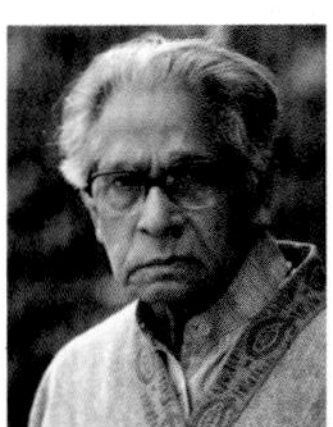

Harivansh Rai Bachchan (1907–2003) was born in Uttar Pradesh. He learned Urdu, as was the family tradition, to pursue a career in law; however, he changed his mind and taught English at Cambridge University. He was a noteworthy Hindi poet and belonged to the Nayi Kavita literary movement. He is best known for his book *Madhushala*. He later became more well known due to the fame of his son Amitabh Bachchan. In 1966 he joined the Rajya Sabha. He was awarded the Padma Vibhushan, a prestigious civilian award given for contribution to society.

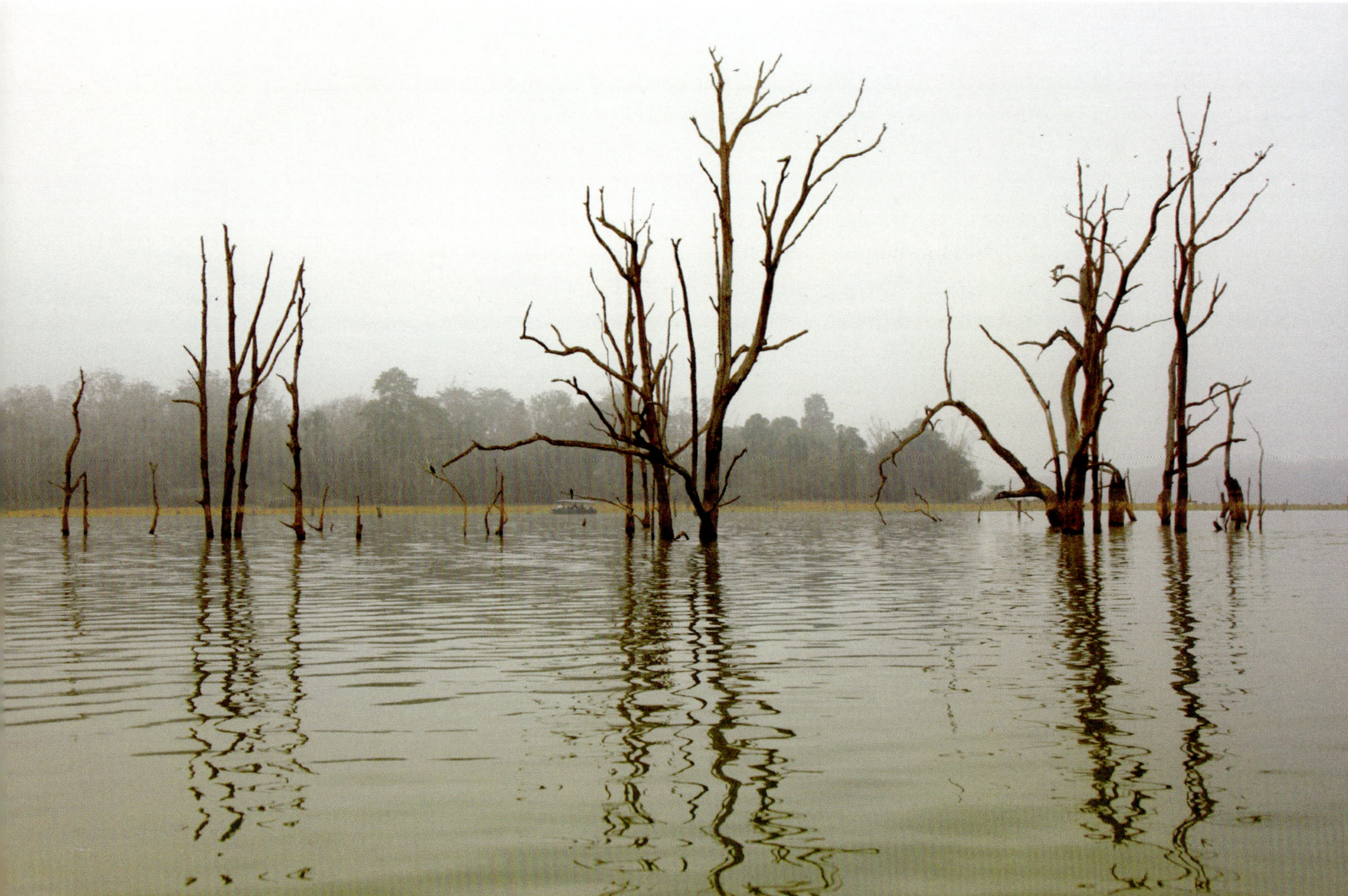

“

I know quite clearly what I want out of my life. Life and my emotions are the only things I am conscious of. I love the consciousness of life and I want as much of it as I can get. But the span of one's life is limited. What comes after death no one knows. Nor do I care. Since, therefore, I cannot increase the content of life by increasing its duration, I will increase it by increasing its intensity. Art, music, poetry and everything else...I do have this one purpose—increasing the intensity of my consciousness of life.

~

I seriously say to you that business or a job as an engineer is not the thing for me.
It is totally foreign to my nature and radically opposed to my temperament and opinions.
Physics is my line. I know I shall do great things here. For, each man can do best and excel in only that thing of which he is passionately fond, in which he believes,
as I do, that he has the ability to do it, that he is in fact born and destined to do it...
I am burning with a desire to do physics. I will and must do it sometime.
It is my only ambition. I have no desire to be a “successful” man or the head of a big firm.
There are intelligent people who like that and let them do it.

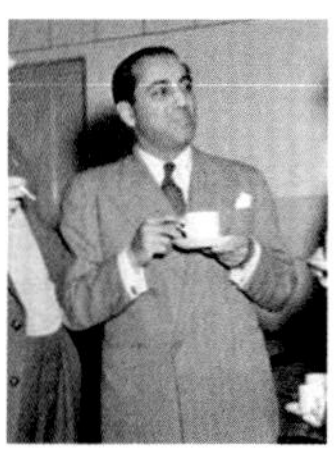

Homi J. Bhabha (1909–1966). Homi J. Bhabha was an Indian nuclear scientist and physicist, and contributed to research on quantum theory. He was from a wealthy, influential Parsi family, and was related to Sir Dorabji Tata. He was the founding director of Tata Institute of Fundamental Research (TIFR). From childhood, he was an intelligent and hardworking student. He is called the “father of the Indian nuclear programme.” After attaining much fame abroad he came back to India in 1940. Because of his prominence, devotion, and comradeship with Prime Minister Nehru, he was able to procure resources for scientific research. He promoted nuclear control and also worldwide prohibition of atomic bombs. He was opposed to making bombs and was in favour of using nuclear power for peaceful ends.

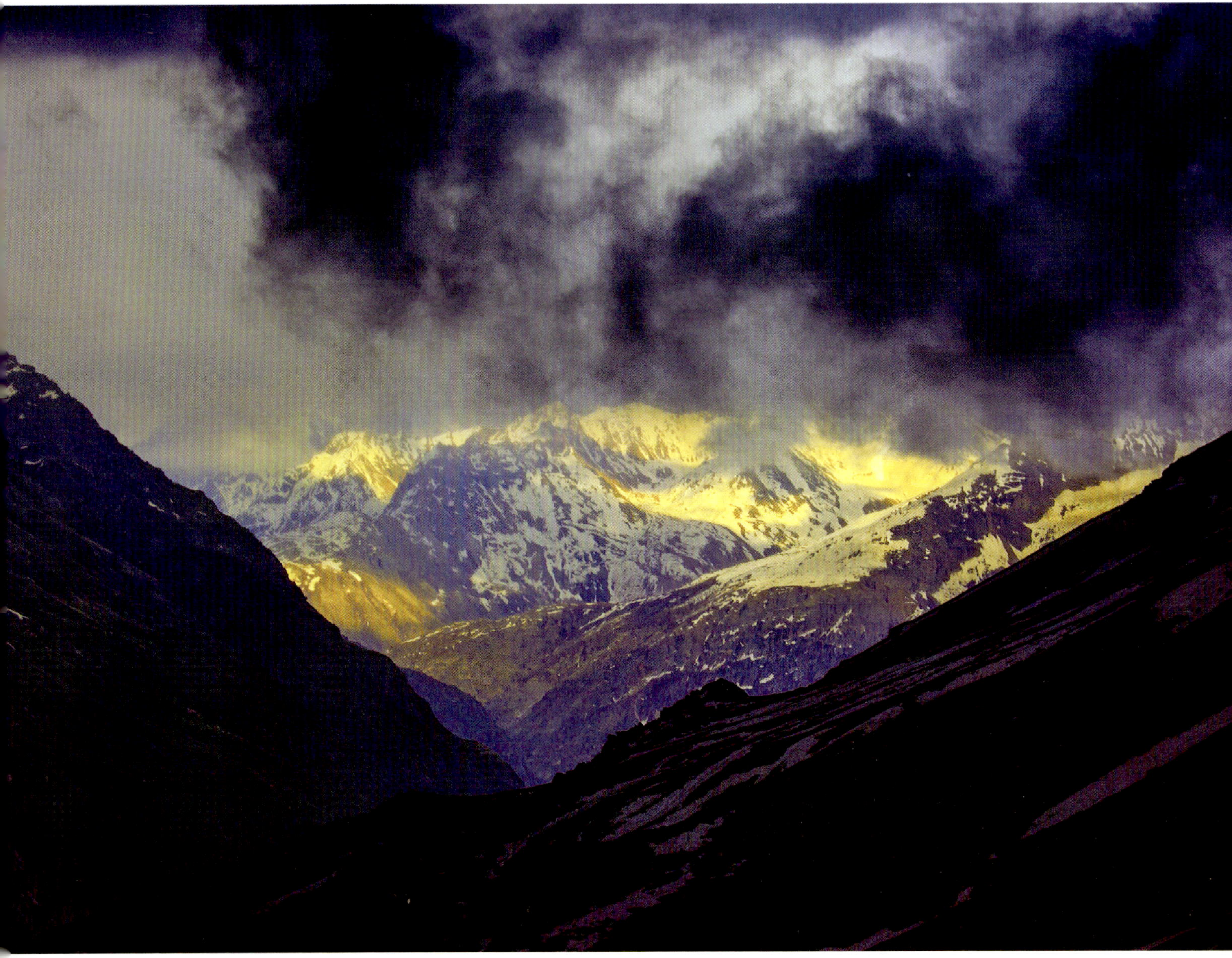

"

We live in a wonderful world that is full of beauty, charm and adventure. There is no end to the adventures that we can have if only we seek them with our eyes open.

~

Life is like a game of cards. The hand you are dealt is determinism; the way you play it is free will.

~

The person who talks most of his own virtue is often the least virtuous.

~

The only alternative to coexistence is codestruction.

~

Culture is the widening of the mind and of the spirit.

~

Socialism is...not only a way of life,
but a certain scientific approach to social and economic problems.

~

Loyal and efficient work in a great cause,
even though it may not be immediately recognised, ultimately bears fruit.

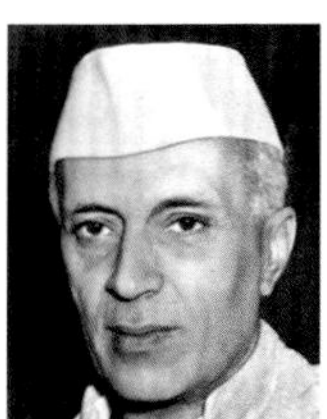

Jawaharlal Nehru (1889–1964). He served as the first prime minister of India and, both before and after independence in 1947, was pivotal in Indian politics. From an early age he was a firm nationalist. He graduated from Trinity College, Cambridge. Under Gandhi's patronage, he became an important leader of the Indian independence movement. He was the architect of the modern Indian nation state: a sovereign, socialist, secular, and democratic republic. He loved the company of children and was fondly called Chacha Nehru (Uncle Nehru).

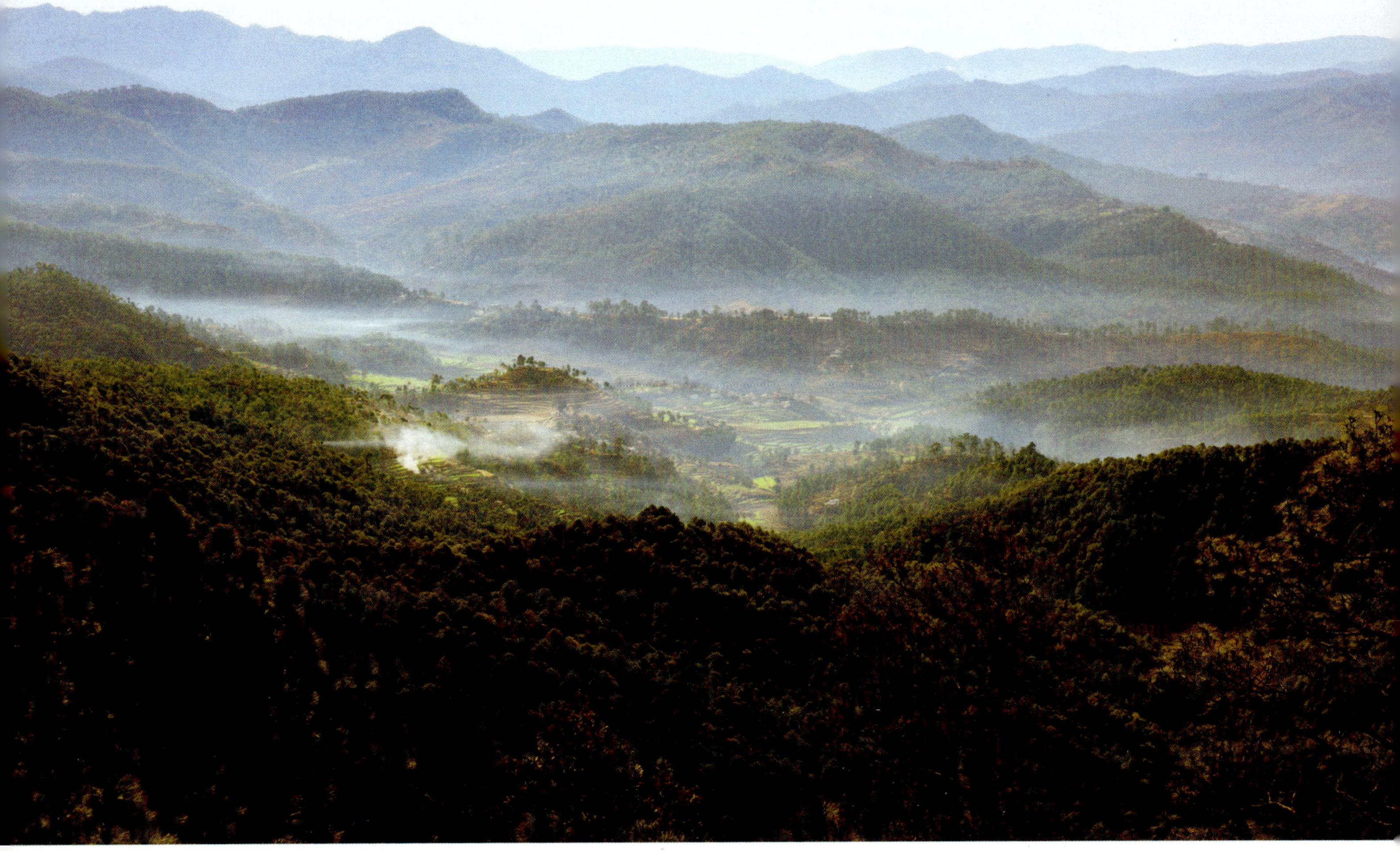

It is no measure of health to be well adjusted to a profoundly sick society.

~

The ability to observe without evaluating is the highest form of intelligence.

~

Tell your friend that in his death, a part of you dies and goes with him. Wherever he goes, you also go. He will not be alone.

~

One is never afraid of the unknown; one is afraid of the known coming to an end.

~

Governments want efficient technicians, not human beings, because human beings become dangerous to governments—and to organised religions as well. That is why governments and religious organisations seek to control education.

~

The constant assertion of belief is an indication of fear.

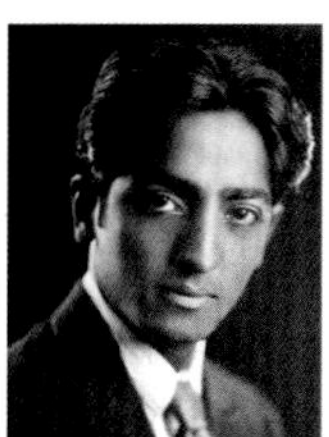

Jiddu Krishnamurti (1895–1986) was a well-known writer and speaker on many matters that related to humankind and the development of its intellect. He was adopted by Dr Annie Besant. He was a free-minded personality who believed in intellectual freedom. He wrote on wide-ranging spiritual subjects. His works are characterised by simplicity and straightforwardness of language; they aimed to revolutionise the psyche of individuals. He emphasised that such a change cannot come from outside but must come from within.

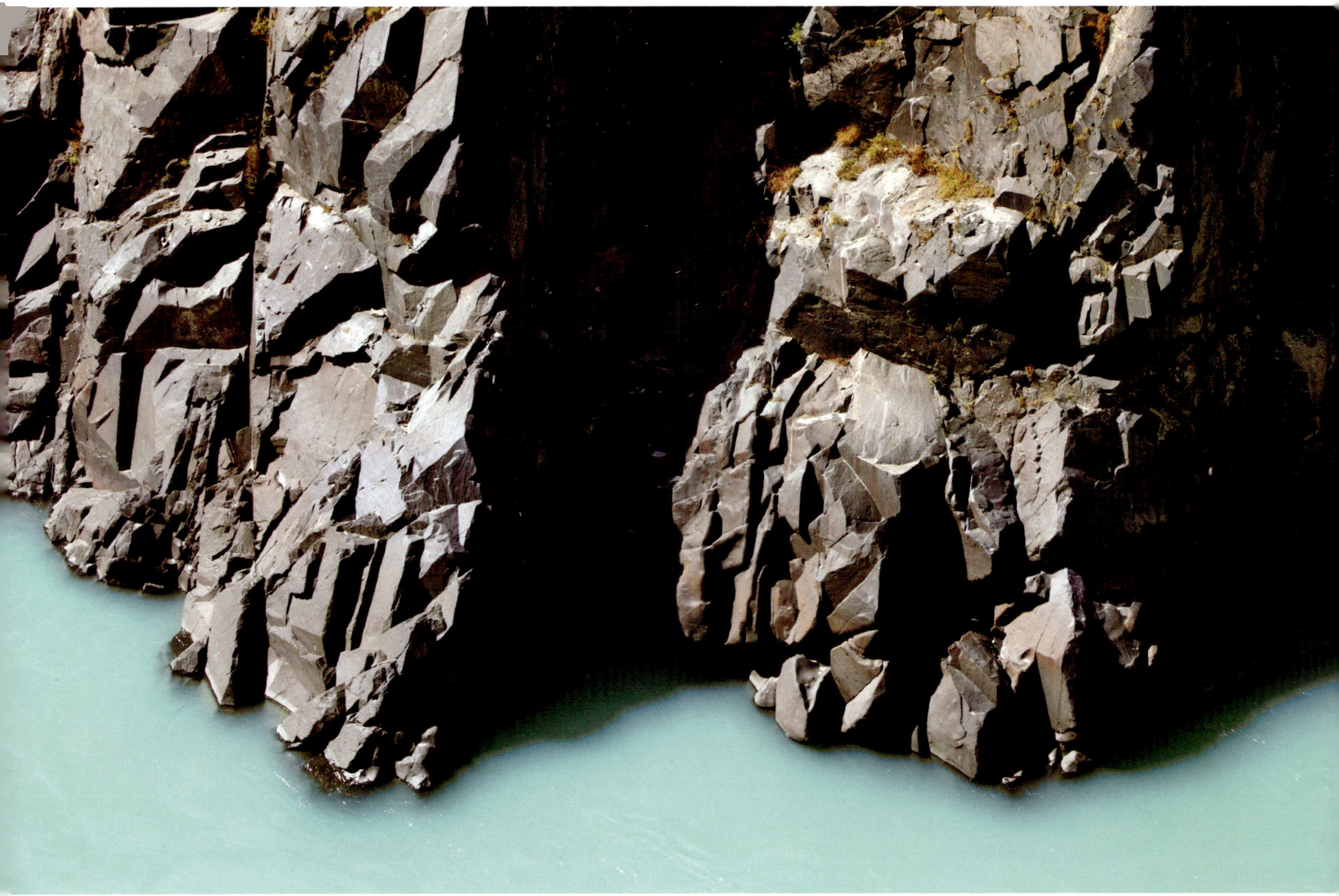

JAMSETJI N. TATA

“

There is one kind of charity common enough among us...It is that patchwork philanthropy which clothes the ragged, feeds the poor, and heals the sick. I am far from decrying the noble spirit which seeks to help a poor or suffering fellow being...

~

Be sure to lay wide streets planted with shady trees, every other of a quick-growing variety. Be sure that there is plenty of space for lawns and gardens. Reserve large areas for football, hockey and parks. Earmark areas for Hindu temples, Mohammedan mosques and Christian churches.

~

Freedom without the strength to support it and, if need be, defend it, would be a cruel delusion. And the strength to defend freedom can itself only come from widespread industrialisation and the infusion of modern science and technology into the country's economic life.

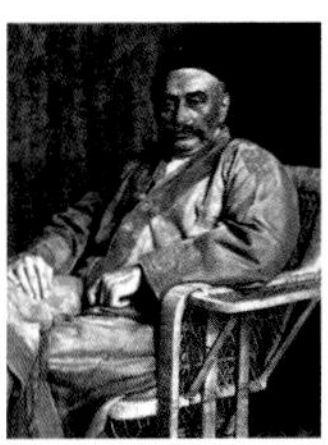

Jamsetji N. Tata (1839–1904). He was charismatic and had a keen business sense. He began his business career at a young age, and his enthusiasm helped him to succeed. As an entrepreneur he is lauded for his groundbreaking work in the Indian industry. After working with his father till the age of 29, he branched out to establish several cotton mills. He always emphasised the importance of the working environment and the welfare of the employees. The foundations laid by him and the hard work of his descendants made each of his key ideas a reality. Today, Tata Group is one of the largest and most prominent companies in the world. Jamsetji Tata was called the “Father of Indian Industry”.

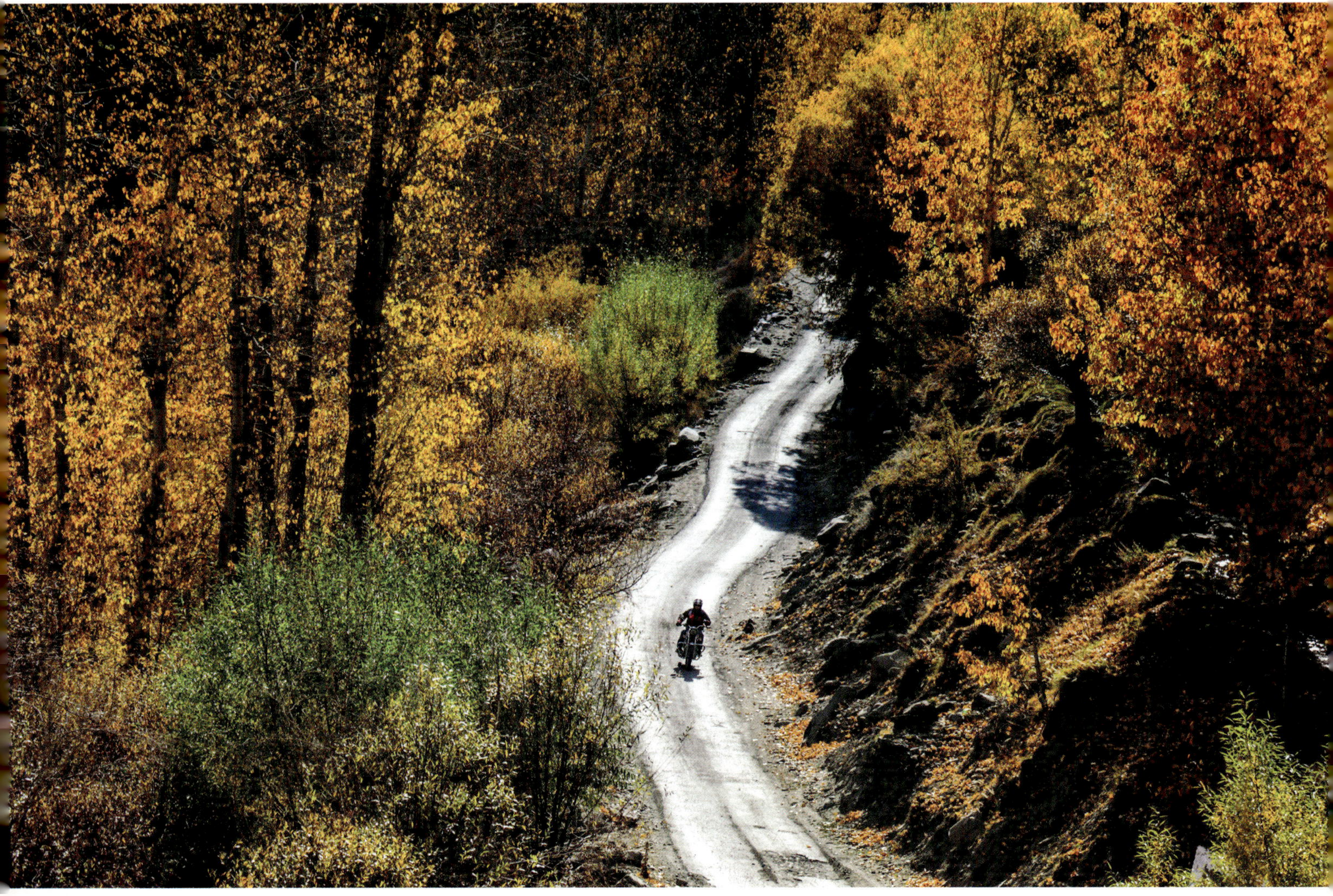

“

All men and women should live together on this earth as one family, with honesty and without discrimination, no matter to which village, province, country, continent or religious beliefs they adhere to.

~

The Creator created man to be independent and capable of enjoying equal rights as others. The Creator has given freedom to all men and women to express themselves freely, but without causing harm on account of their thoughts or views. This is known as true (righteous) conduct.

~

The Creator has endowed everyone with human rights. Hence it follows that an individual or a group cannot dominate another. To follow this principle is to practise righteous conduct.

~

The Creator has given all men and women religious and political freedom. One who does not harm another in any way and does not usurp another's rights is a practitioner of righteous conduct.

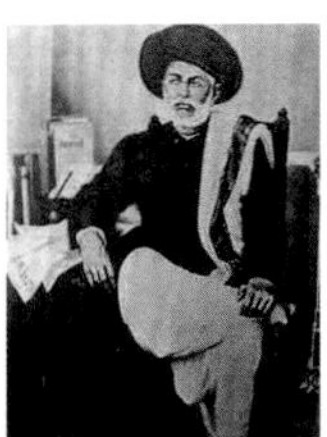

Jyotirao G. Phule (1827–1890). He was a significant social reformer. He led the operation against caste restrictions in Indian society. He then started a campaign of serving people of lower castes, who were deprived of all their rights as human beings. He opened schools for girls. He founded the Satya Shodhak Samaj, the purpose of which was to liberate peasants from the suppression of Brahmins. He and his wife, Savitribai Phule, were pioneers of women's education in India. He refused to regard the Vedas as sacrosanct and advocated the spread of rational thinking.

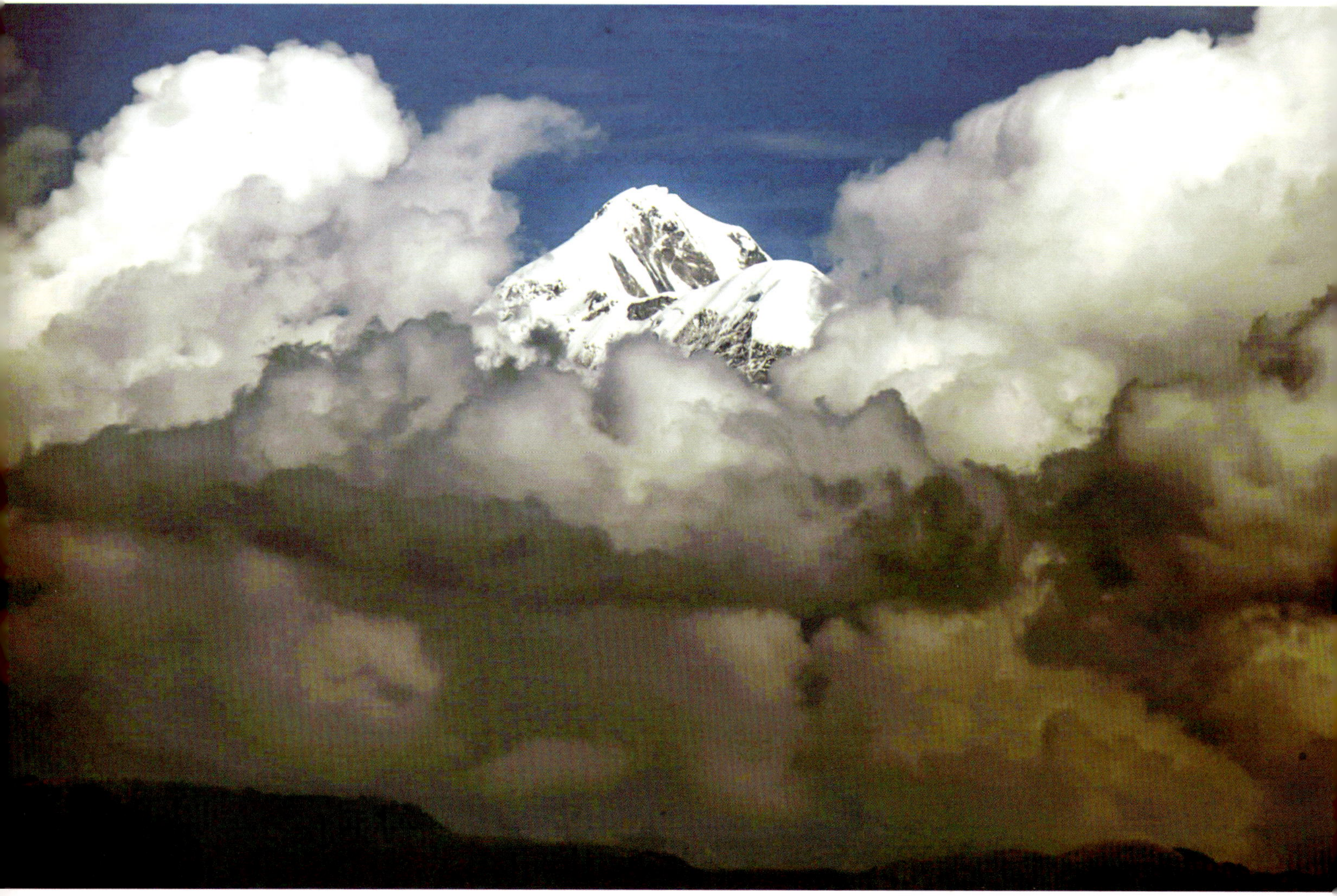

"

If you want the truth, I'll tell you the truth:
Listen to the secret sound, the real sound, which is inside you.

~

Love is not grown on trees or bought in the market, but if one wants to be loved one must first know how to give (unconditional) love.

~

The Lord is in me, the Lord is in you, as life is in every seed,
put false pride away and seek the Lord within.

~

The Kazi is searching the words of the Koran, and instructing others:
but if his heart be not steeped in that love, what does it avail, though he be a teacher of men?

~

So long as man clamours for the I and Mine, his works are as naught: When all love of the I and the Mine is dead, then the work of the Lord is done.

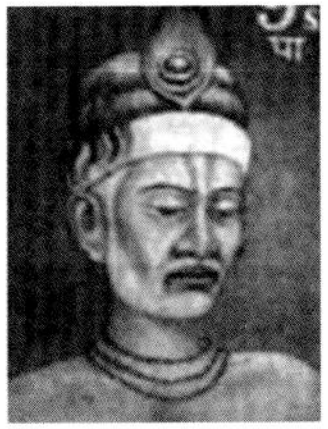

Kabir (1440–1518) stands among the greatest poets of the world, let alone of India. He is quoted most frequently and ranks with Tulsidas, who is called the Shakespeare of India. Despite criticising each sect of faith, he is respected and revered by all. He left an enormous impact on Indian philosophy and Hindi poetry. His birth and death are surrounded by myths and legends. There are conjectures about him and his origins. Some believe he was the son of a Muslim weaver, while others believe he was the son of a Brahmin widow and adopted by a childless couple. He was dear to both Hindus and Muslims alike. In Maghar, his tomb and samadhi stand side by side.

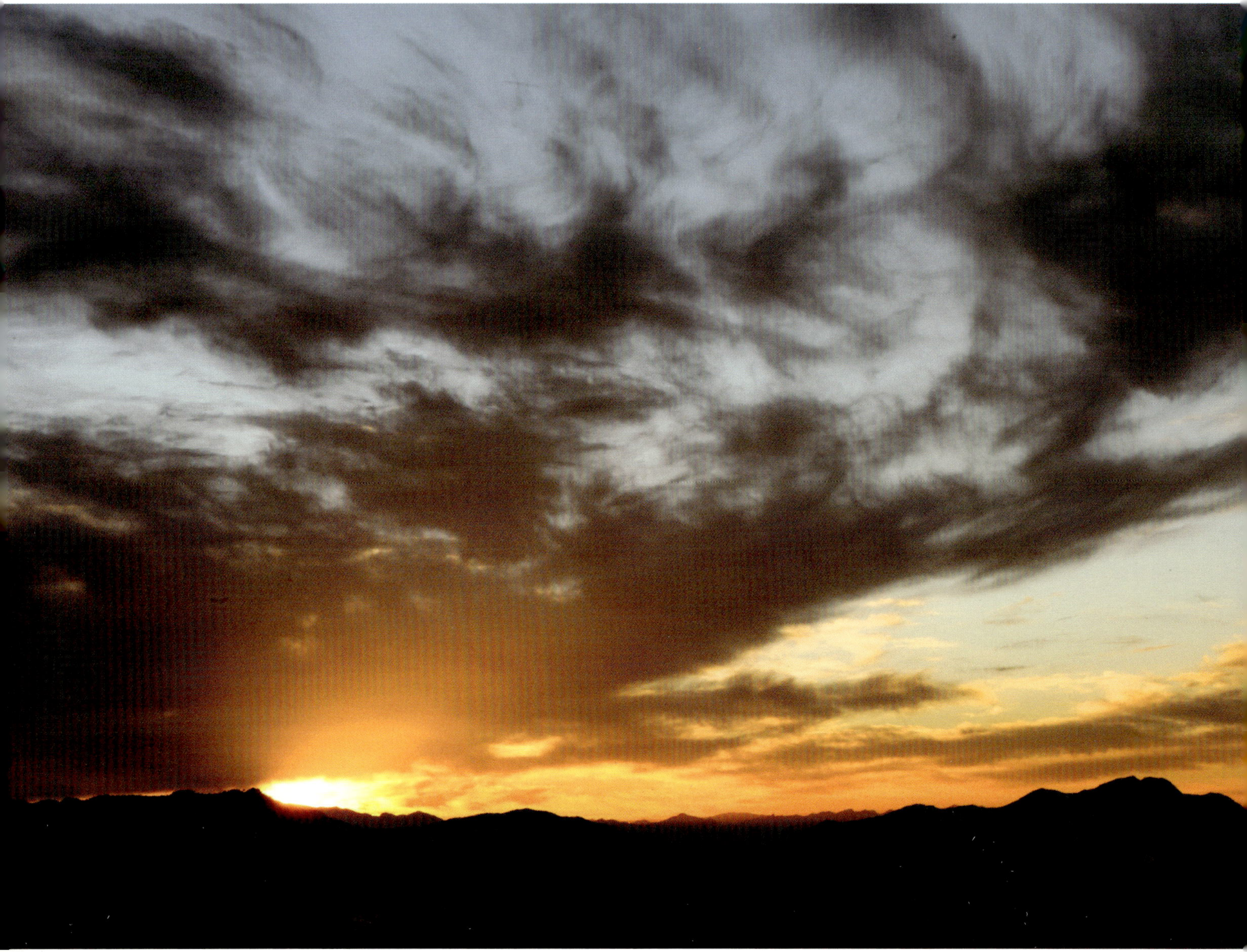

"

Flowers continuously bloom and die, just like love.

~

Love is that to life what wind is to a windmill.

~

Love gives eyes to see what the eye without love cannot see.
Be luminous. Don't adapt yourself to the circumstances around you, but change them to be better.
Always take your sunshine wherever you go.

~

Those who happily leave everything in Allah's hand will eventually see Allah's hand in everything.
Because worry ends where faith begins.

~

Who can destroy iron but its own rust, and who can destroy a person but his own mind?

~

Be content with what Allah has given you, and you will be among the richest of people.

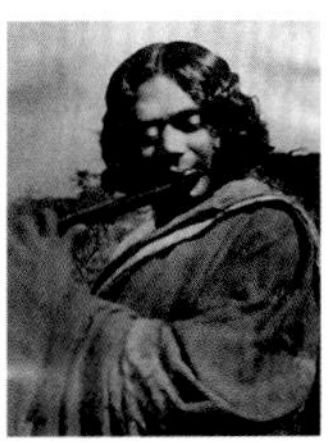

Kazi Nazrul Islam (1899–1976) is known to the public as Nazrul. He hailed from Bengal (now Bangladesh) and was a well-known musician, writer, and revolutionary. Initially he received praise for his poetry collections, but later the British Empire detected a sense of hostility and rebellion in his writings, for which he was jailed. He protested fascism and oppression of all forms and was for spiritual freedom. For his multifaceted work, he earned the title of "Rebel Poet". He has as large a following in India as in Bangladesh. Opposed to bigotry in all forms, he focused on themes of love, freedom and revolution.

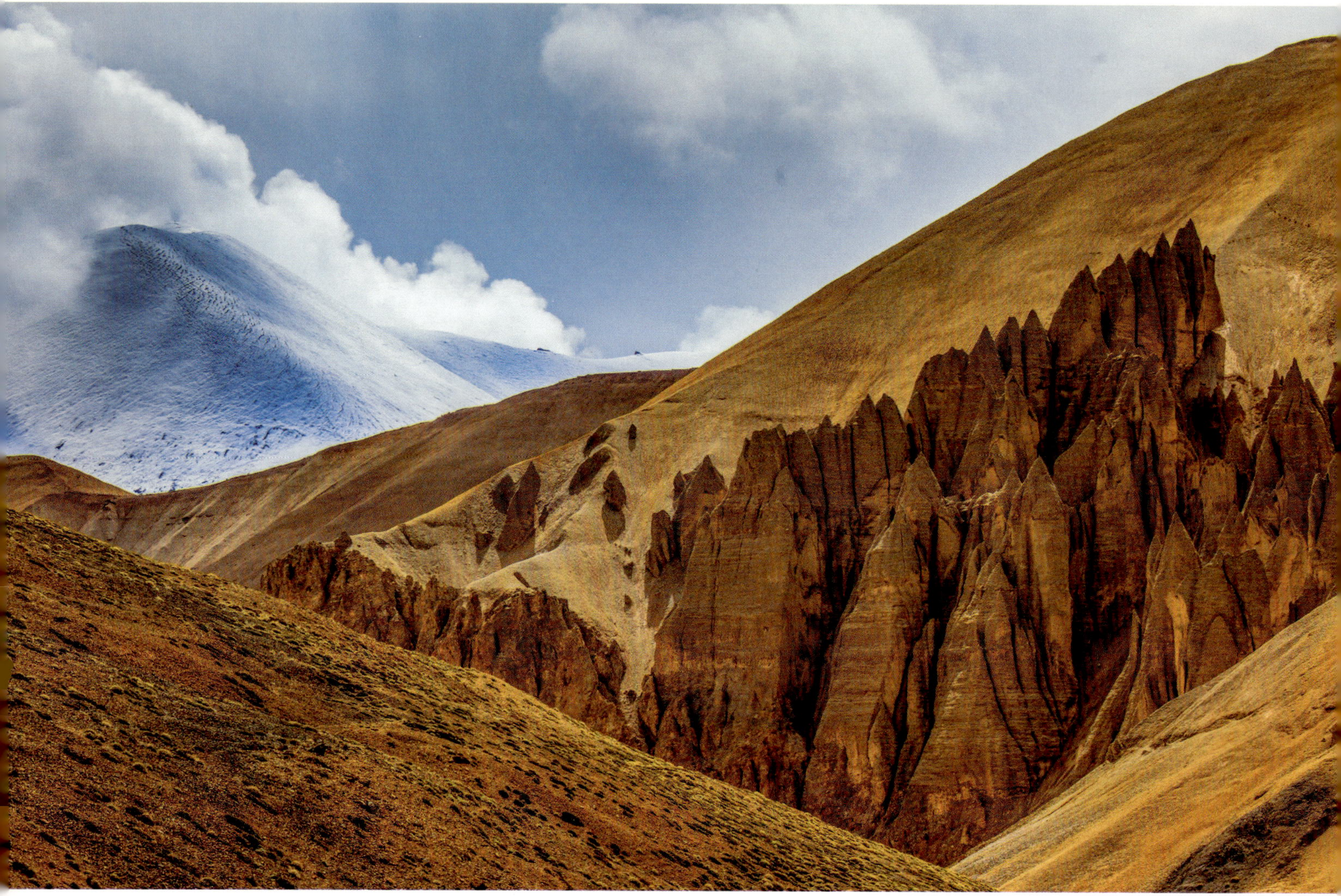

"

Let individual liberty be recognised: let individual rights be fully vindicated and respected; but still at the same time, while we recognise differences of opinion, let us feel, and let us declare, that it is possible to have a common platform of action where we can exchange our sympathies with each other as brethren.

~

The truths which are represented in England and Western countries generally are those which refer to force of character, earnestness of purpose, conscientious strictness, noble charity, practical duty, whilst the truths which I find peculiarly developed in India—developed to a greater extent than anywhere else—and in the Eastern countries generally, are those which have reference to sweetness of communion, sweetness of temper, meekness and resignation unto God.

~

Her (India's) great curse is caste; but English education has already proved a tremendous power in levelling the injurious distinctions of caste.

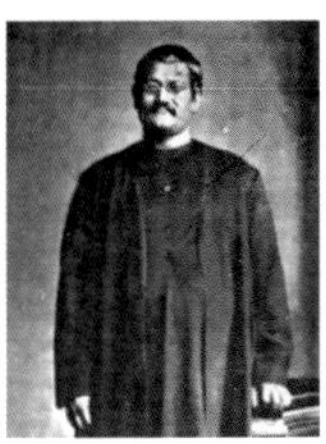

Keshub Chandra Sen (1838–1884). He was born in Calcutta. He was a great Hindu philosopher who tried to blend Christian and Hindu thought. At the tender age of 19 he joined Brahmo Samaj (Society of God). The main aim of this society was to put a new vigour in the Hindu faith and revitalise it. To achieve this large task, he felt that the help of Christian doctrines was essential, and he did everything to achieve this goal for the betterment of Hinduism, which was facing an onslaught by the British government. He launched several radical reforms such as the giving up of caste names, advocating inter-caste marriage, and denouncing child marriage. He was responsible for the passage of the Native Marriage Act, legalising the Brahmo Samaj marriages and fixing the minimum marriageable age for boys and girls.

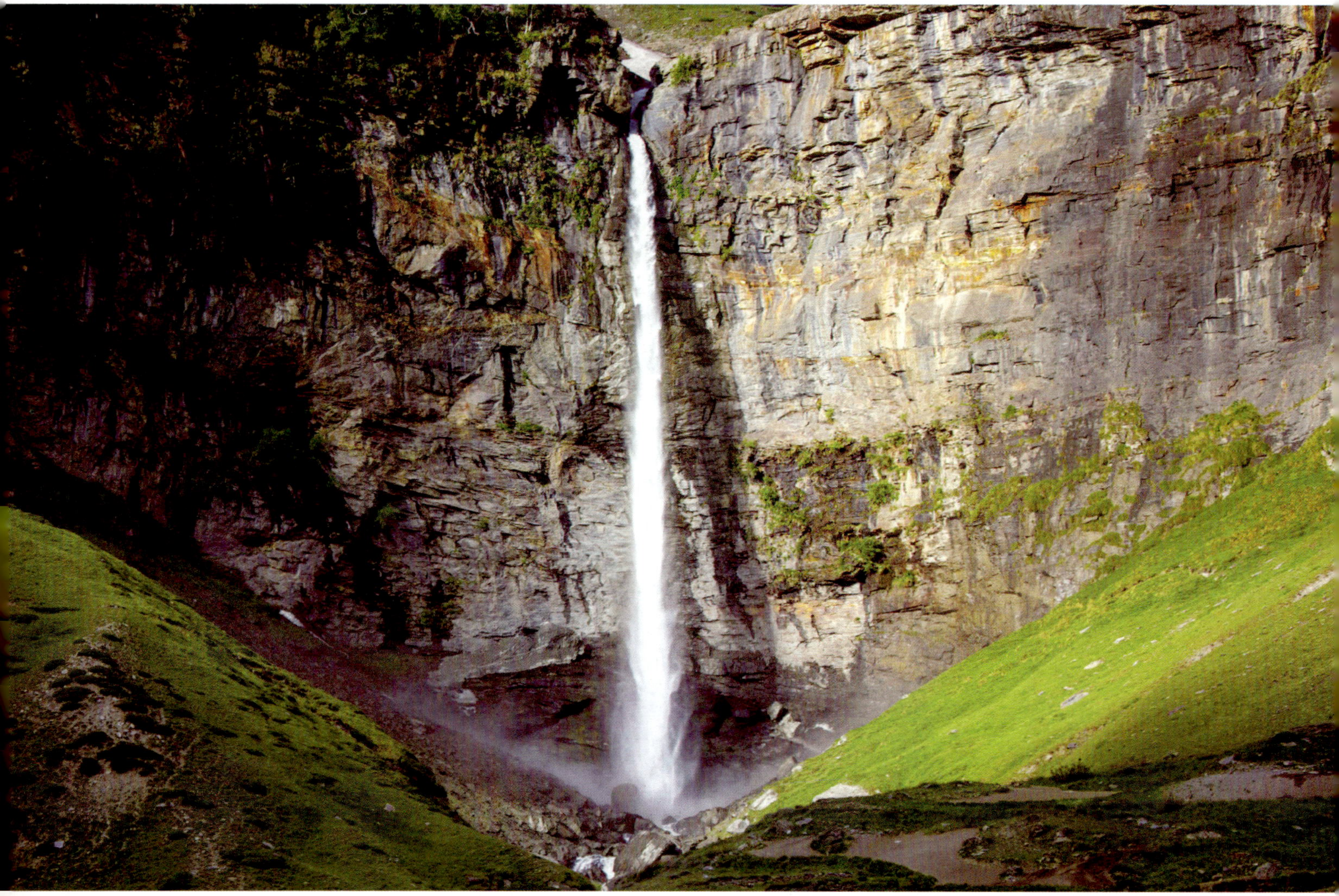

LAL BAHADUR SHASTRI

“

We believe in peace and peaceful development,
not only for ourselves but for people all over the world.

~

The basic idea of governance, as I see it, is to hold the society together
so that it can develop and march towards certain goals.

~

India will have to hang down her head in shame if
even one person is left who is said in any way to be untouchable.

~

We all have to work in our respective spheres with the same dedication, the same zeal and the same determination which inspired and motivated the warrior on the battle front.
And this has to be shown not by mere words, but by actual deeds.

~

Among the major tasks before us none is of greater importance for our strength and stability than the task of building up the unity and solidarity of our people.

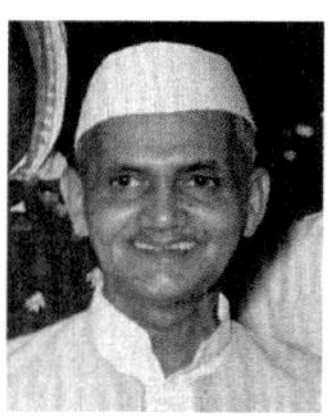

Lal Bahadur Shastri (1904–1966). He took over as prime minister of India in 1964 after the death of Jawaharlal Nehru. He played an important role as a freedom fighter and was a prominent leader in the Indian National Congress. He was a deep and ardent follower of Gandhiji and became his loyal subordinate. On the death of Gandhiji he turned all his loyalty to Nehru, won his confidence and turned into a trusted lieutenant. He was chosen as prime minister as he too was a believer in Nehru's socialism. He proved his mettle during the Indo-Pakistan war in 1965, during which his slogan of "Jai Jawan, Jai Kisan" (Hail the Soldier, Hail the Farmer) became very well known and till date is remembered.

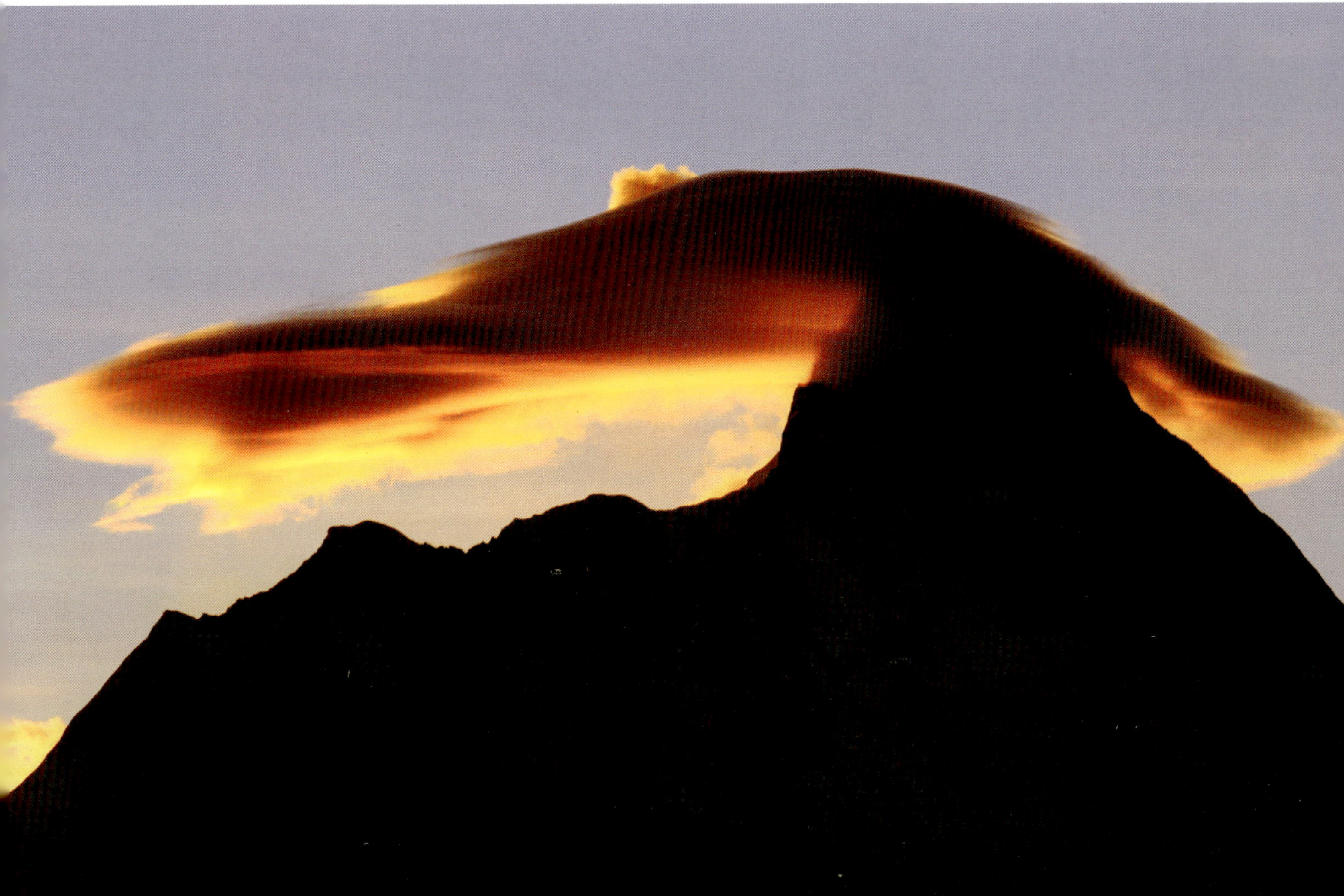

"

Science is the result of and the instrument for acquiring more and more knowledge, which enables man to outgrow progressively the limitations set to the development of his mind and spirit by old ideas, ideals and notions which resulted from the primitive ignorance of humanity in its infancy.

~

The renaissance is a rebirth of man. Man must remember that everything that exists in society was created by men who preceded him, and it was created for the progress and happiness of mankind. Confronted with social institutions or political organisations which are antagonistic to the progress and happiness of mankind, which bind men instead of liberate them, man must feel the necessity of breaking those bonds, so that he can make further progress. But in order to have the confidence that he can do that, man must remember himself. That is the rebirth of man as man. Men have been either slaves of gods or the servants of kings or of the best devotees of some religion. But man must be man for himself, if he wants to work his own salvation.

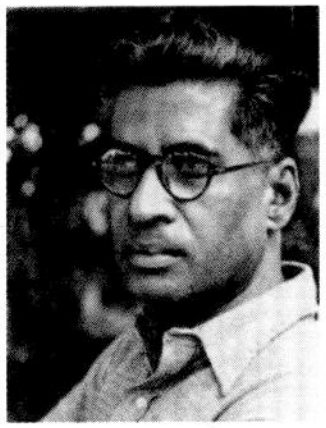

M.N. Roy (1887–1954), though he began his career as a political activist for the freedom of India, eventually was recognised as a 20th-century philosopher with leftist leanings. He left India in 1915 to gather arms for the struggle but did not succeed in the mission. In 1916 he landed in the USA and there developed friendships with some radical Americans. He changed his course mid-stream when, instead of fighting socialism, he turned in its favour. He met Lenin, the prominent Russian leader, and became an ardent Communist leader. He returned to India in 1930 and was sentenced to six years for his anti-national role in the Kanpur Communist Conspiracy Case.

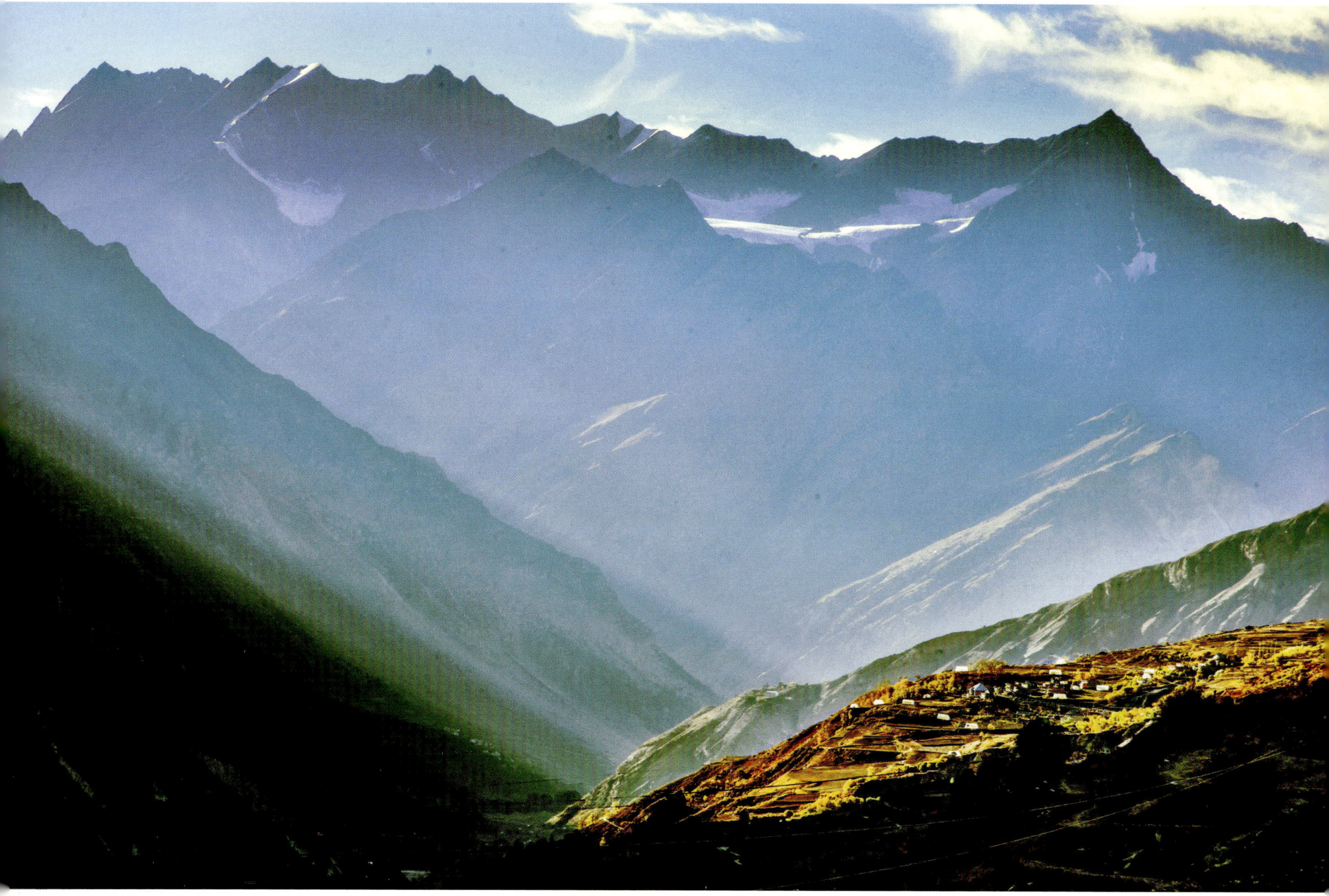

"

All breathing, existing, living, sentient creatures should not be slain, nor treated with violence, nor abused, nor tormented, nor driven away.

~

Kill not, cause no pain. Non-violence is the greatest religion.

~

A living body is not merely an integration of limbs and flesh, but the abode of the soul which potentially has perfect perception.

~

Anger begets more anger, and forgiveness and love lead to more forgiveness and love.

~

Start the practice of self-control with some penance; begin with fasting.

~

One who neglects or disregards the existence of earth, air, fire, water and vegetation disregards his own existence, which is entwined with them.

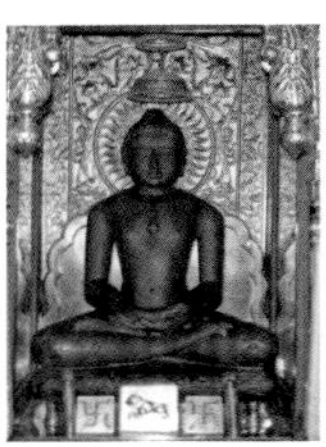

Mahavira (599–527 BC) was an Indian philosopher and one of the most crucial figures of Jainism. He was the 24th and final *tirthankara* of the religion. He was born into a royal family of Kshatriyas in what is now Bihar. Since he was the son of a king he was raised in luxury. As time passed he realised that his luxurious life did not provide him any satisfaction and at the age of 30 he gave up all his worldly ties and began a search for spiritual truth. He underwent severe penance for over 12 years, after which he attained *kevala jnana*, the highest stage of perception. He established the rules of religious life for Jain monks and nuns. He preached non-violence under all circumstances and his teachings strongly influenced several great personalities like Mahatma Gandhi and Rabindranath Tagore.

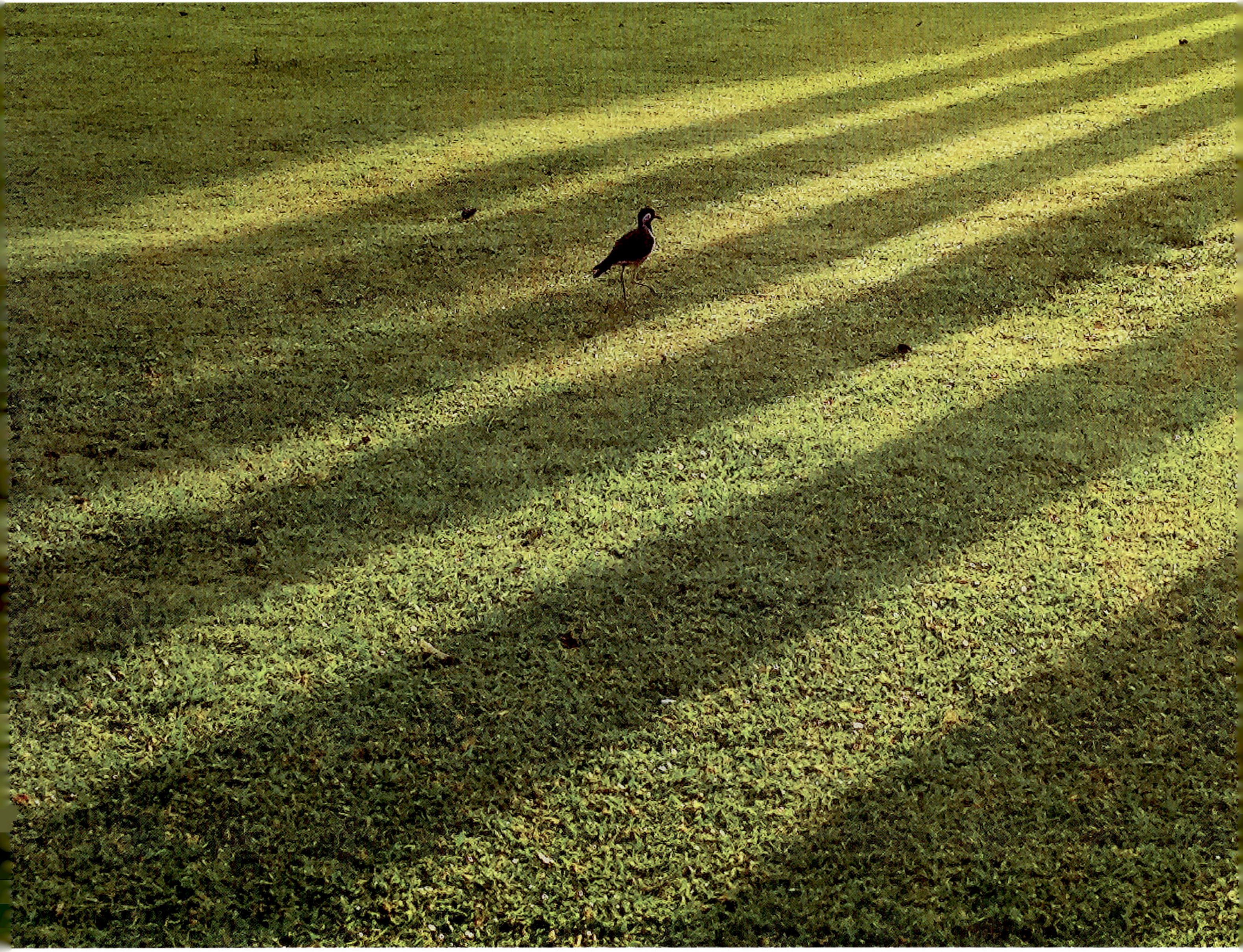

Slavery is the worst even if it bears beautiful names.

~

Education imparted by heart can bring revolution in society.

~

I am proud of being an Indian. I am a part of the indivisible unity that is Indian nationality. I am indispensable to this noble edifice, and without me this splendid structure of India is incomplete. I am an essential element which has gone to build India. I can never surrender this claim.

~

To succeed in your mission you must have single-minded devotion to your goal.

~

The light of knowledge is strong enough to brighten the darkest recesses of humanity.

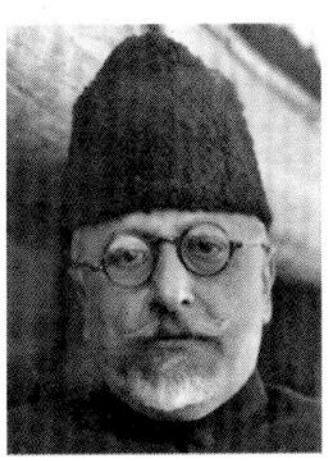

Maulana Abul Kalam Azad (1888–1958) was a leading Muslim scholar and a well-known political leader who played a significant part in the struggle for independence. After independence in 1947 he became the first minister of education in the Union Cabinet. In 1992 he was given the highest civilian award, the Bharat Ratna, for his noteworthy services to the nation. He was known as Maulana Azad in day-to-day speech. His birthday is celebrated as National Education Day.

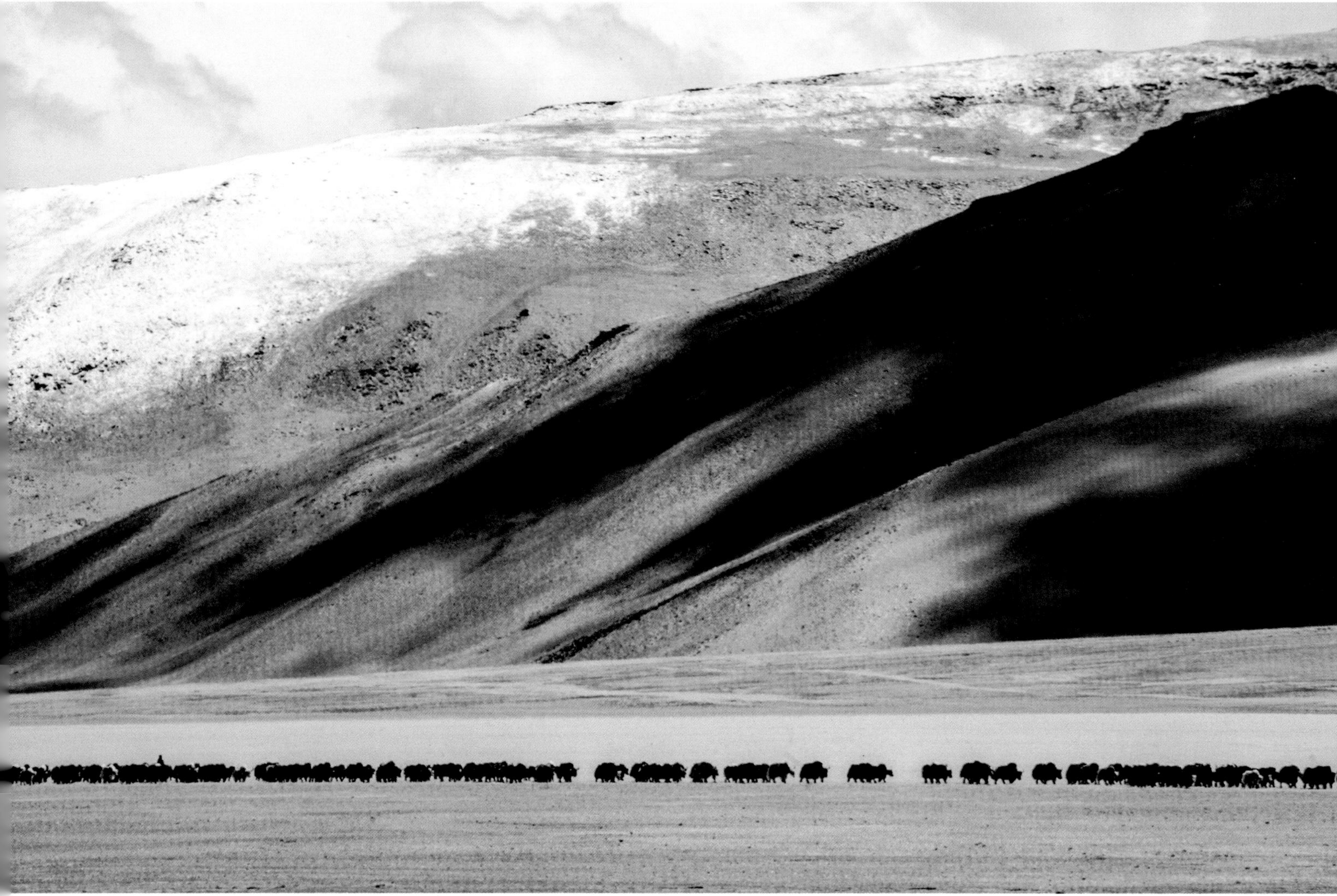

"

Don't forget love; it will bring all the madness you need to unfurl yourself across the universe.

~

I want you to have this, all the beauty in my eyes, and the grace of my mouth, all the splendour of my strength, all the wonder of the musk parts of my body, for are we not talking about real love, real love?

~

I have felt the swaying of the elephant's shoulders;
and now you want me to climb on a jackass? Try to
be serious.

~

I came for the sake of love-devotion; seeing the world, I wept.

~

Let people say good things or bad things; I will bear them all!
Meera cannot love even a moment without her beloved Lord Krishna.
O my companion,
Worldly comfort is an illusion,
As soon you get it, it goes.

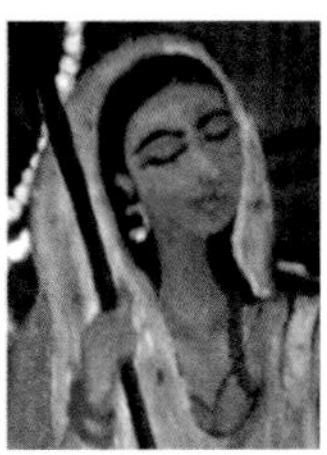

Meerabai (1498–1546) was a famous devotee of Lord Krishna and a Hindu poet. She was born into a royal family in Rajasthan. Even today, her poetry and bhajans are highly relevant and sung with much reverence. Her name figures prominently among the spiritual leaders of the Bhakti Movement. She was a courageous and unconventional lady who disregarded many familial and social norms. For her, devotion to Krishna meant everything and she treated Krishna as her husband. For these actions she was persecuted by her in-laws. Myriad folk tales and legends surround her name.

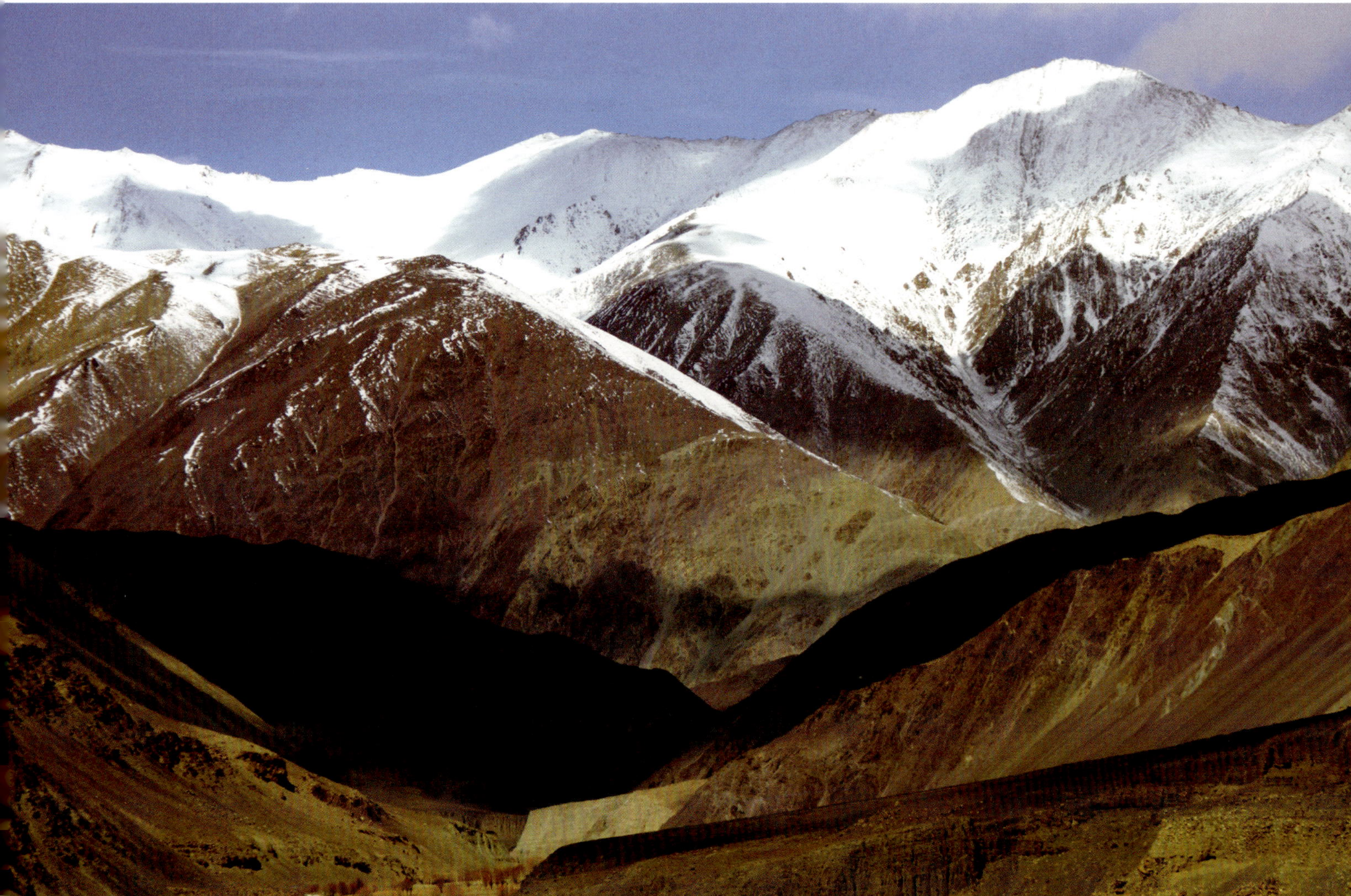

“

It’s the beginning of Love, why do you wail; just wait and watch how things unveil.

~

Every leaf and bud knows my situation, the flower doesn’t know but the whole garden knows it.

~

O Mir, he came to my grave after I’d died; my messiah thought of a medicine after I’d died.

~

Mornings come, evenings come, thus our life passes away.

~

Where has selflessness taken me? I’ve been waiting for myself for long.
What can I tell you about Mir’s faith or belief? A tilak on his forehead in a temple he resides, having abandoned Islam long ago.

~

From my eye, when doesn’t a tear fall, blood falls when it doesn’t fall.

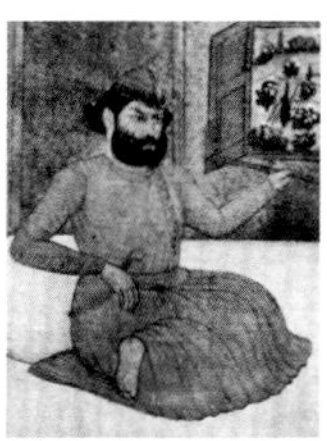

Meer Taqi Meer (1722–1810) was born in Agra and lived in the 18th century. He was a renowned Urdu poet. He is also known as the “God of Poetry”, *Khuda e Sukhan*. He wrote an autobiography, *Zikr-e-Mir*, from which many details of his life are taken. His father, Meer Muttaqi, was a famous Sufi saint. Meer Taqi Meer was touched by the influence of Sufis and Sufism in the family, and did not show any desire for worldly things. Because of how his family treated him, he wandered homeless for a while.

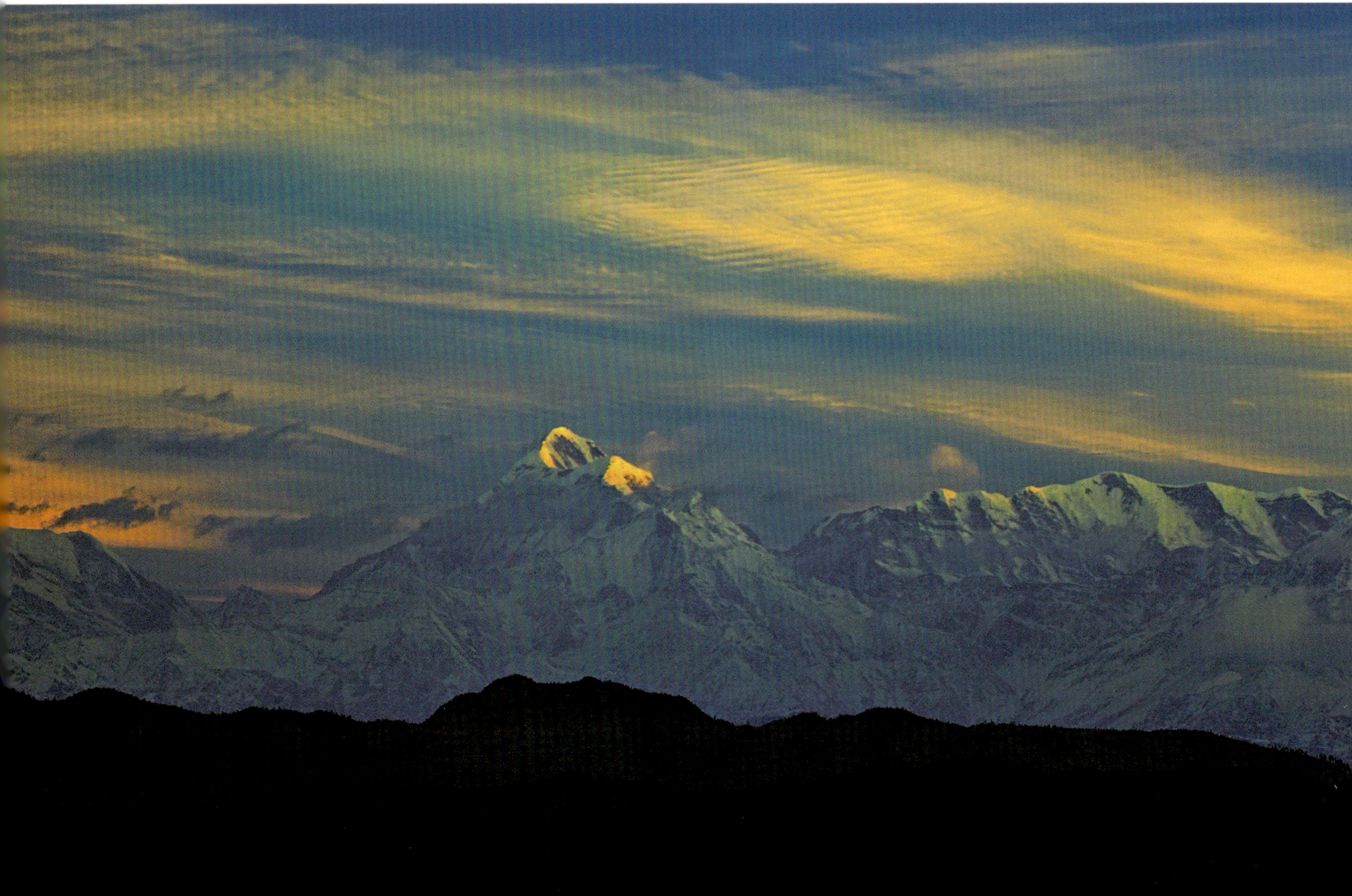

"

Do not pretend—be. Do not promise—act. Do not dream—realise.

~

Love is not sexual intercourse. Love is not vital attraction and interchange. Love is not the heart's hunger for affection. Love is a mighty vibration coming straight from the One. And only the very pure and very strong are capable of receiving and manifesting it.

~

It is the Divine Presence that gives value to life. This Presence is the source of all peace, all joy all security. Find this Presence in yourself and all your difficulties will disappear.

~

Widen your consciousness to the dimension of the earth and you will have a place for everything.

~

There should be somewhere upon Earth a place that no nation could claim as its sole property, a place where all human beings of good will, sincere in their aspiration, could live freely as citizens of the world, obeying one single authority, that of the supreme truth.

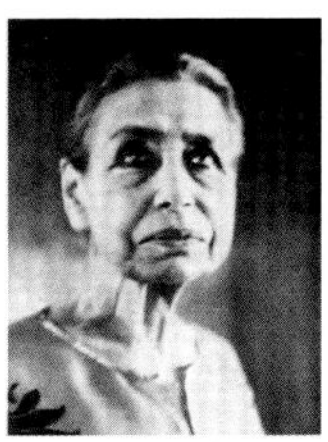

Mirra Alfassa (1878–1973). She was known as "the Mother". She had heard of Sri Aurobindo, and in 1914, she travelled to Pondicherry (now Puducherry) and met him. She recognised him as the person she had encountered in her visions, and decided that her future work had to be with him. She organised the group of followers of Sri Aurobindo into the Sri Aurobindo Ashram, and founded the Sri Aurobindo International Centre of Education. This was done to fulfill his desire to provide a different type of education for Indian youth. In 1968 she founded the international township project of Auroville as another attempt to implement Sri Aurobindo's vision, paving the way towards a brighter future for humanity.

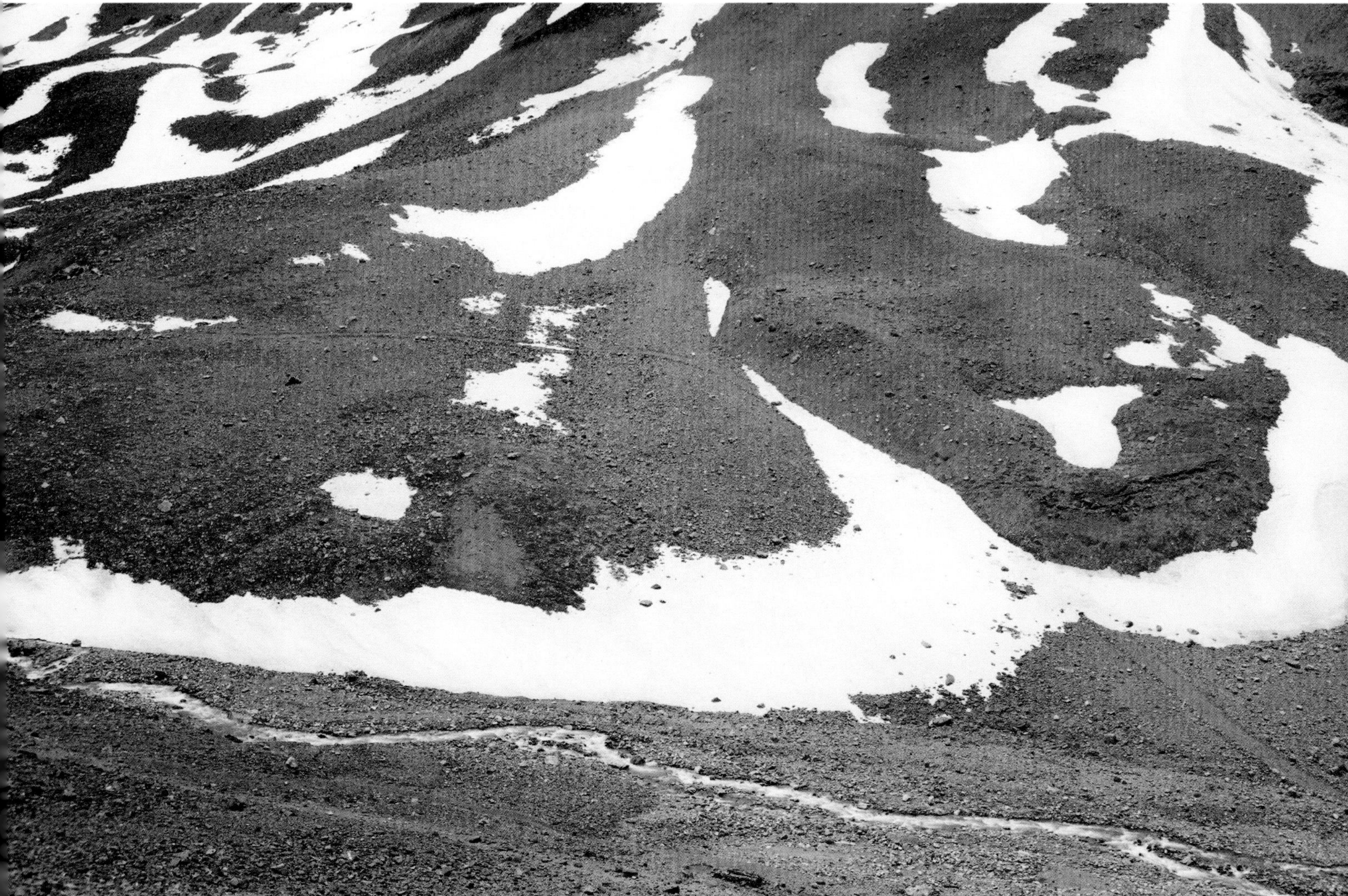

"

Whereas it is difficult for everything to work out easily,
a man cannot even afford to be a human.

~

Love demands patience, desire is restless; what colour shall I paint the heart, until you savage it? You shall not ignore me when the time comes, I know, but I may turn to dust before the news reaches you.

~

In Paradise it is true that I shall drink at dawn the pure wine mentioned in the Koran, but where in Paradise are the long walks with intoxicated friends in the night, or the drunken crowds shouting merrily? Where shall I find there the intoxication of monsoon clouds?

~

In love, there is no difference between living and dying,
one lives by watching the beloved on whom life is lost,
if your prayers are potent, Mullah, move this mosque my way,
else have a drink or two with me, and we'll see its minarets sway.

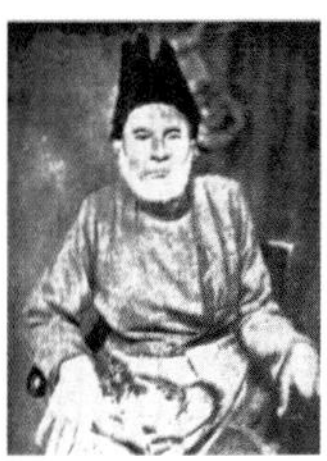

Mirza Ghalib (1797–1869). During the final years of the Mughal Empire in India, Ghalib was the peerless poet of Delhi, and was fluent in both Persian and Urdu. Ghalib wrote many *ghazals* that have been sung and interpreted by many people. It would not be a stretch to say that there will never be a greater poet of Urdu than him. He has a lot of influence and is respected not only in India but all over the world. Success came late to him, and he lived much of his life as a poor man.

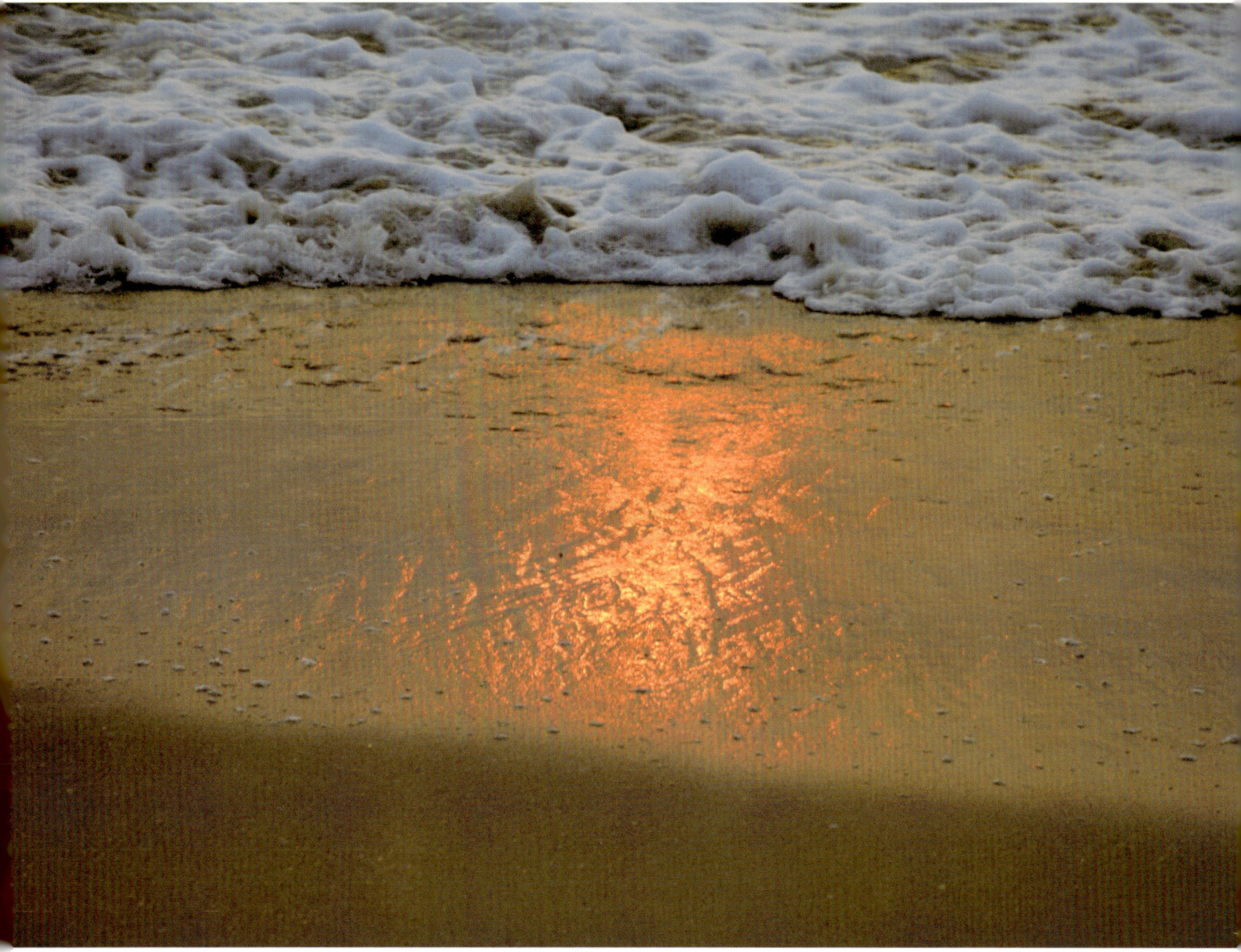

"

Live as if you were to die tomorrow; learn as if you were to live forever.

~

The weak can never forgive. Forgiveness is the attribute of the strong.

~

Happiness is when what you think, what you say, and what you do are in harmony.

~

My life is my message.

~

When I admire the wonders of a sunset or the beauty of the moon, my soul expands in the worship of the creator.

~

I object to violence because when it appears to do good, the good is only temporary; the evil it does is permanent.

~

An eye for an eye only ends up making the whole world blind.

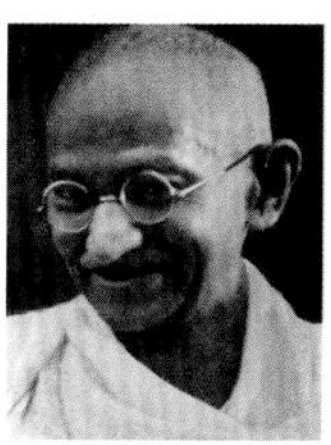

Mohandas Karamchand Gandhi (1869–1948), known as Gandhiji, is the most prominent Indian of modern times. With immense love, affection and esteem, he is also called Bapu (meaning "father" in Gujarati). For his great contributions to the independence of the country, he is acknowledged as the "Father of the Nation". He used the weapon of non-violence against oppression and country-wide agitations, and in this way brought about the downfall of the colonial rule. A countless number of books have been written about him and his life in politics. He was assassinated in 1948. Hindu-Muslim riots pained him immensely as he always felt that religion should teach love to all. He staged many agitations for the freedom of India in his long career.

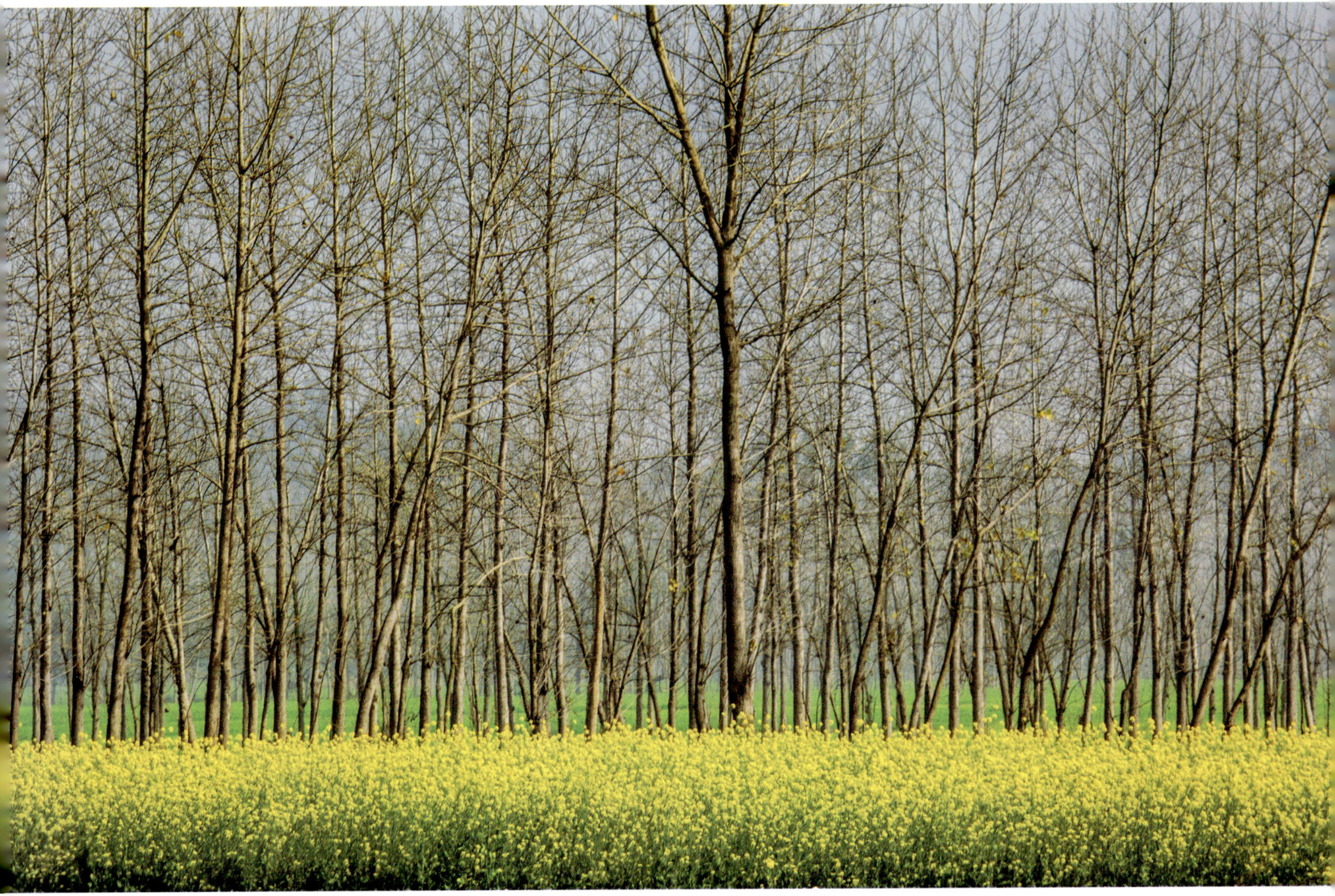

"

There is only one thing present in the entire universe and that is the Noor (Divine Effulgence) of the Most Holy, glorious is He; everything else is absent.

~

The basis (for spiritual endeavours) must be a sound intention, because while people note what you do, God almighty takes note of what you intend to do. When your intention is fixed on God, then a little amount of work will be greatly rewarded.

~

To look lovingly towards your parents is also a reason to gain the grace of your Lord.

~

There is only one veil standing between man and his creator and it is called nafs (soul).

~

Hoarding of wealth and food for profit has become a destructive disease in the body of the nation. To fight and eradicate this disease lies within each citizen.

Moinuddin Chishti (1141–1230). He is one of the most famous Sufi saints of the Chishti Order of India. He established the order in South Asia. Moinuddin Chishti practised peace to all to promote harmony between Muslims and non-Muslims. He never made a book out of his teachings, and neither did his immediate disciples, but they laid emphasis on the renunciation of material goods, a strict regime of discipline and prayer, and generosity to others, particularly by sharing food and wealth. He viewed religion in terms of human service. The highest form of devotion, according to him, was to fulfill the needs of the helpless and to feed the hungry.

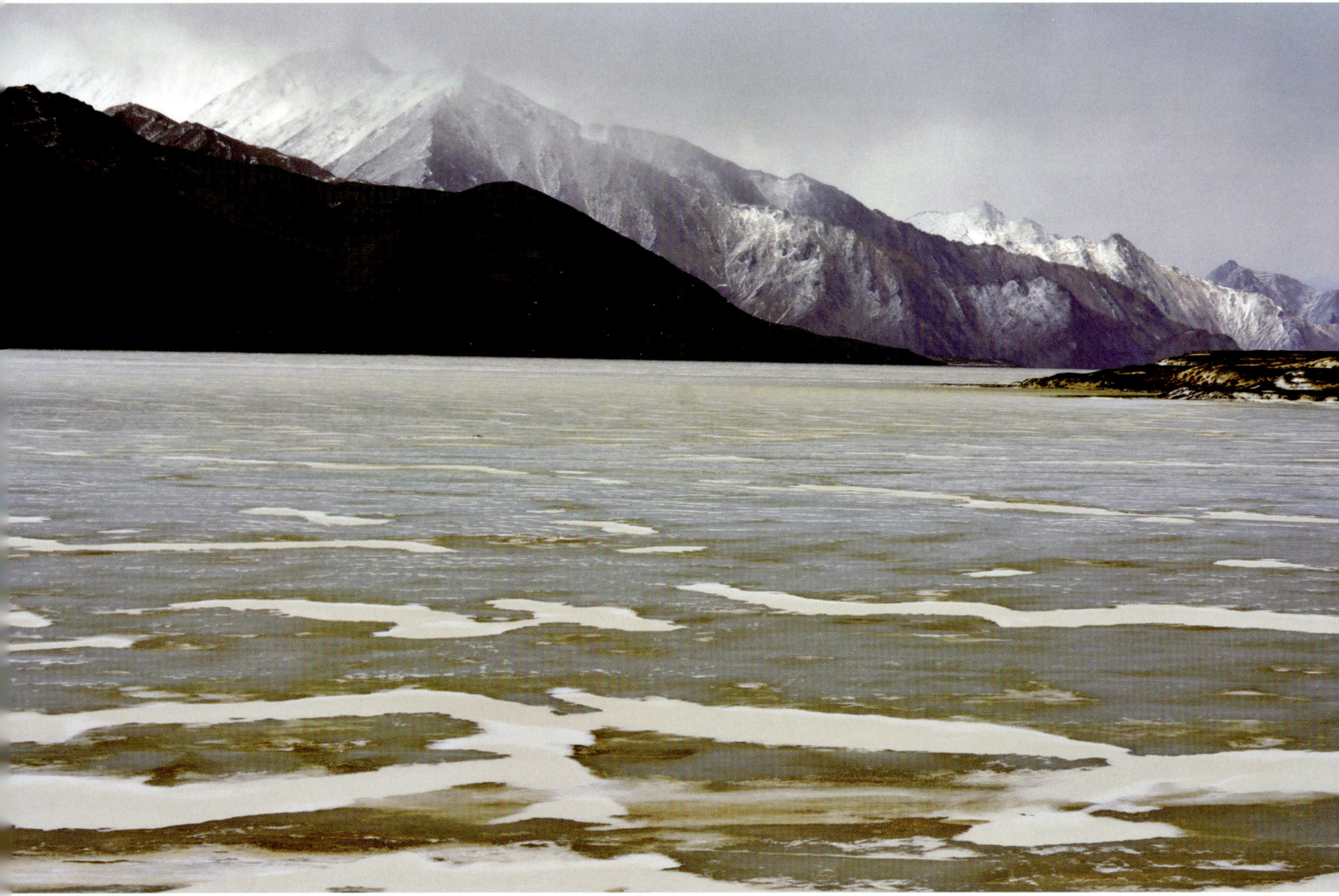

"

True wisdom is to renounce the world.

~

Salik achieves greatness from four things: Less eating, less talking, less sleep, and less socialising.

~

Benediction drops at three times: in the state of hearing music,
eating for purpose of obedience, speaking about mendicants.

~

In making a deal, one should not talk as to make veins stand on his neck viz.
symptoms of prejudice and anger.

~

Patience is: When a man experiences a thing not to his liking, and does not complain.

~

The joys neither make a mendicant happy nor sufferings grieve him.

~

Forgive the person who has committed a wrong and thus eliminate your anger.

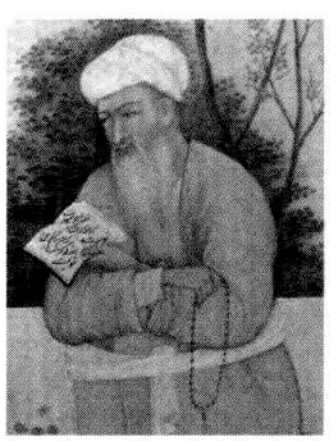

Nizamuddin Auliya (1238–1325). Chishti Nizamuddin Auliya was renowned for his humanitarianism, frugality, generosity, and wit. He was a famous Sufi saint of the Chishti Order in India. At his langar, praiseworthy food was served. His order of Sufism believes in being close to God by service to humanity and renunciation of the world. He felt love was key to the attainment of bliss and realisation of God. Each year his shrine in Delhi is visited by thousands of pilgrims. Qawwalis are organised daily. The food served is only vegetarian. Hazrat Nizamuddin believed in equal rights for women, that food should be served to people of all religions, that people should always think of humankind, and that love should be the prayer for your master.

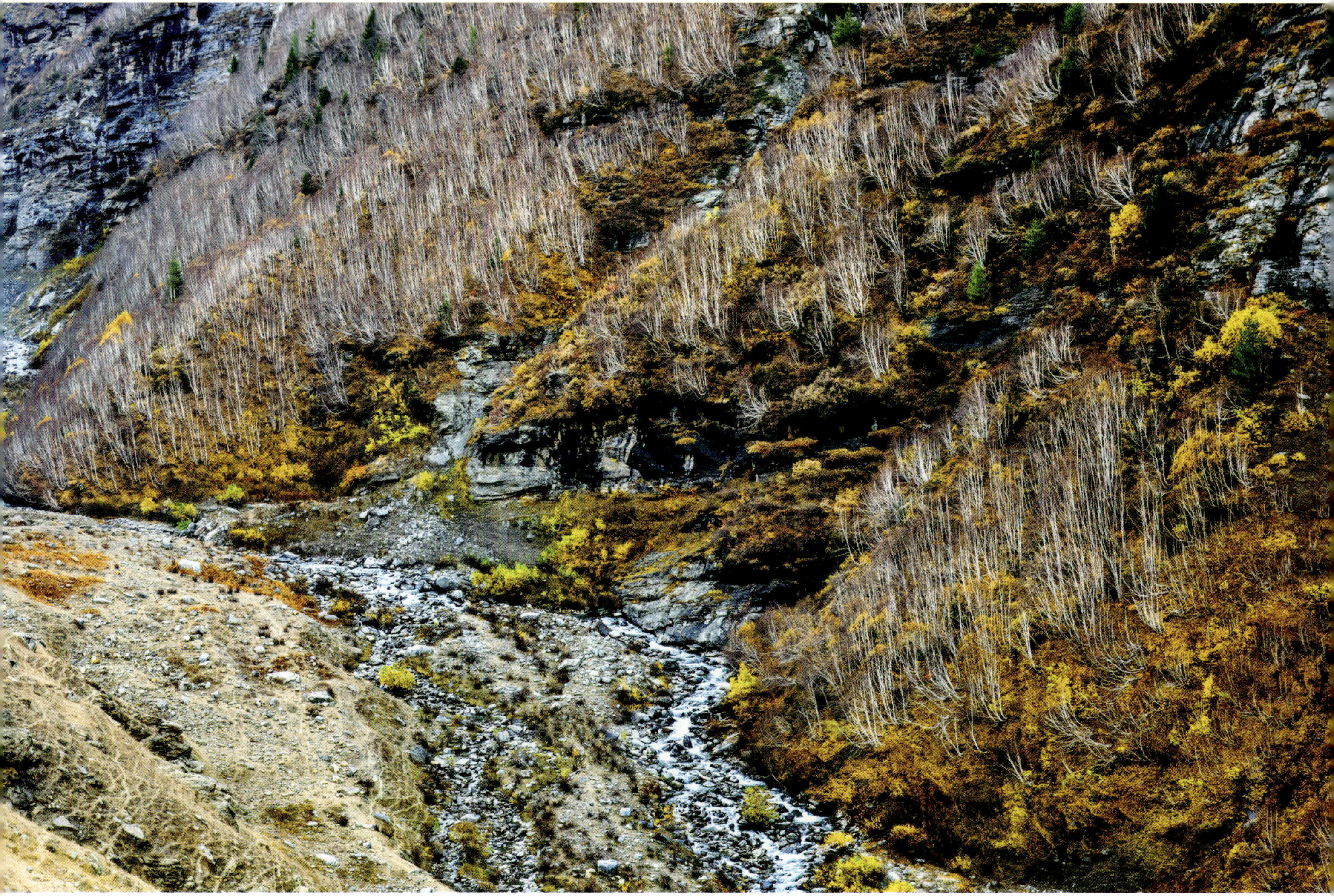

“

Man has nothing else to do but surrender—in deep trust, in deep love.
Don’t be a doer, just surrender. Let there be a let-go.

~

Respect your uniqueness, and drop comparison. Relax into your being.

~

You say that in heaven there is eternal beauty. The eternal beauty is here and now, not in heaven.

~

All the Buddhas of all the ages have been telling you a very simple fact: Be—don’t try to become.

~

It does not matter if you are a rose or a lotus or a marigold. What matters is that you are flowering.

~

Ecstasy is our very nature; not to be ecstatic is simply unnecessary.
To be ecstatic is natural, spontaneous. It needs no effort to be ecstatic,
it needs great effort to be miserable.

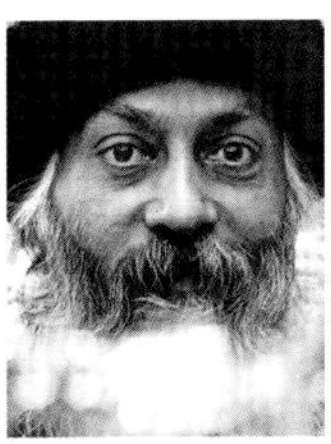

Osho (1931–1990). Osho Rajneesh was a controversial leader. He was an Indian mystic, guru and spiritual teacher, and created the practice of dynamic meditation. He had thousands of followers around the world, and also many people who opposed him. Over a period of time he established himself as a popular spiritual guru not just in India but also internationally. When members of his community committed several crimes, he made headlines. In the mid-1980s, relations between the commune and the local governmental community became strained, and it was revealed that the commune members had been engaging in a variety of serious crimes including murder. His health deteriorated considerably during the late 1980s and he breathed his last on 19 January 1990 at age 58 due to a cardiac arrest.

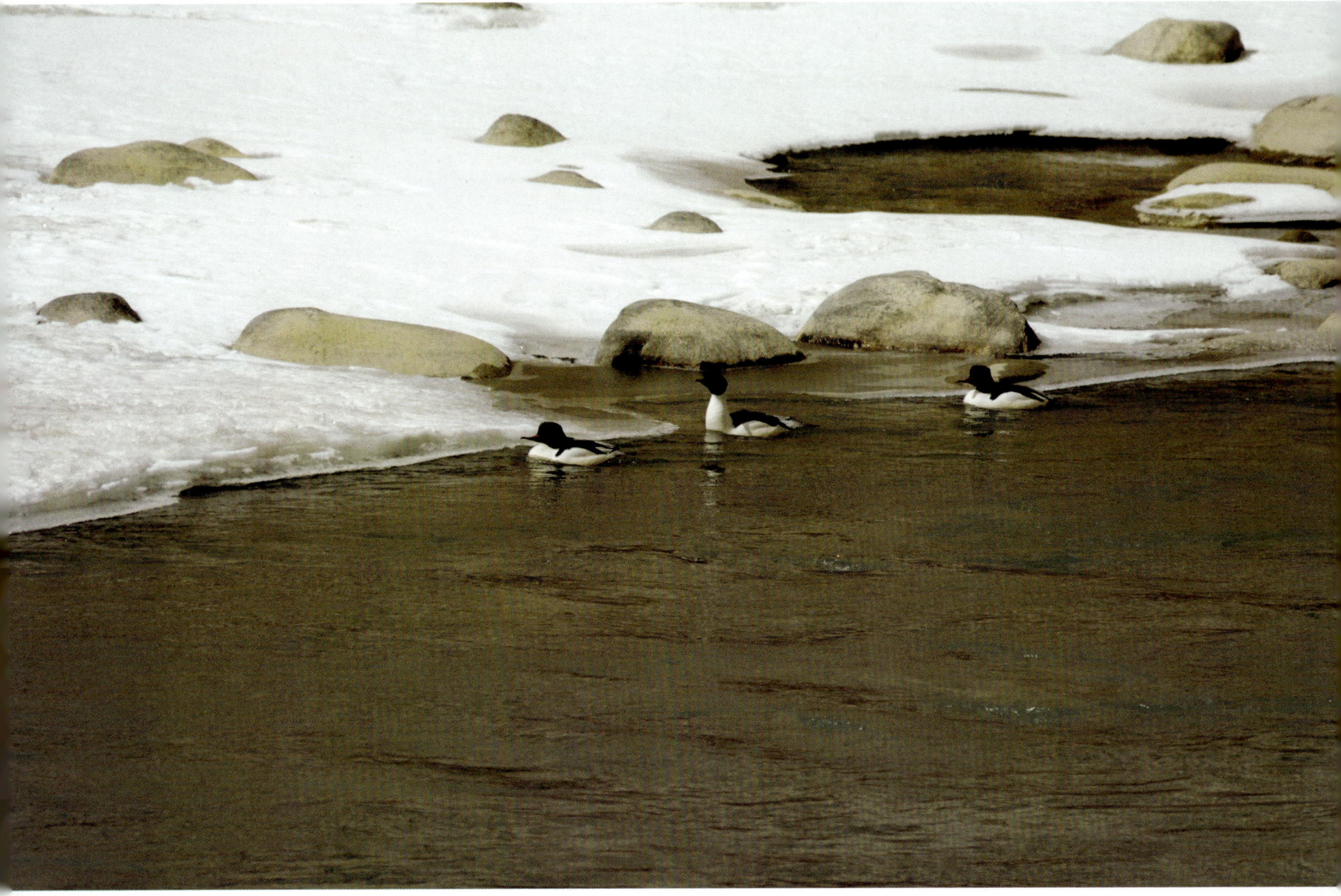

"

People must not only hear about the kingdom of God, but
must see it in actual operation, on a small scale perhaps and in imperfect form,
but a real demonstration nevertheless.

~

A life totally committed to God has nothing to fear, nothing to lose, nothing to regret.

~

I realised after reading the fourth chapter of St. John's Gospel that
Christ was truly the Divine Saviour he claimed to be, and no one but
He could transform and uplift the downtrodden women of India...
Thus my heart was drawn to the religion of Christ.

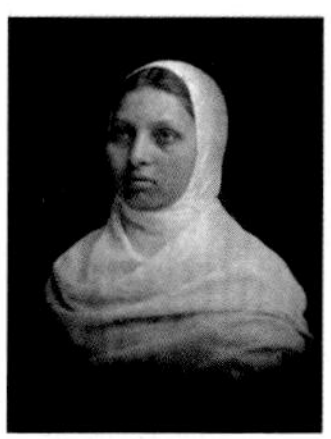

Pandita Ramabai (1858–1922) was an Indian social reformer. She played a large role in women's rights and was a trailblazer in education. She was also a renowned Sanskrit scholar. Her parents passed away during the 1877 famine. It was then that she and her brother decided to continue their parents' work, for which they travelled to several parts of the country. Her fame reached Kolkata and she was invited to speak at Calcutta University. Impressed by her, Calcutta University bestowed on her the title of "Pandita", as well as the highest title of "Saraswati", for her interpretation of various Sanskrit works. She was presented with a copy of the Vedas by Keshab Chandra Sen himself.

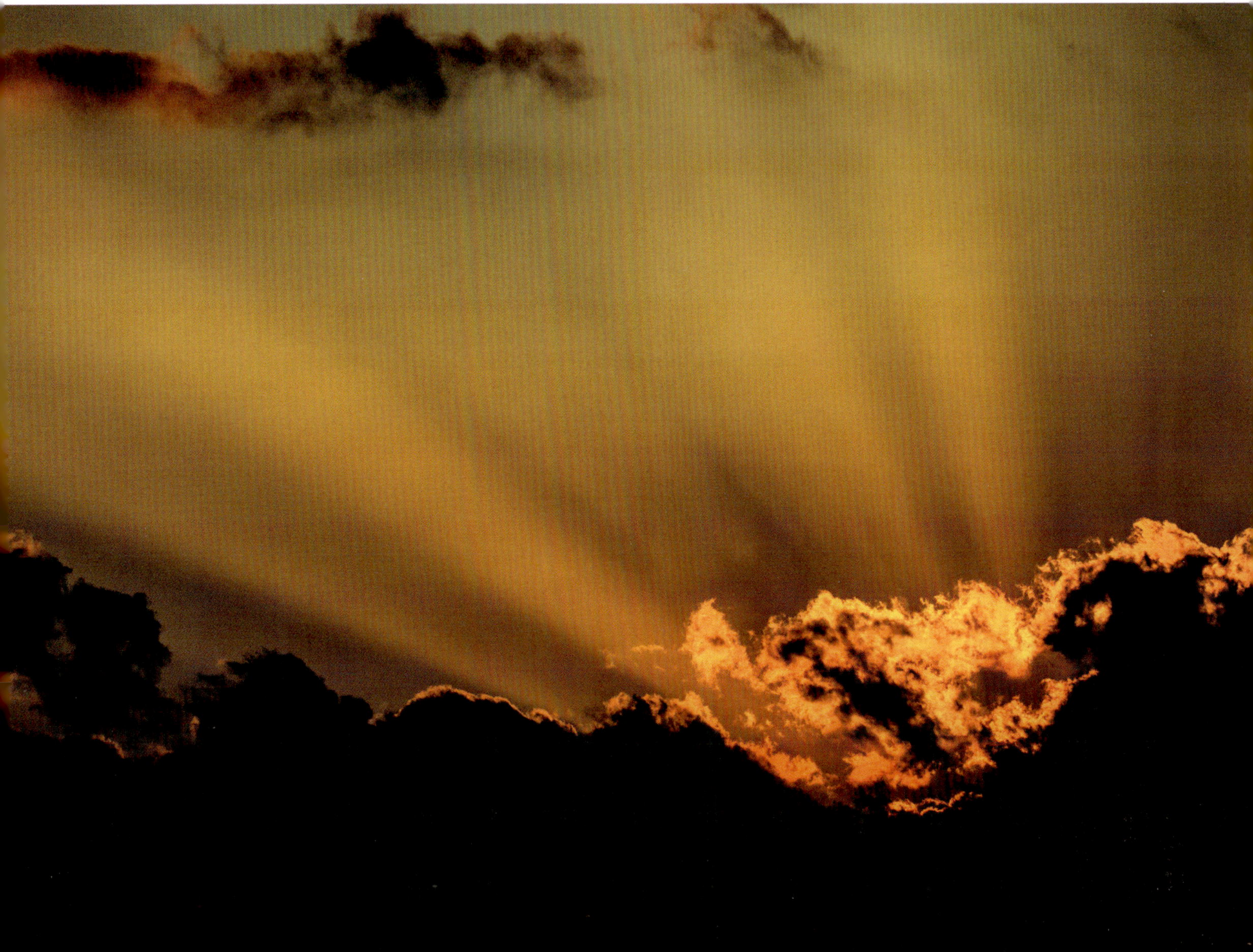

“

The season of failure is the best time for sowing the seeds of success.

~

Remain calm, serene, always in command of yourself.
You will then find out how easy it is to get along.

~

The happiness of one’s own heart alone cannot satisfy the soul;
one must try to include, as necessary to one’s own happiness, the happiness of others.

~

Let my soul smile through my heart and my heart smile through my eyes,
that I may scatter rich smiles in sad hearts.

~

There is a magnet in your heart that will attract true friends. That magnet is unselfishness,
thinking of others first; when you learn to live for others, they will live for you.

~

As often as you fail, get up and try again. God will never let you down,
so long as you don’t let Him down, and so long as you make the effort.

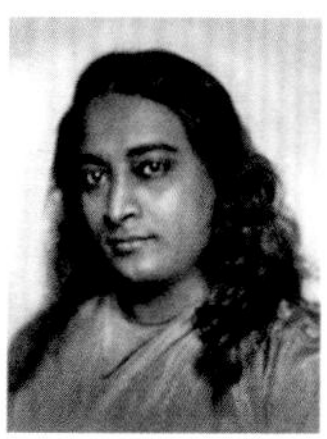

Paramahansa Yogananda (1893–1952). He was born as Mukunda Lal Ghosh into a religious family and showed a keen interest in spirituality from an early age. A few years after entering the Monastic Swami Order, he travelled to America and founded the Self-Realisation Fellowship (SRF) to spread his teachings on India’s spiritual practices like yoga. He spent the rest of his life teaching in America. He took a brief trip to India, during which he established the Yogoda Satsanga Society. His life story, *Autobiography of a Yogi*, was published in 1946 and listed on “100 Most Important Spiritual Books of the 20th Century”.

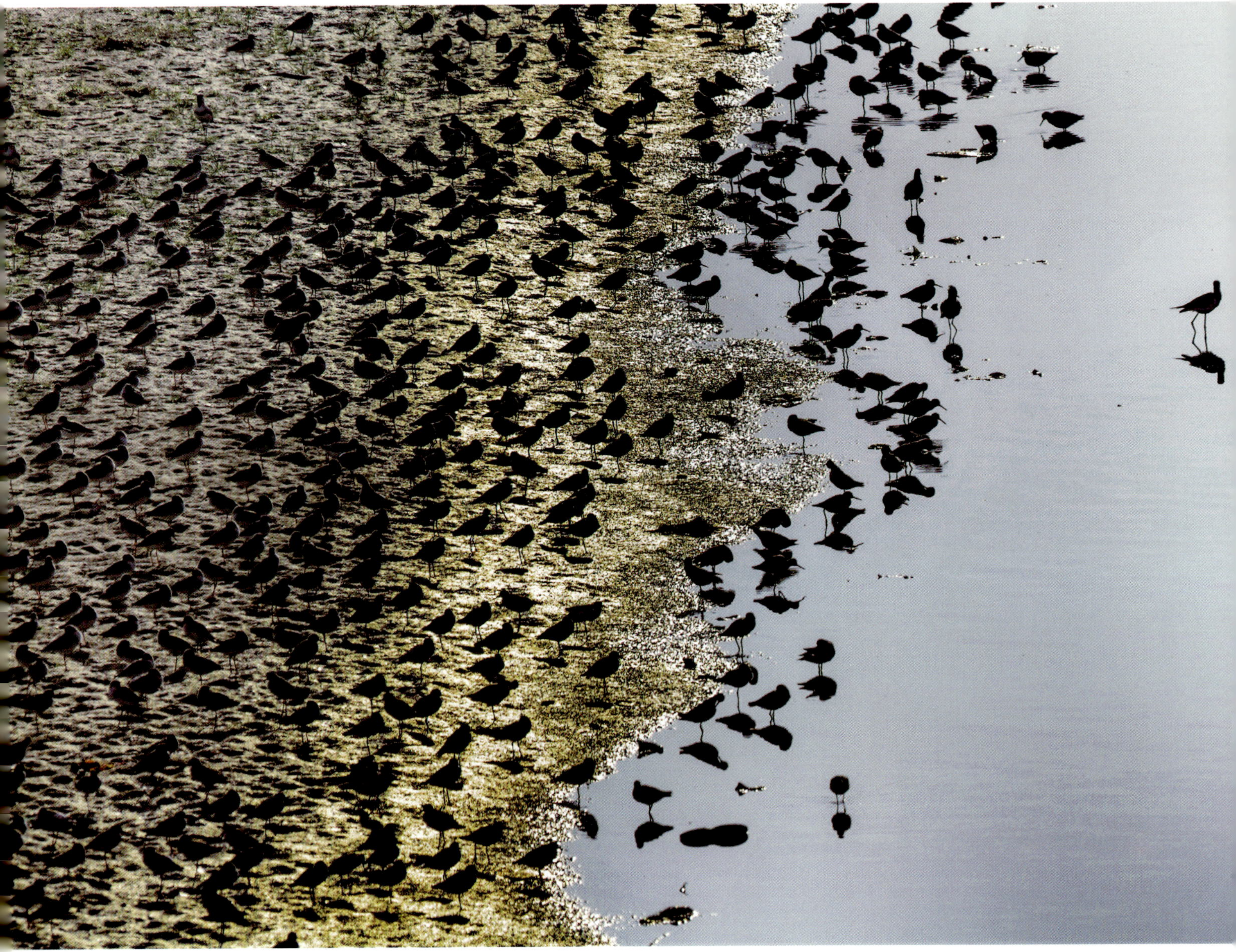

"

By helping the poor, we must be able to remove their poverty. By extending help to one here and one there in the form of providing food will not remove poverty.

~

Man is equal to man. There should not be exploitation. One should help the other. No one should harm anybody. Generally there should be no room for grievance or complaint from anybody. Everyone should live and let others to live, with a national spirit.

~

It gave me extraordinary pleasure to fling at the pundits their own contradictions and thus perplex them. It also gave me the reputation, among our neighbours, of being a clever speaker. I believe that it was this experience, which deprived me of faith in castes and communities, in religion, in the Puranas, in sastras and in God.

~

While all men are born as equals, to say that Brahmins alone are the highest and all others are low as Pariah (the Untouchables) or Panchama is sheer nonsense. It is roguish to say so. It is a big hoax played on us.

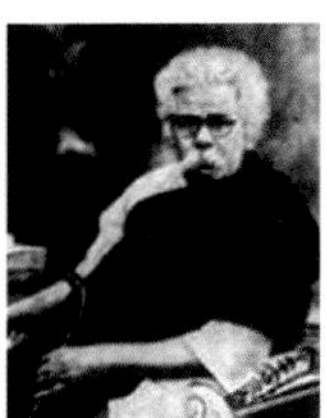

Periyar (1879–1973). Periyar, or Erode Venkata Ramasami, was one of the most inspiring politicians and activists. He fought for the establishment of principles such as equality of castes and genders, realisation of fundamental rights for women and an end to the exploitation of the non-Brahmin Dravidians of South India. Periyar was always against the Brahmins in Tamil society, and often made controversial statements about them. His satyagraha and non-cooperation movements got him thrown into prison numerous times. He is best known for leading the movement for the creation of the state of South India or Dravidistan.

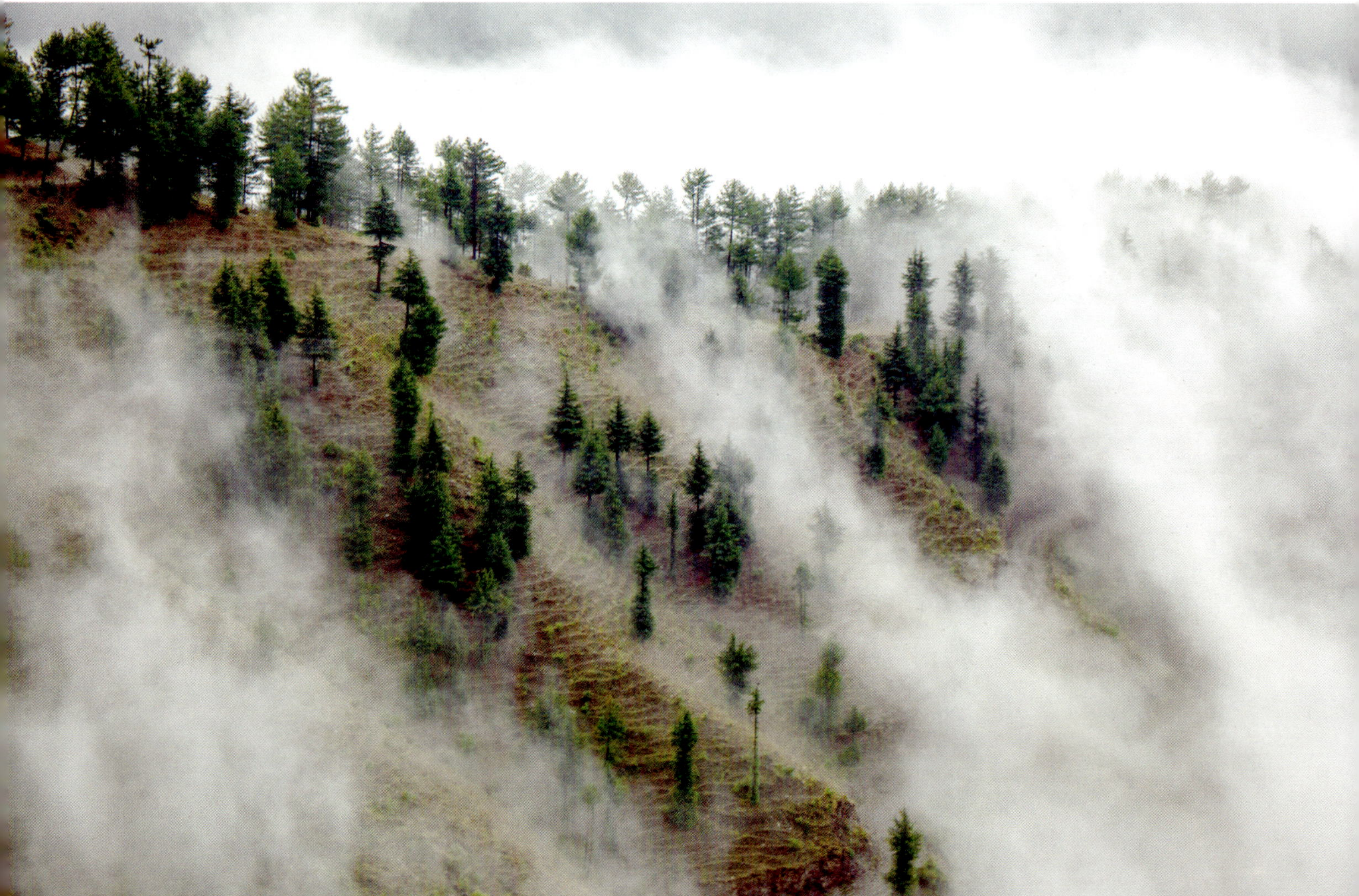

"

Clouds come floating into my life, no longer to carry rain or usher storm, but to add colour to my sunset sky. Let us not pray to be sheltered from dangers but to be fearless when facing them.

~

I slept and dreamt that life was joy. I awoke and saw that life was service. I acted and behold, service was joy.

~

The highest education is that which does not merely give us information but makes our life in harmony with all existence.

~

Depth of friendship does not depend on length of acquaintance.

~

Those who own much have much to fear.

~

We live in the world when we love it.

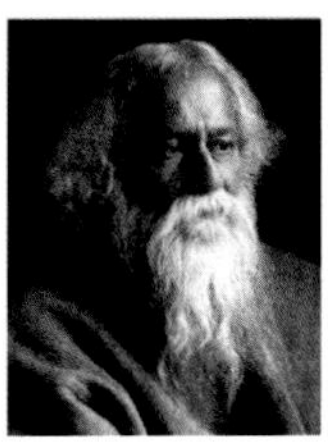

Rabindranath Tagore (1861–1941) is known for his literature, paintings and music. He was awarded the Nobel Prize in 1913 for his book of poetry, *Gitanjali*. He was the first non-European to win this prize, a matter of immense pride for our country. He received universal applause for his spiritual work. He created a new poetic style that was different from the models based on classical Sanskrit. He is rightly credited with spreading Indian culture in the West and vice versa, and was universally acclaimed as an outstanding creative artist. He also supported freedom from the British Raj and modernised Bengali art by diverging from rigid classical forms. His novels, stories, songs, dance drama, and essays are read with great interest all over the world.

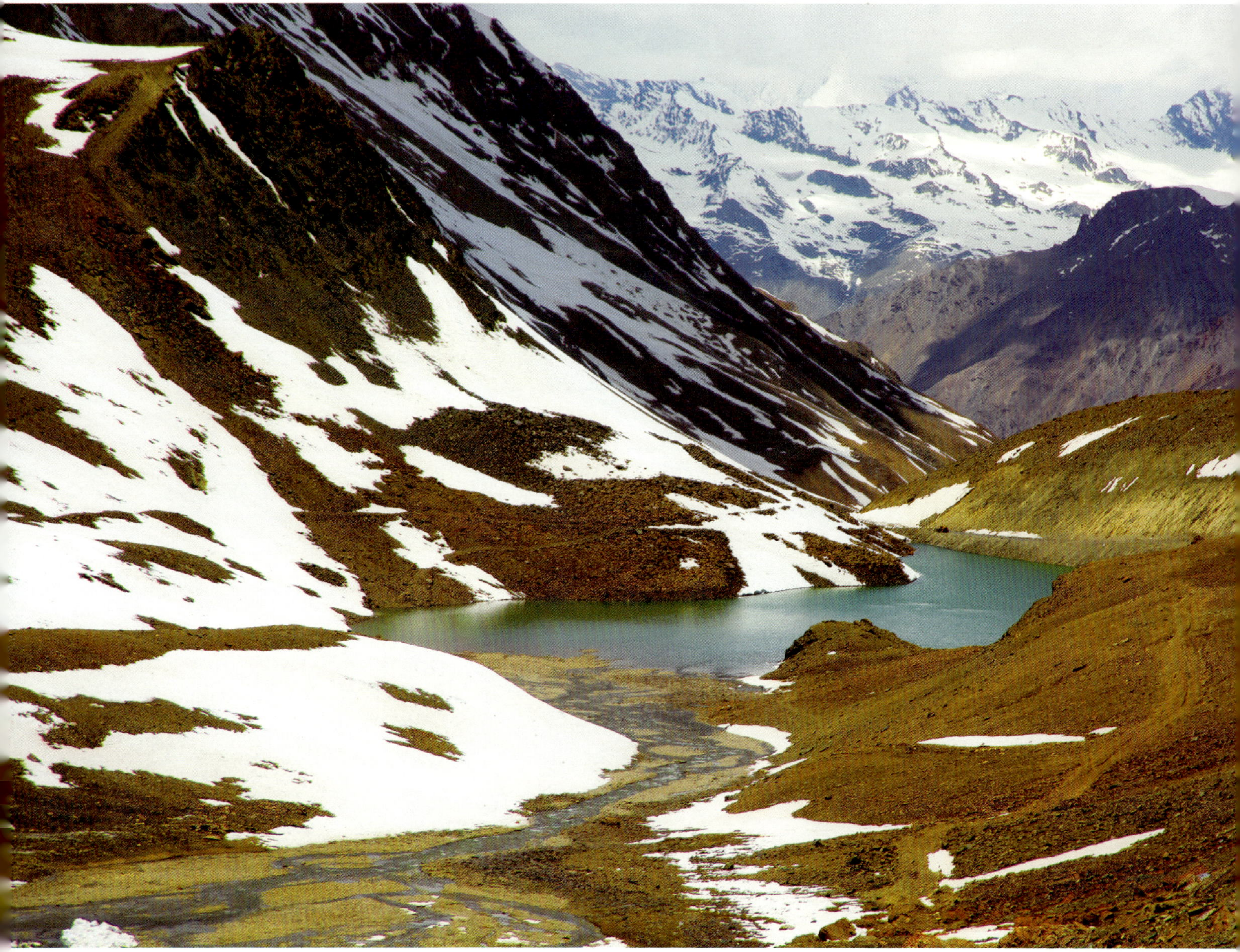

“

Your speech should be such that it should please everyone. Others should feel happy listening to you and you yourself should also feel happy and content.

~

Rahim says, don't allow the delicate thread of love between people to snap. If it breaks once, it cannot be mended; even if you mend it there will be a knot in it, which means there will always be some awkwardness in the relationship.

~

Rahim says, if good people get angry with you, you should reconcile with them as many times as it happens. As you repair a pearl necklace as many times as it breaks.

~

Trees do not eat their own fruits, pools don't drink their own water. Rahim says, good people accumulate wealth to do good to others.

~

Rahim says that wanting things is the root of all worries and if one can abolish all wants there will be no worry. People who do not want anything are the kings of kings as they are happy in all circumstances.

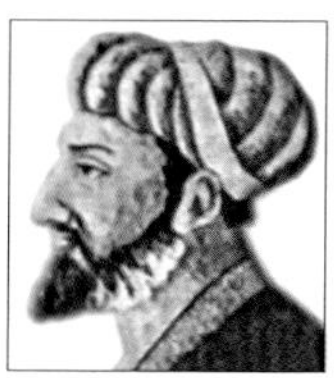

Rahim (1556–1627). He was a famous poet, known for his *dohas* (couplets). He was born in Lahore and lived during the reign of Mughal emperor Akbar. He earned the honour of being counted among the *Navratnas*, the nine most important ministers in Akbar's court. For his important contributions to literature, the village Khankhana in Punjab is named after him. His tomb is situated near Humayun's tomb in Delhi.

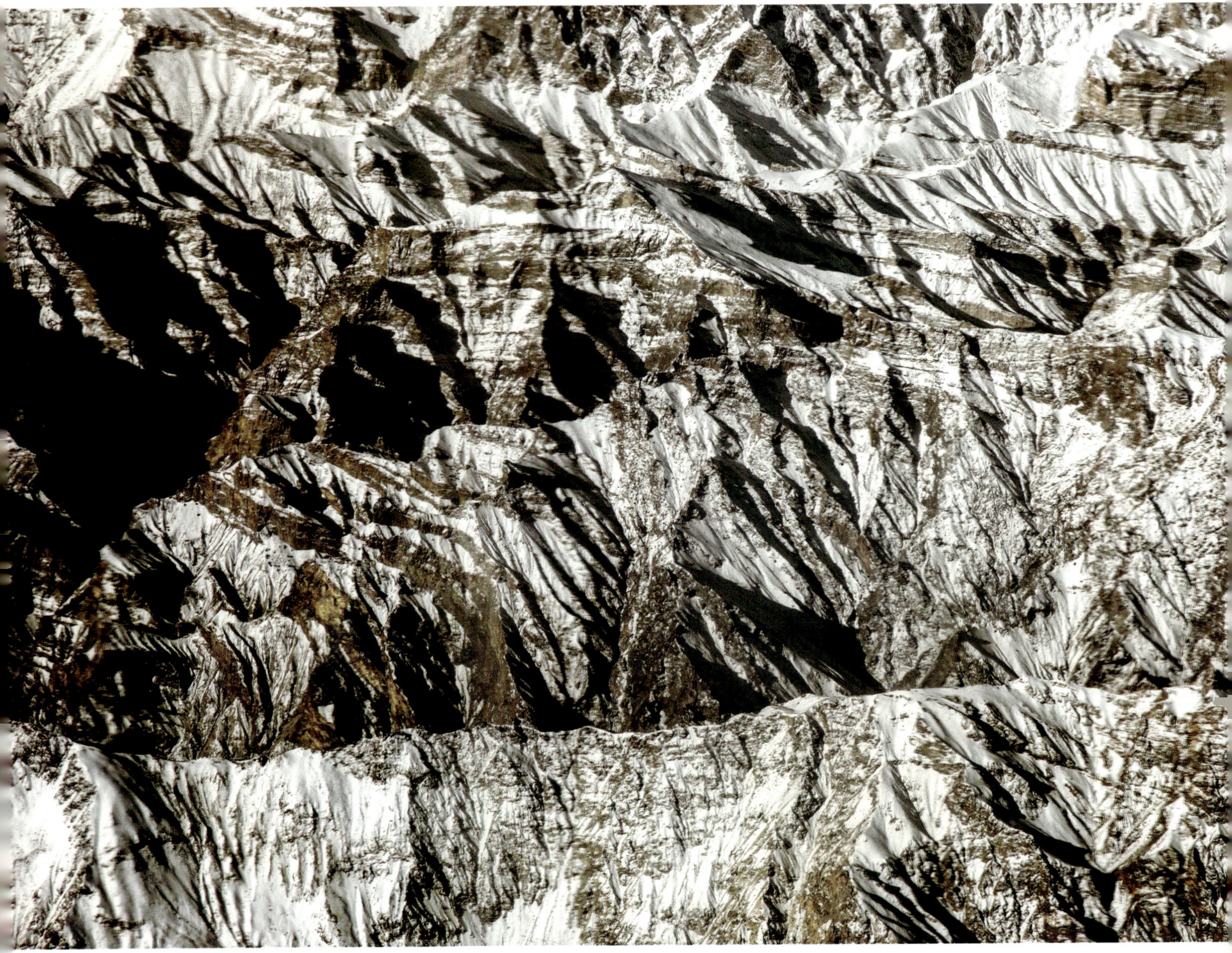

"

I believe the most important thing in this world to be traveling. There can be no one who would think better for society than a person who travels a lot. Whether the world is steeped in joy or mired in sadness, it only finds refuge in the wisdom of the travellers.

~

Ancient Man was a great traveller. It is necessary to speak of the great contribution to human civilisation by the travellers in the modern age, because people stole from the writings of the great travellers of history and published their writings in their names, which led to the misconception that only frogs of the well are able to do something worthwhile in this world.

~

Charles Darwin occupies a pivotal place in the growth of modern science. He not only carried out important and unparalleled research in the origin of species and of the human race, but it could be said that all sciences had to change their direction in the light of Darwin's contributions.

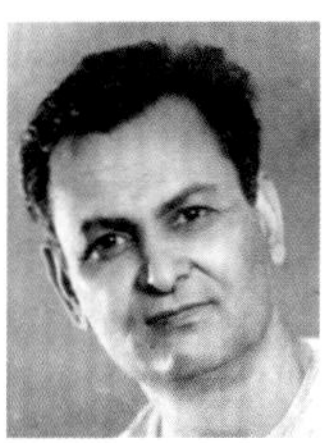

Rahul Sankrityayan (1893–1963) is known as the "Father of Hindi Travelogue Literature". He travelled extensively, spending almost 45 years of his life away from his home. This scholar, on the move, wrote many travelogues. His writings are known for their authenticity, and his notes are respected by all. His book *Meri Ladakh Yatra* contains wonderful descriptions about Ladakh's historical and cultural past. The place influenced him so much that he became a Buddhist monk and also turned to Marxist socialism. The British government was disturbed by his activities and put him in jail for three years, apprehensive of his anti-British writings and speeches. He is often referred to as a *mahapandit* (great scholar).

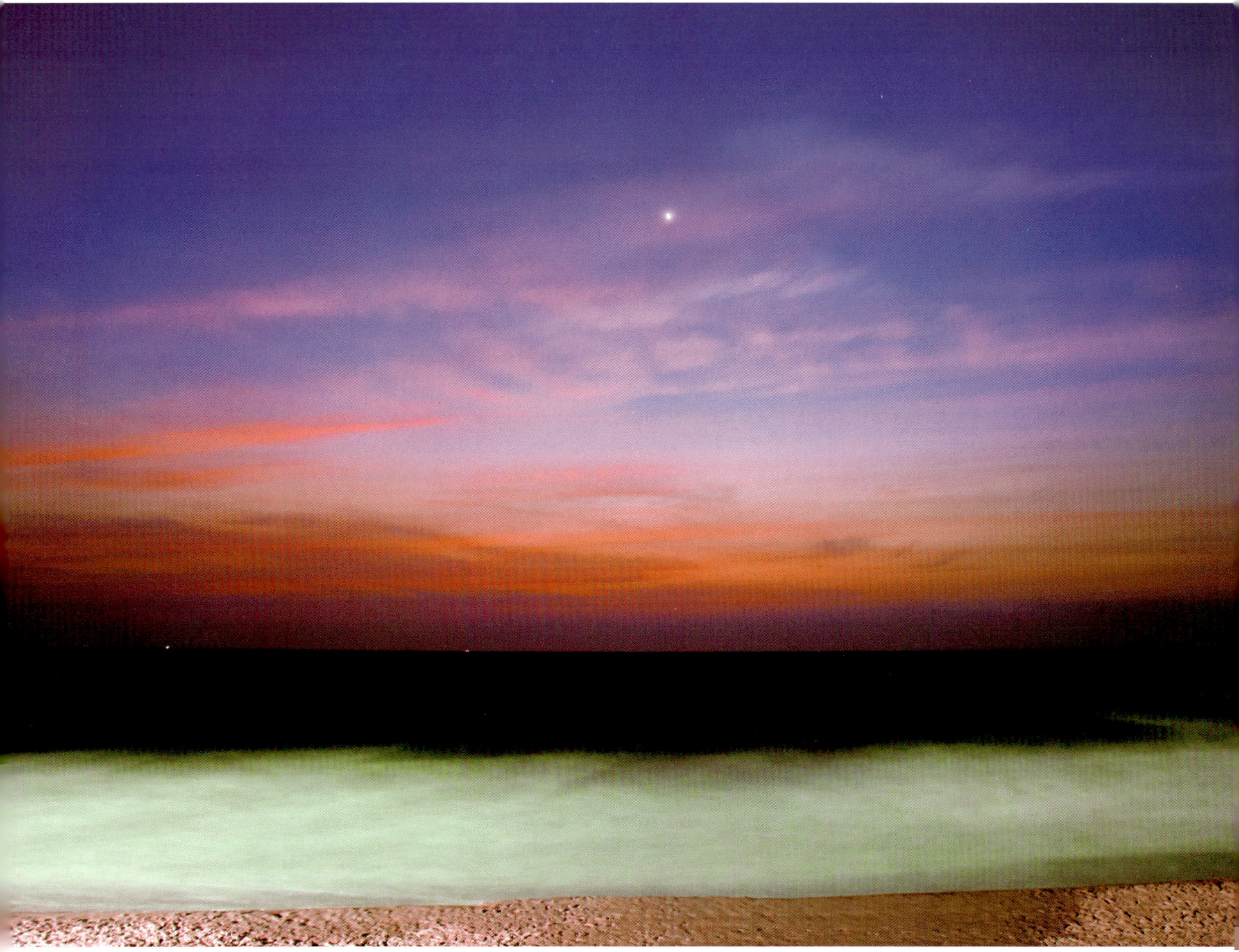

“

Despite seeing old age, birth and death, our mind does not fear anything. This proves that the entire world has drunk the wine of attachment and greed and is not in its senses. This is indeed the glory of time that despite realising the truth we tend to neglect or overlook it.

~

Wisdom, indeed, is the highest ornament that a man possesses. It is a valuable to be carefully guarded, for wisdom gains food, glory, and blessing. Wisdom is as a friend to a man travelling in a distant land. Wisdom is honoured among kings even more than wealth. The man devoid of wisdom is but an animal.

~

Intercourse with wise men takes away dullness of mind, elevates the intellect, inspires the speech with truthfulness. What will it not do for men?

~

There are two uses both for a garland of flowers and also for a wise man: they may be exalted on the head or wither in the forest.

Raja Bharthari lived in the 1st century BC. He was the king of Ujjain. He abdicated the throne to allow Vikramaditya, his younger brother, to rule. He became a religious beggar. Along with Gopi Chand, his nephew, he became a follower of Guru Gorakhnath in the north of Punjab. Several of his life details are given in *Baital Pachisi* (“Twenty-Five Tales of Baital”). He was also known as Sant Bharthari.

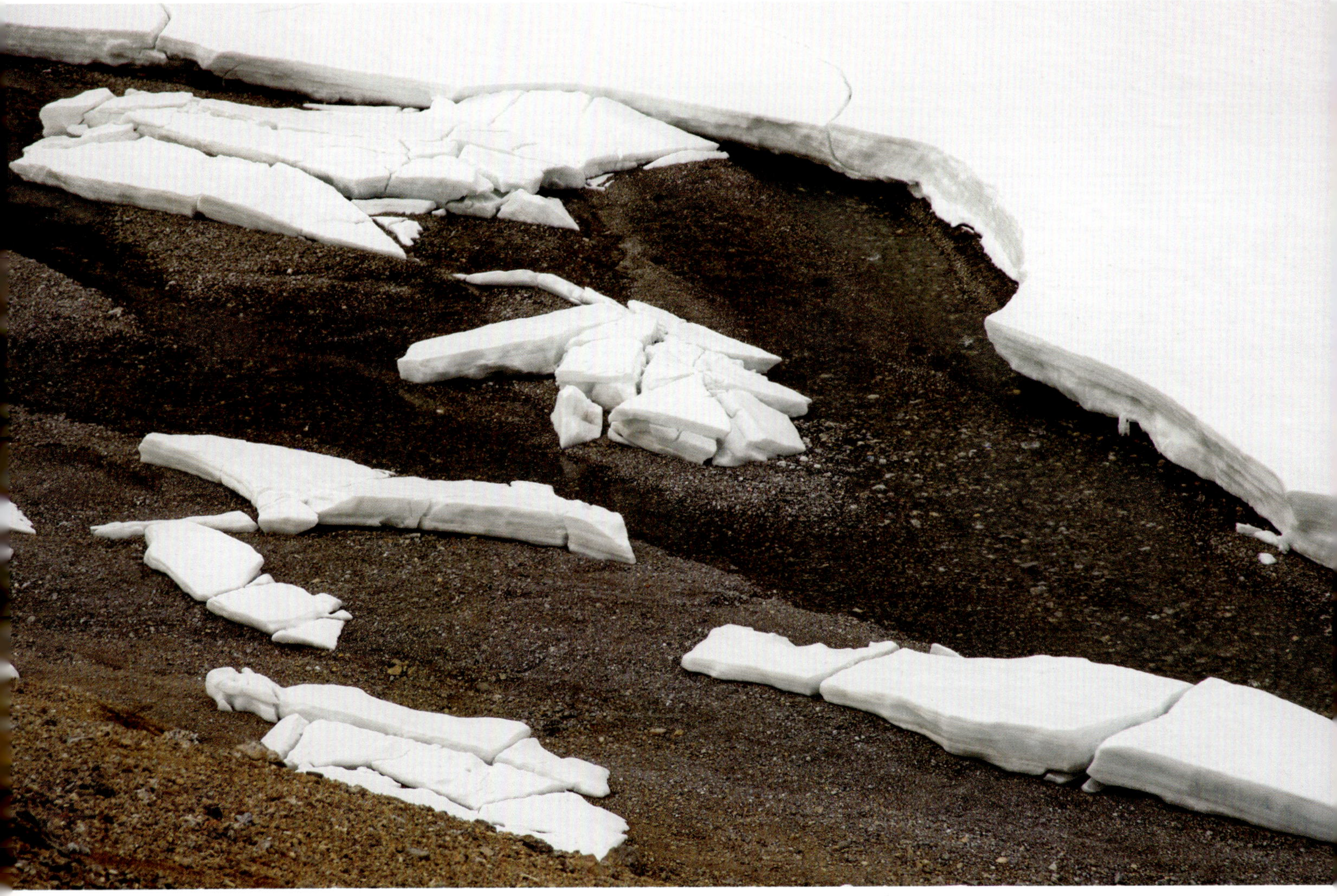

"

Physicists have always wondered if there is a direct interaction between two conscious human beings without the aid of the sense organs. I believe I have some verification of its possibility.

~

What better inspiration can there be for the pursuit of science and philosophy? The material world has its laws but human consciousness has a higher reality which can be understood only when ignorance is destroyed by real knowledge, even as the great Adi Sankara himself achieved.

~

To the person whose ignorance is destroyed by real knowledge, God gives light equal to the light of the Sun.

~

If one has to realise something of Advaita from the feet of the acharya himself, the atmosphere around must be consistent with the aim of acquiring supreme knowledge. I had not understood the need to such consistencies and this was my second lesson.

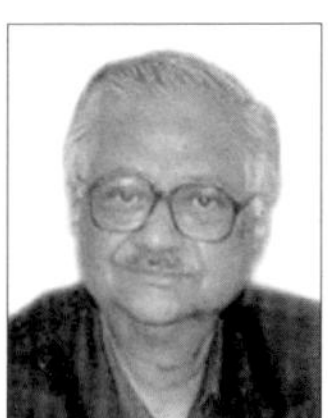

Raja Ramanna (1925–2004). He was an eminent physicist, a highly accomplished technologist, an able administrator, an inspiring leader, a gifted musician, and a scholar of Sanskrit literature and philosophy. He is well known for his work in the Indian Nuclear Programme. During the early stages of the development of the programme, he played a key role. He was responsible for expanding and supervising scientific research on nuclear weapons, and in 1974 conducted the test of nuclear device, code-named "Smiling Buddha", at Pokhran. He is also credited with installing the country's first series of nuclear reactors, Apsara, Cirus and Purnima. He initiated industrial defence programmes for the Indian Armed Forces. He received the Padma Vibhushan, India's second-highest civilian award. He died at the age of 79 in 2004.

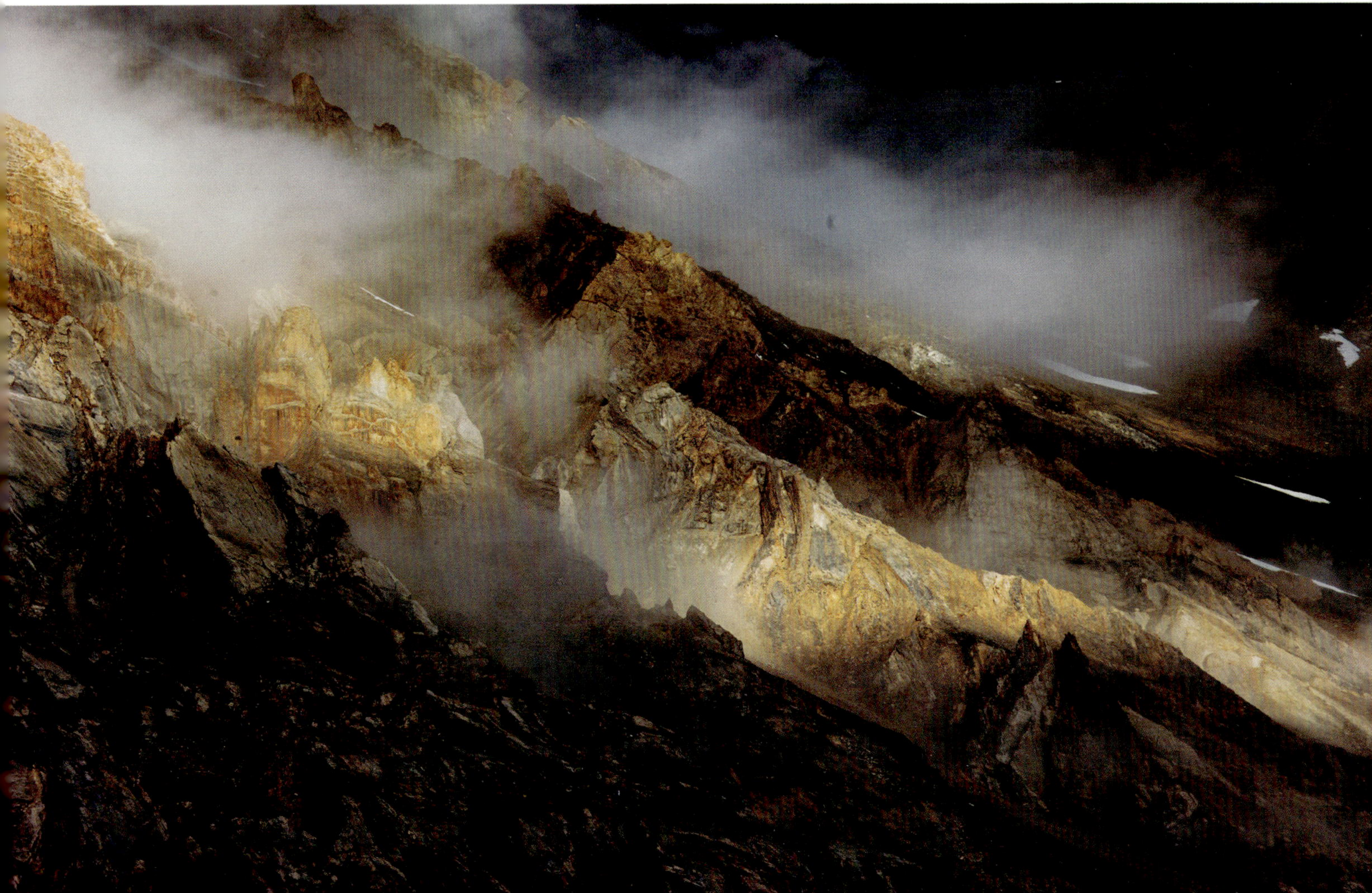

“

Today, for the first time in our long and chequered history, we find the whole of this vast land...brought together under the jurisdiction of one constitution and one union which takes over responsibility for the welfare of more than 320 million men and women who inhabit it.

~

Our constitution is comparatively a new constitution. It is based largely on the model of the British Constitution. As such it has history if not ancestry, which may well go back to centuries. It is being worked I venture to presume, successfully and to the satisfaction of all concerned although within the short period of ten years, it has had to undergo not less than one amendment...The constitution is largely founded on the British Constitution.

~

In attaining our ideals, our means should be as pure as the end!

~

I know I cannot do all the stuff that I did ten years ago. More importantly, I also understand my age and am in a better position to appreciate it.

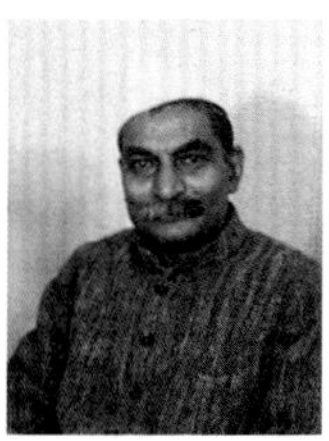

Rajendra Prasad (1884–1963). He was the first president of India. Educated as a lawyer, he joined the Indian independence movement as a prominent leader from his home state of Bihar. Affectionately called Rajan Babu, he firmly supported Gandhi. He was sent to prison in 1931 for taking part in the Salt Satyagraha and in 1942 for his active role in the Quit India Movement. He also served as president of the Indian National Congress from 1934 to 1935, when it was deeply involved with problems of the partition of the country. When independence finally came in 1947, Rajendra Prasad was instrumental in the preparation of the Constitution of India.

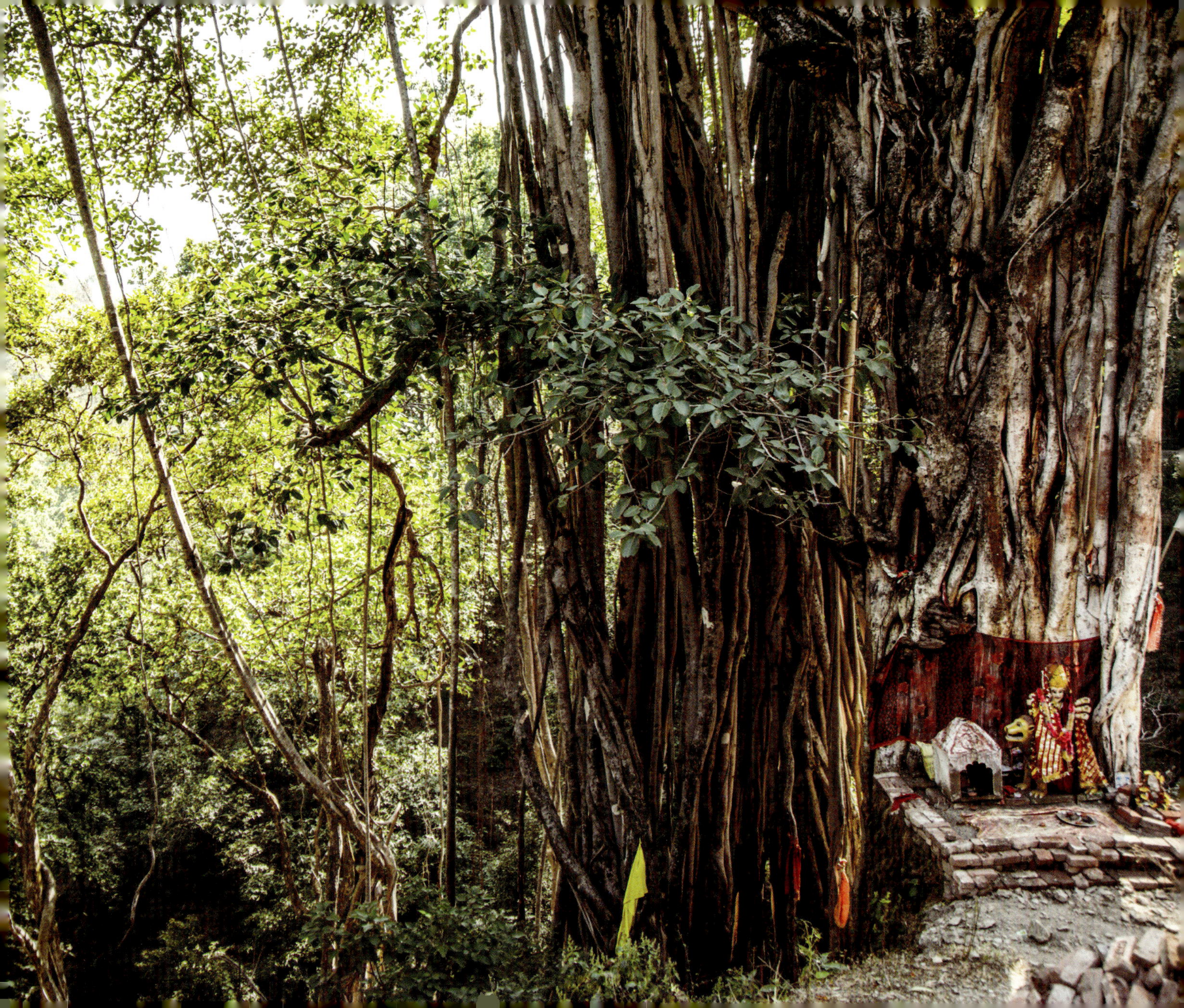

"

When there are thoughts, it is distraction: when there are no thoughts, it is meditation.

~

One must realise his Self in order to open the store of unalloyed happiness.

~

It is the Higher Power which does everything, and the man is only a tool. If he accepts that position, he is free from troubles; otherwise, he courts them.

~

Self-reform automatically brings about social reform.

~

No one succeeds without effort...Those who succeed owe their success to perseverance.

~

Let come what comes, let go what goes. See what remains.

~

All activities and events that a body is to go through are determined at the time of conception.

~

I am not the perishable body, but the eternal Self.

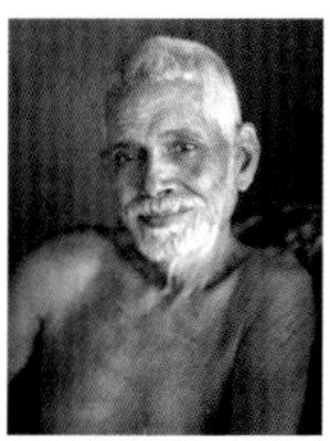

Ramana Maharshi (1879–1950). Maharshi was well known for his saintly life, for being fully realised, and for the powerful transmissions that often occurred to visitors in his presence. At the age of 16 he understood his true path and settled in Arunachala, where he remained till his death. When people were in his presence, their minds were affected. Ramana Maharshi always said that his most important teaching was done in silence. Another important teaching was self-awareness, which aimed to achieve diminished thoughts and heightened awareness. Sri Ramana summarised his method in a pamphlet called *Who Am I?*, which was for years his most widely circulated writing.

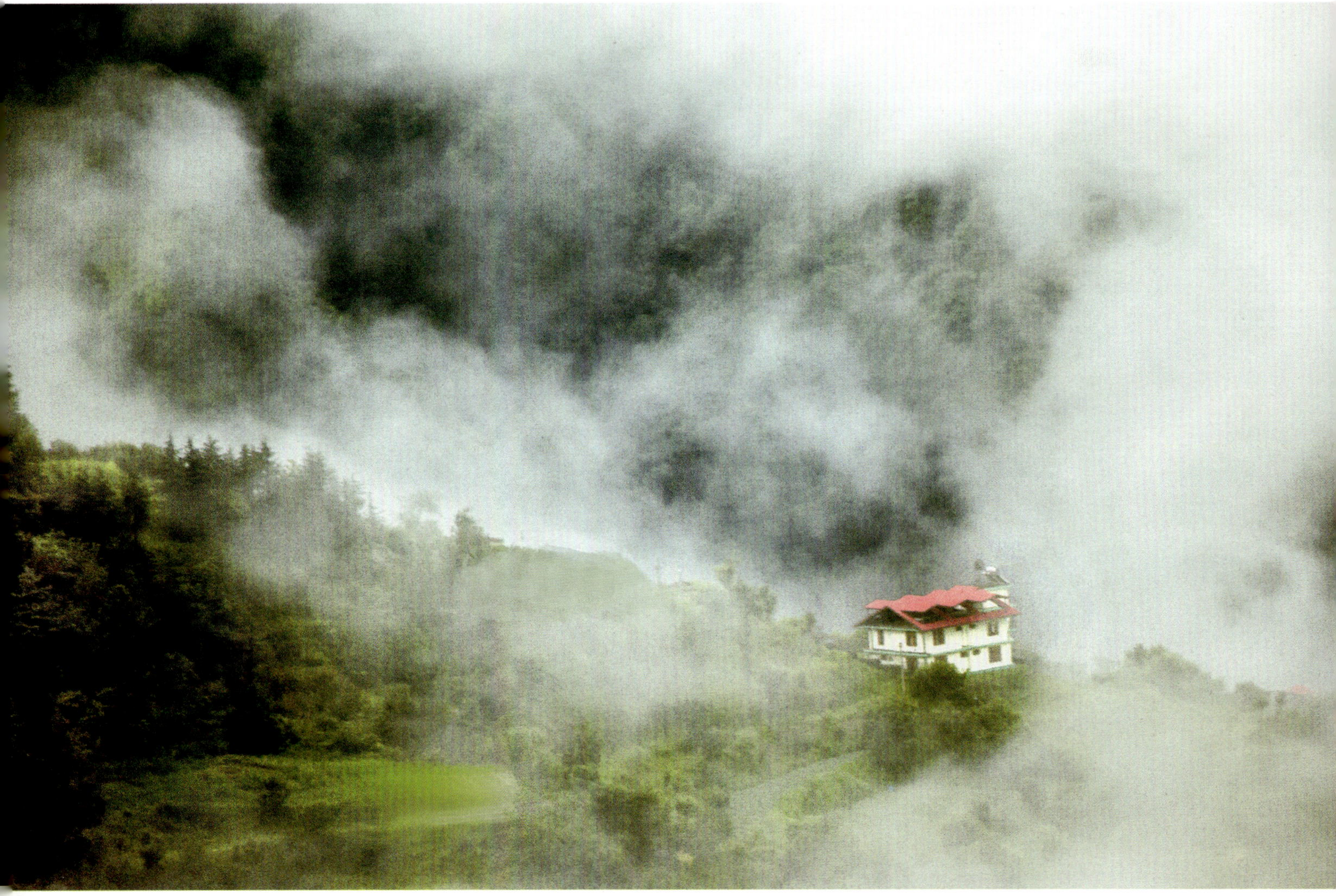

"

When the divine vision is attained, all appear equal;
and there remains no distinction of good and bad, or of high and low.

~

The fabled musk deer searches the world over for the source of the scent which comes from itself.

~

One must be very particular about telling the truth. Through truth one can realise God.

~

Travel in all the four quarters of the earth, yet you will find nothing anywhere.
Whatever there is, is only here.

~

Many good sayings are to be found in holy books,
but merely reading them will not make one religious.

~

Many are the names of God and infinite the forms through which He may be approached.

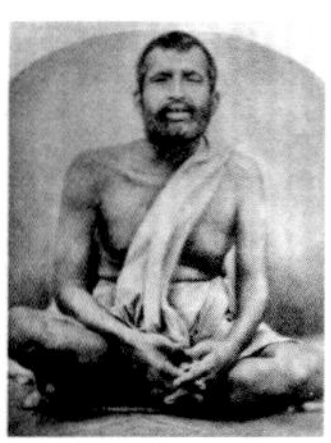

Ramakrishna Paramhansa (1836–1886). He played a highly important role in the Bengali Renaissance. A child prodigy, his parents had spiritual visions while he was in the womb and, as expected, he started having mystical experiences while he was still a child. His statement, 'If you must be mad, be it not for the things of the world. Be mad with the love of God,' suitably describes his life as a whole. He was mentored by several gurus. Notably, unlike other religious leaders of his era, Ramakrishna acknowledged all forms of worship.

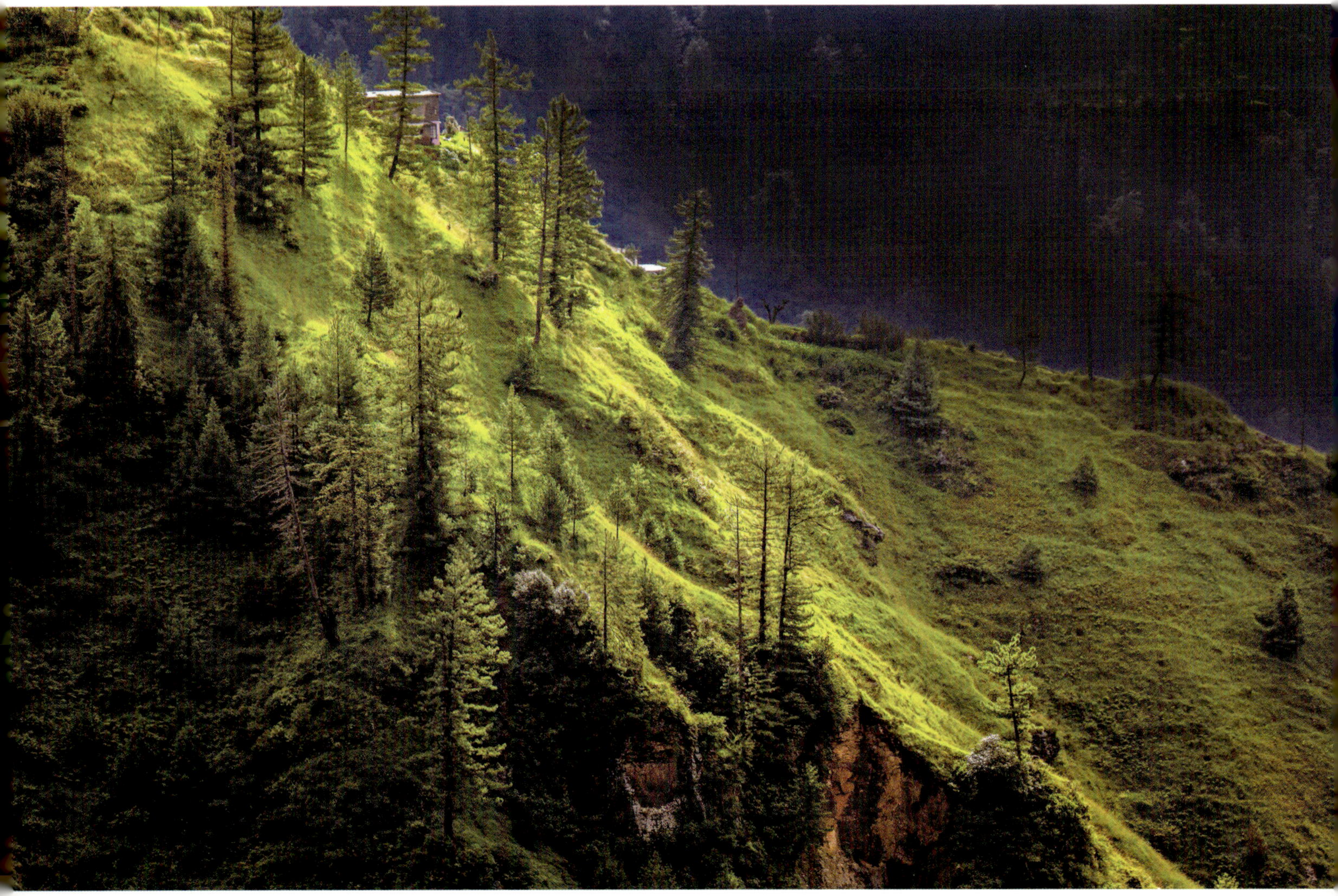

"

Satyagraha without constructive work is like a sentence without a verb.

~

Caste restricts opportunity. Restricted opportunity constricts ability.
Constricted ability further restricts opportunity.

~

Where caste prevails, opportunity and ability are restricted to ever-narrowing circles of the people.

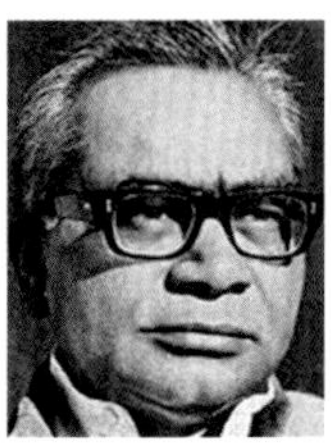

Ram Manohar Lohia (1910–1967). He was a socialist-political leader as well as a noted freedom fighter. He began his activities by organising a hartal after the death of Tilak and later led protests against the Simon Commission. He founded the Congress Socialist Party and was imprisoned on two occasions by the British government for his anti-national activities. After independence he came into limelight for his insistence on making Hindi the national language. He rigorously wrote articles to spread the message of toppling the British imperialistic governments from Asian and African countries. Dr Lohia was the first to introduce the idea unification of some 650 Indian princely states to form larger states, an idea later adopted by Sardar Patel. He argued that the welfare of the country depended on economic robustness.

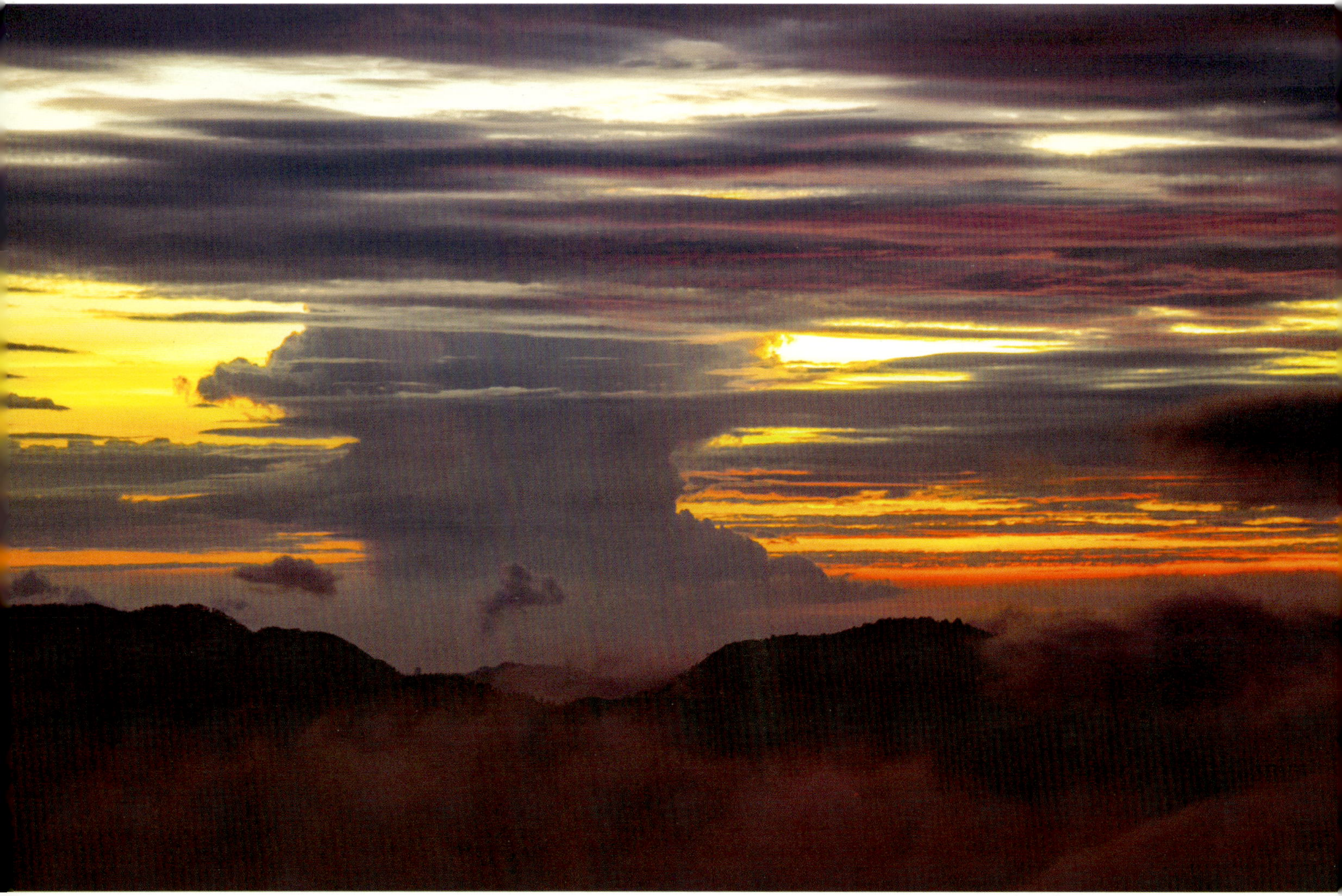

"

Just consider how terrible the day of your death will be.
Others will go on speaking and you will not be able to argue back.

~

If Science and Mathematics are necessary for them, why are they not necessary for us?

~

If this conch can give all the wealth of the world, it must be Goddess Lakshmi herself.
I can't understand why this poor fellow wishes to sell Goddess Lakshmi!

~

Enemies of liberty and friends of despotism have never been,
and never will be, ultimately successful.

~

There is only one God. None equals Him. He has no end.
He is present in all living beings.

~

Innumerable revolutions have taken place in all parts of the world
where no freedom of the press existed.

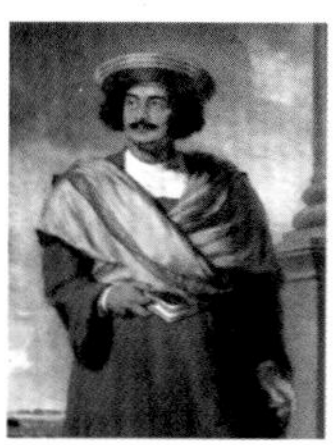

Ram Mohan Roy (1772–1833). He is known as the "Maker of Modern India". He established Brahmo Samaj, one of the first Indian socio-religious reform movements, and played a significant role in abolishing the social evil, sati. He discouraged idol worship and orthodox Hindu rituals and stood against conservatism, all sorts of social bigotry, and superstitions. He campaigned for the rights of women, including the rights of widows to remarry. He was also an exceptional scholar and an independent thinker. He promoted the study of English, science, Western medicine and technology. He was highly influential in public administration, politics, religion and education.

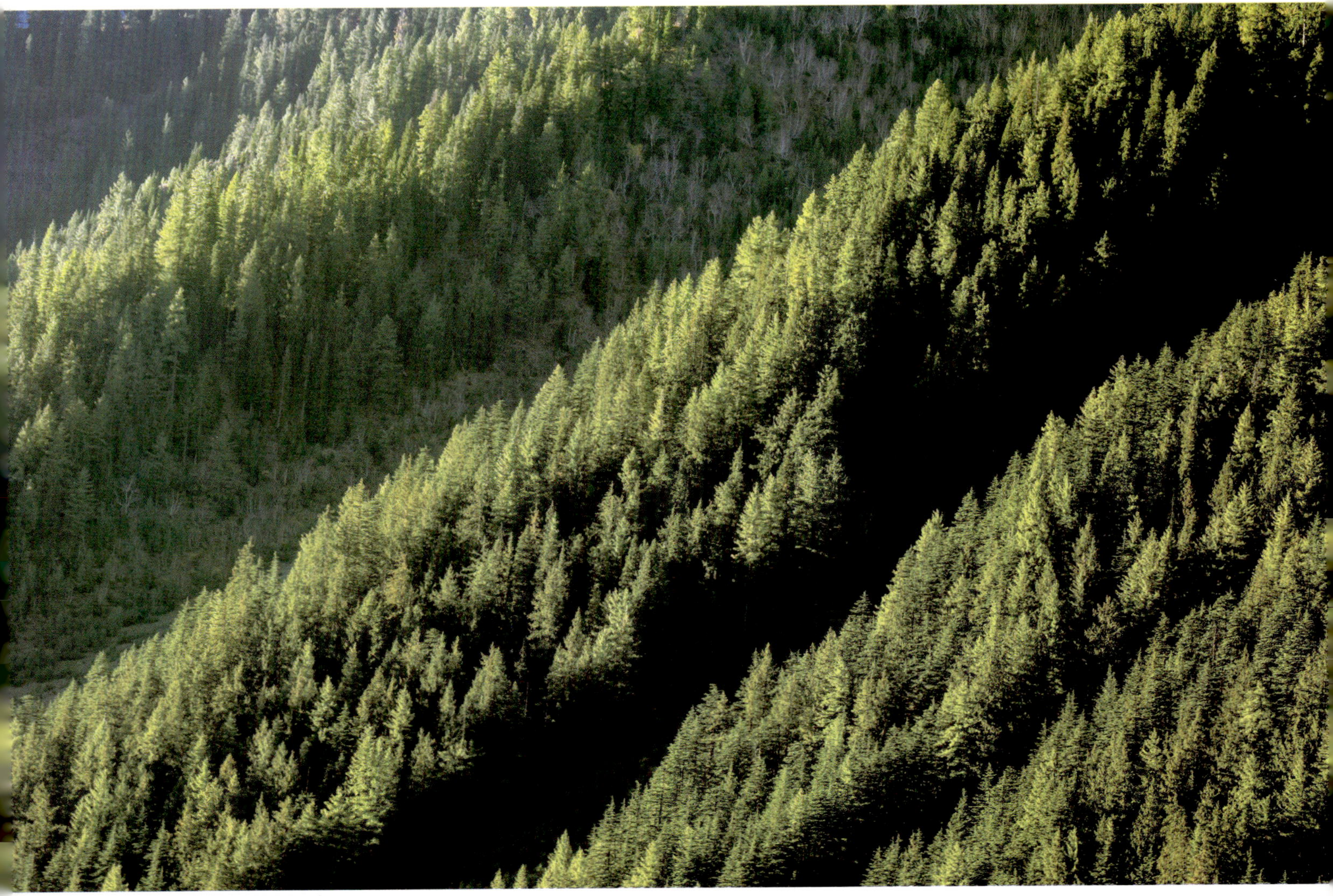

"

What obstacle is there apart from the religious one. There is plenty to do in the world without it.

~

This is the land of religion. Be it be for good or for evil, we cannot do without religion. Religious thoughts are in our blood. If we try to flee from it, it will pursue us.

~

We are but artless folk and not expert in rhythm, time, and tune, but that does not matter. He for whom we sing our hymns understands them all, and he pays no attention to our deficiencies of execution.

~

We have above all to learn what is to bear and forbear—to bear ridicule, insults, even personal injuries at times, and forebear from returning abuse for abuse. In the words of the prophet of Nazareth, we have to take up the cross, not because it is pleasant to be persecuted, but because the pain and injury are as nothing by the side of the principle for which they are endured.

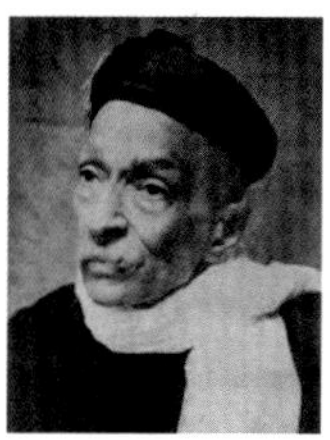

Ranade (1842–1901). Mahadev Govind Ranade was a founding member of the Indian National Congress. He was also a scholar and social reformer. He was one of the foremost people who condemned untouchability and the caste system. He campaigned for social reforms such as the emancipation of oppressed classes, widow remarriage, and liberation of women. He founded Prarthna Samaj, a Hindu movement inspired by Brahmo Samaj, promoting principles of enlightened belief based on the ancient Vedas. He edited a Bombay Anglo-Marathi daily paper *Induprakash*, founded on his ideology of social and religious reform. He was the mentor of renowned freedom fighters Gopal Krishna Gokhale and Bal Gangadhar Tilak.

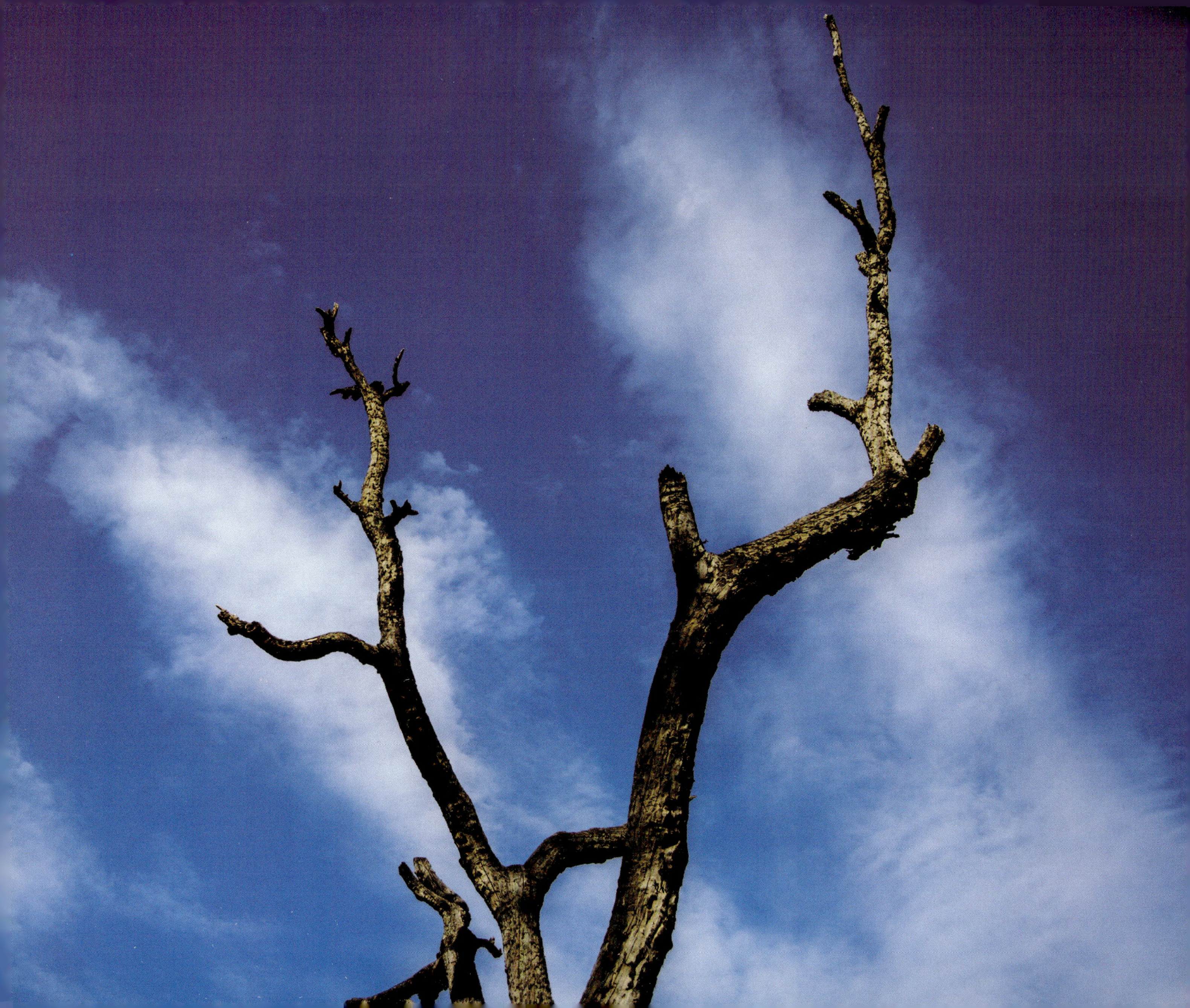

“

An equation means nothing to me unless it expresses a thought of God.

~

I have not trodden through a conventional university course,
but I am striking out a new path for myself. I have made a special investigation of
divergent series in general and the results I get are termed by
the local mathematicians as “startling”.

~

While asleep, I had an unusual experience. There was a red screen formed by
flowing blood, as it were. I was observing it. Suddenly a hand began to write on the screen.
I became all attention. That hand wrote a number of elliptic integrals.
They stuck to my mind. As soon as I woke up, I committed them to writing.

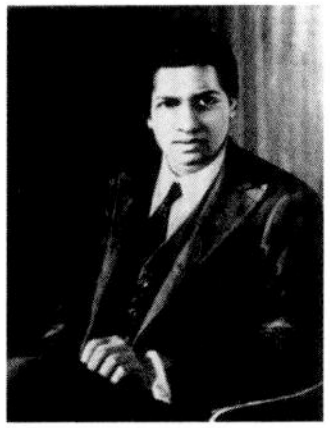

S. Ramanujan (1887–1920) was a famous self-taught mathematician. He lived a short but productive life, and continues to be an inspiration for mathematicians across the world; his work has inspired a lot of research over the years. He was born in Tamil Nadu. It is remarkable that without any formal training, he made extraordinary contributions to mathematics. He did this all on his own till Indian mathematicians discovered him. His fame spread to Europe, and then he had a partnership with the English mathematician, G.H. Hardy of Cambridge. He was the second Indian to be included as a Fellow of the Royal Society. A follower of his family goddess Mahalakshmi, Ramanujan credited her for his abilities. His birth anniversary, December 22, is celebrated as National Mathematics Day.

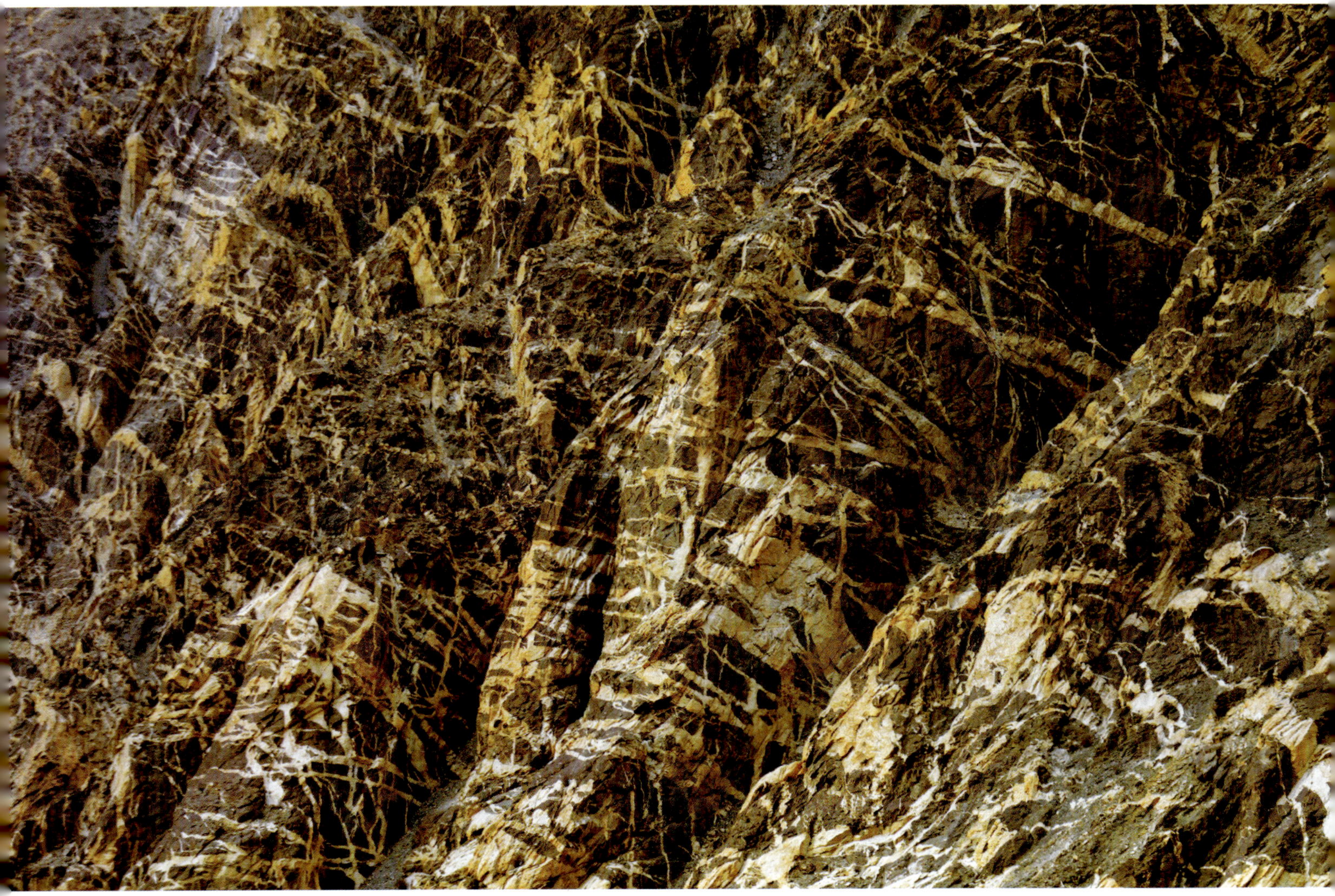

"

Be ashamed of your hatred. Give up hatred and be quiet.

~

Wealth is really a means to work out dharma.
If one uses it merely for personal enjoyment, it is vainly spent.

~

Gain and loss, birth and death, are in the hands of God.

~

All gods are one. There is no difference between a Hindu and a Muslim.
Mosque and temple are the same. Satsang, that is, associating with the good, is good.
Dussaya, or associating with evil-minded people, is evil and must be avoided.

~

Choose friends who will stick to you till the end, through thick and thin.

~

Distinguish right from wrong and be honest, upright and virtuous.

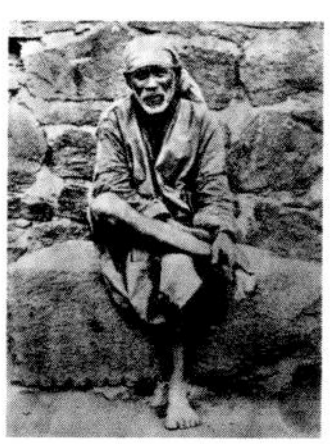

Sai Baba Of Shirdi (1835–1918). He is generally called Shirdi Sai Baba. His simple language and his devotion to solving the problems of poor and destitute people made him known as Shri Sai Baba. There is a mystery about him as to whether he was a Muslim or a Hindu, as both communities revere him deeply. Sai Baba considered the faith of his followers a matter of no concern. He believed that the path through the complexities of life lay in spiritual training by surrendering to a *satguru* or murshid. He was against the love of perishable things and urged people towards self-realisation. His moral code stood for love, forgiveness, helping others, charity and contentment. Today, he is worshipped by people all around the world. He is regarded by his followers as a fakir, saint, and *santguru*, according to their beliefs.

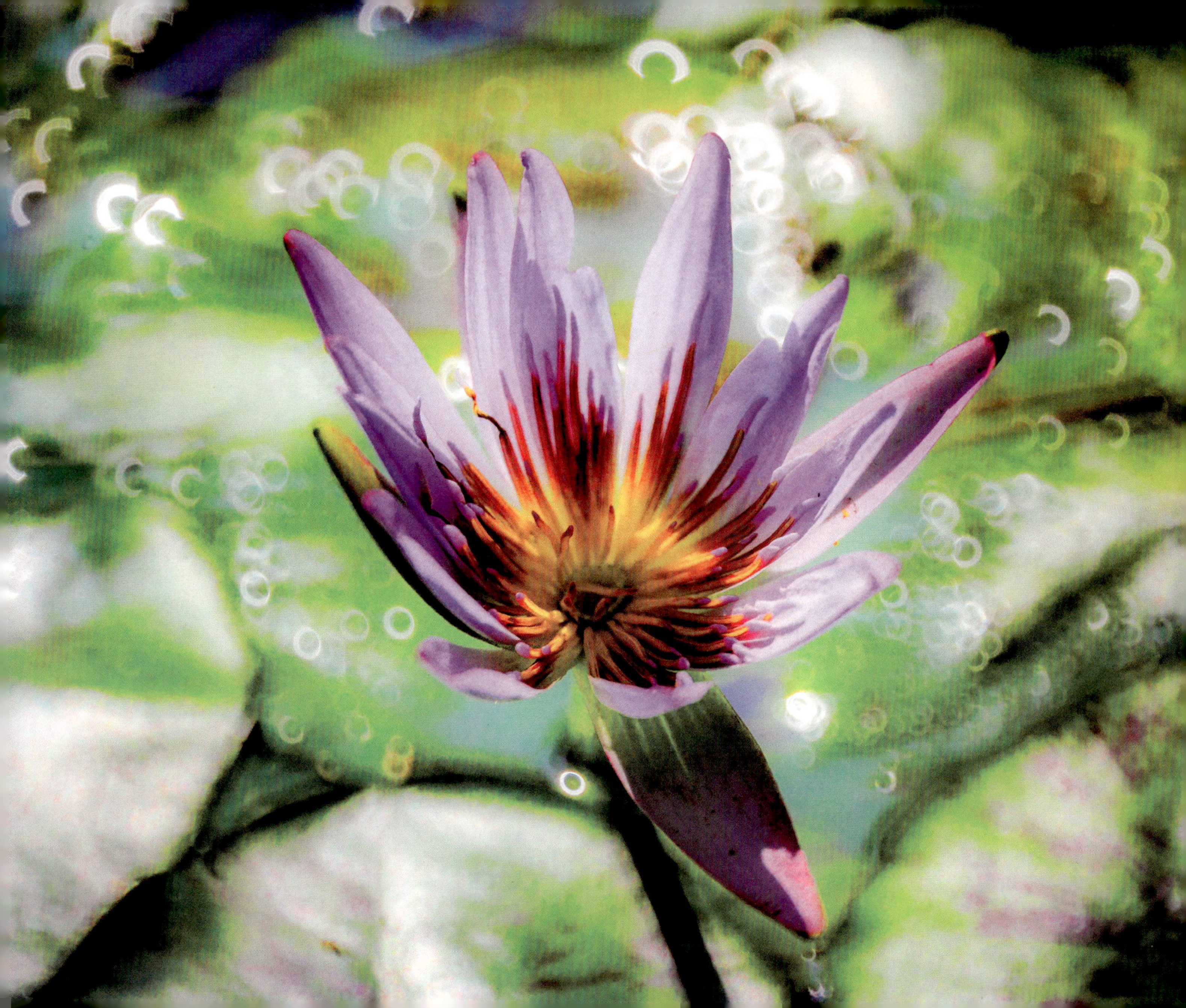

"

The sayings of a man who practised what he preached must be of special interest to us.

~

Duty well performed purifies the mind, and qualifies one for Bhakti.

~

The Vedas should be followed as long as one has not risen above attachment and duality, just as a watchman is needed to guard the fruits of a mango tree until the fruits are removed, and then he can be dispensed with.

~

So when a man transcends body consciousness he is beyond the Vedic Order.

~

Through Love, the devotee can even become God.

~

God and His devotees are akin to the ocean and its waves.

~

To emaciate one's body with fasts and the like is not true penance. So long as evil passions persist in man, all external appliances are useless.

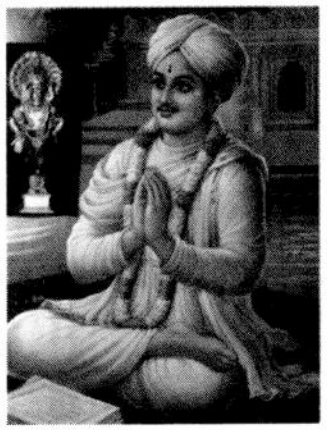

Sant Eknath was one of the great rishis of Maharashtra, and his work on the Bhagavad Gita was groundbreaking. This renaissance transformed society completely, culminating in independence from Islamic rule for most of India. Born into a Brahmin family near Aurangabad, he was dedicated to devotional practices. The precise dates of his birth and death are uncertain, but it is believed he lived in the 16th century. He went on to become a scholar fluent in Marathi, Sanskrit, Persian and Arabic. He fought against the social evil of untouchability and this made many enemies for him in his own community of Brahmins. He wrote many treatises like the *Bhavartha Ramayana, Rukmini Swayamvara* and *Eknath Bhagavatam.*

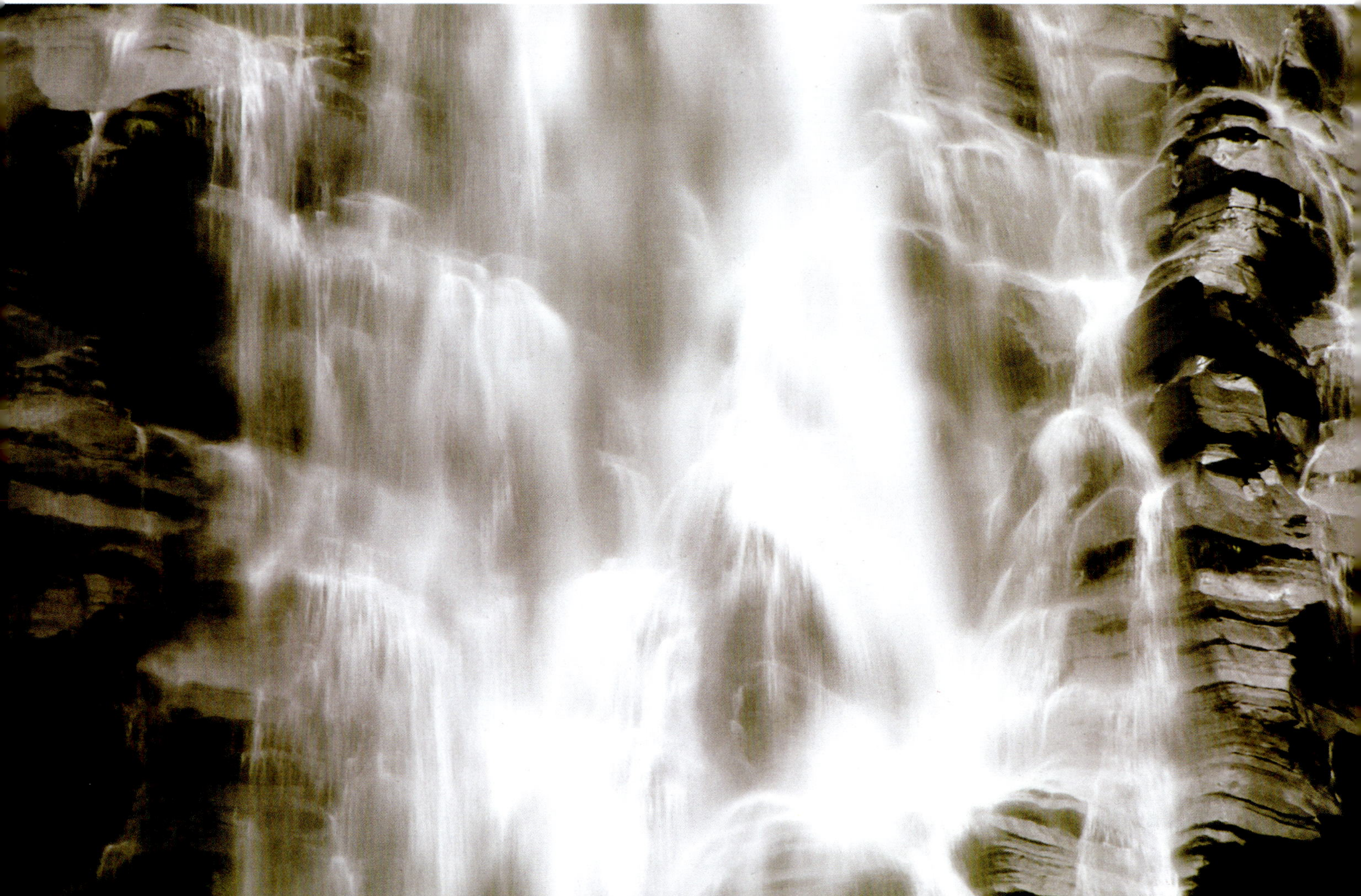

"

I am blunt and uncultured. To me there is only one answer to this question. That answer is not that you should shut yourselves in colleges and learn history and mathematics while the country is on fire and everybody is fighting freedom's battle. Your place is by the side of your countrymen, who are fighting the freedom's battle.

~

We have to shed mutual bickering, shed the difference of being high or low, develop a sense of equality and banish untouchability. We have to restore the conditions of Swaraj prevalent prior to British rule. We have to live like children of the same father.

~

In a domestic government unity and cooperation are essential requisites.

~

No distinctions of caste and creed should hamper us. All are the sons and daughters of India. We should all love our country and build our destiny on mutual love and help.

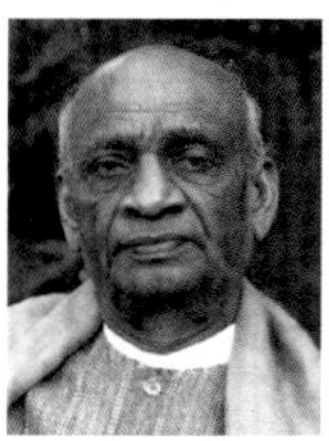

Sardar Patel (1875–1950). Though his full name was Vallabhai Jhaverbhai Patel, he is generally known as Sardar Patel. He not only played a great role in the movement for Indian Independence but was largely responsible for the transformation of India into a united country. He was a born leader. He began his career as a lawyer in his home state of Gujarat, where he mobilised the local population for non-violent civil disobedience against the British Raj. This made him a popular leader in Gujarat. His popularity eventually led him to be the leader of the Indian National Congress. He participated in the Quit India Movement. For his tough approach to merge princely states into the Indian Republic he was called "The Iron Man of India".

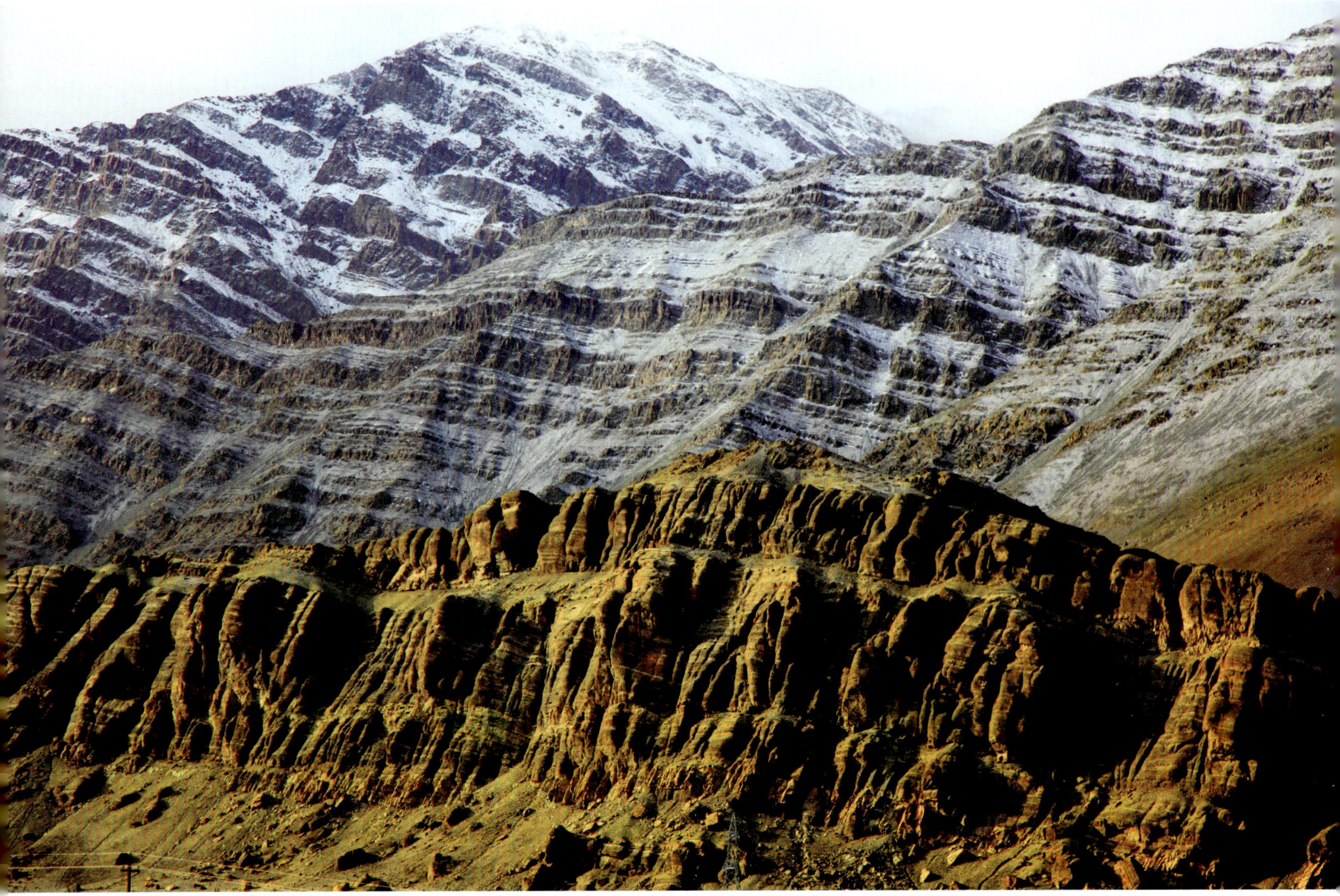

“

We want deeper sincerity of motive, greater courage in speech, and earnestness in action.

~

A country's greatness lies in its undying ideals of love and
sacrifice that inspire the mothers of the race.

~

A sense of justice is one of the most wonderful ideals of Islam,
because as I read in the Qur'an I find those dynamic principles of life,
not mystic but practical ethics for the daily conduct of life, suited to the whole world.

~

When there is oppression, the only self-respecting thing is to rise and say,
this shall cease today, because my right is justice.
If you are stronger, you have to help the weaker boy or girl both in play and in work.

~

Nay, do not grieve tho' life be full of sadness, dawn will not veil her splendour for your grief,
nor spring deny their bright, appointed beauty to lotus blossom and ashoka leaf.
Nay, do not pine, tho' life be dark with trouble, time will not pause or tarry on his way.

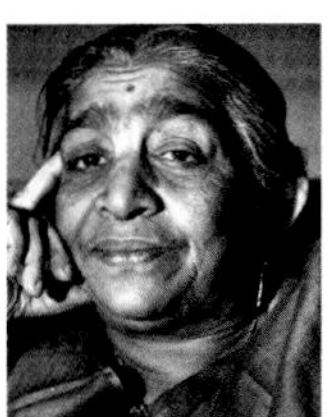

Sarojini Naidu (1879–1949) was born in Hyderabad. She is known as the Nightingale of India. She was a renowned poet and activist who advocated for independence. From 1947 to 1949 she held the position of the first governor of the United Provinces of Agra and Oudh. The first woman to occupy that prestigious post, she also had the distinction of becoming the second woman to hold the post of the President of Indian National Congress in 1925, and the first Indian woman to do so. Her birthday is celebrated as Women's Day as a mark of respect for her role in Indian Independence.

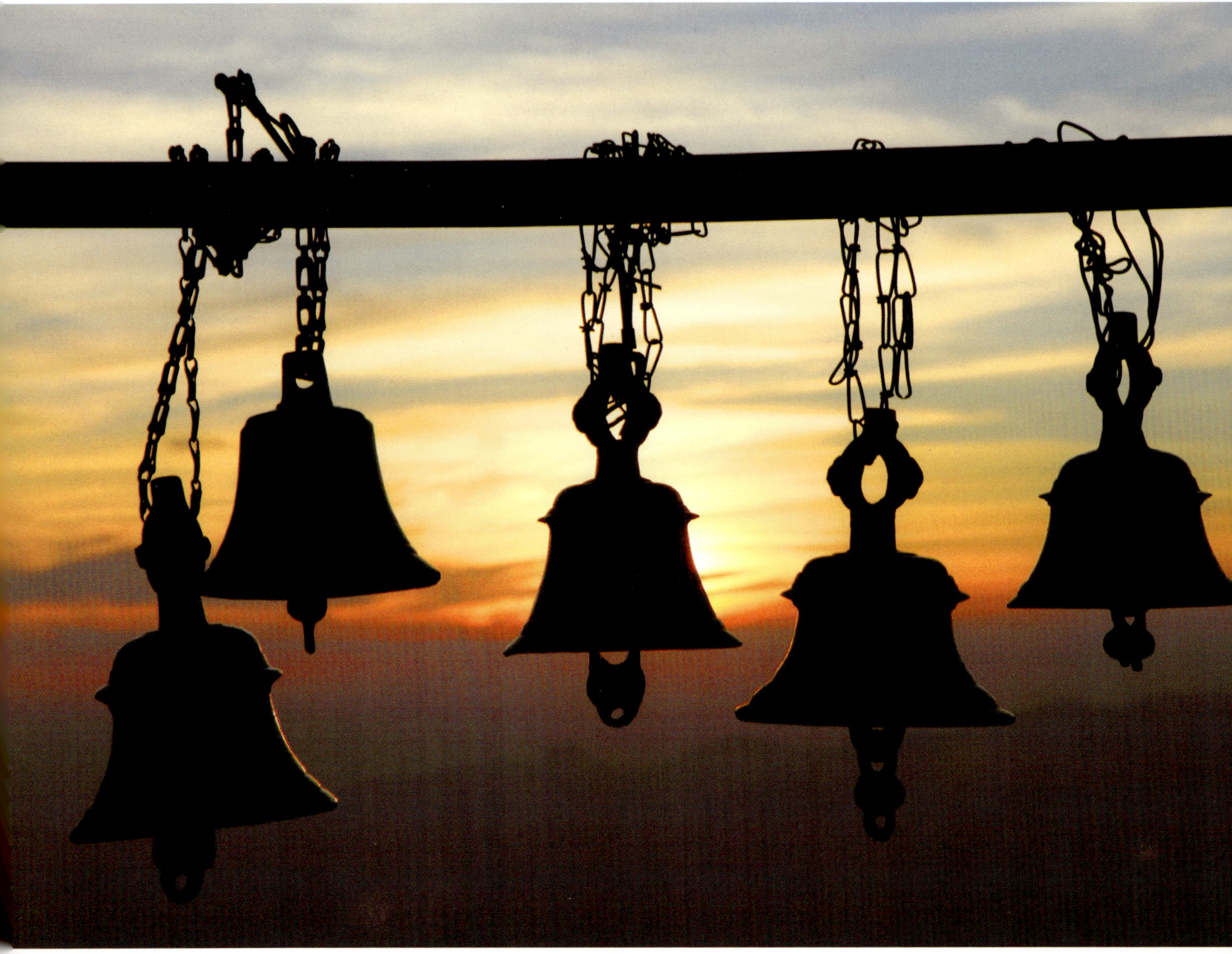

"

It is the intense spirituality of India, and not any great political structure or social organisation, that it has developed, that has enabled it to resist the ravages of time and the accidents of history.

~

The main function of a university is not to grant degrees and diplomas,
but to develop the university spirit and advance learning.
The former is impossible without corporate life, the latter without honours and post-graduate.

~

The true teachers are those who help us think for ourselves.

~

Hinduism is not just a faith. It is the union of reason and intuition that cannot be defined but
is only to be experienced. Evil and error are not ultimate.
There is no Hell, for that means there is a place where God is not,
and there are sins which exceed his love.

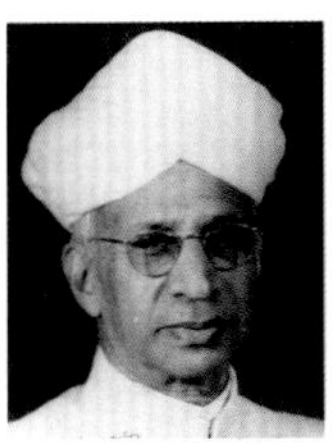

Sarvepalli Radhakrishnan (1888–1975) is one of the most famous and recognised philosophers, academicians and statesmen of the 20th century. All his life the focus of his writings was on his religion, i.e., Hinduism. He dwelt on the spirit of Hinduism and argued that the religion was coherent and of very high ethical standards. As he was familiar with Western philosophy too, he helped bridge the gap between East and West through his extensive writings, teachings and lectures. He drew from knowledge of both worlds and was equally at home on both turfs. His writings have helped the West to appreciate the complexities of Hinduism; otherwise it would have remained obscure to the common man. He also held the highest office in India as president of the country.

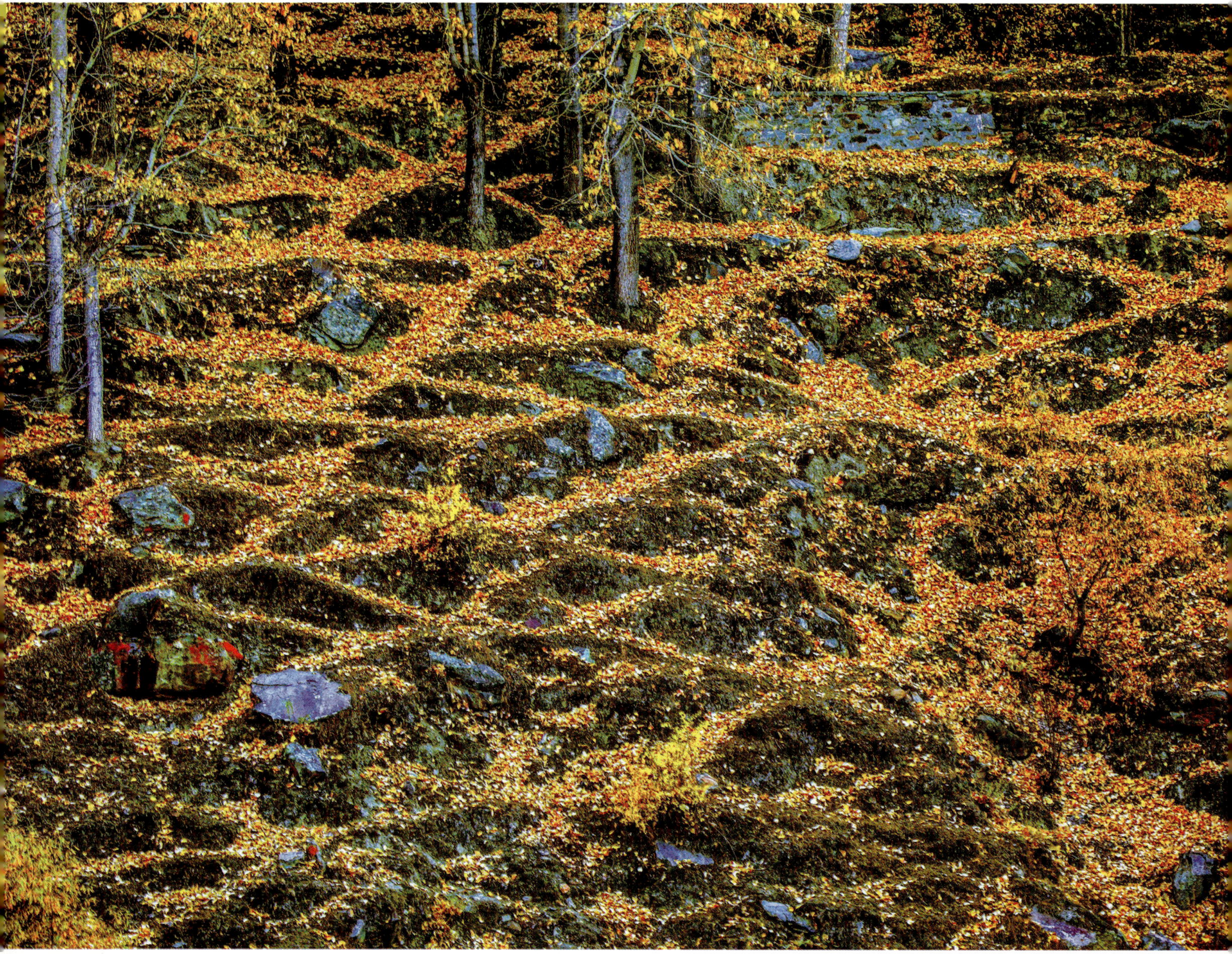

“

Do not follow a truth that resembles a lie.

~

Always find an excuse to do something good.

~

If you want the position of a saint, remain away from the king's family.

~

Look the way you are, otherwise your true face will be unveiled automatically.

~

A person should perform such deeds which keep him alive for ever.

~

Truthful in love is a person who has only love and nothing else in his heart.

~

Do not degrade yourself to achieve a rank.

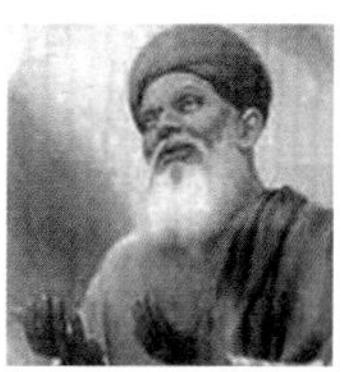

Sheikh Farid (1173–1266). His full name was Fariduddin Masud Ganjshakar. He was a Sufi saint and a Muslim missionary from the Chishti order. He lived in the Punjab region of the subcontinent. He was affectionately called “Baba Farid” and was born in Kothewal, 10 km from Multan, Pakistan. He is broadly considered the first major poet of the Punjabi language. Many famous people have visited his shrine over the years.

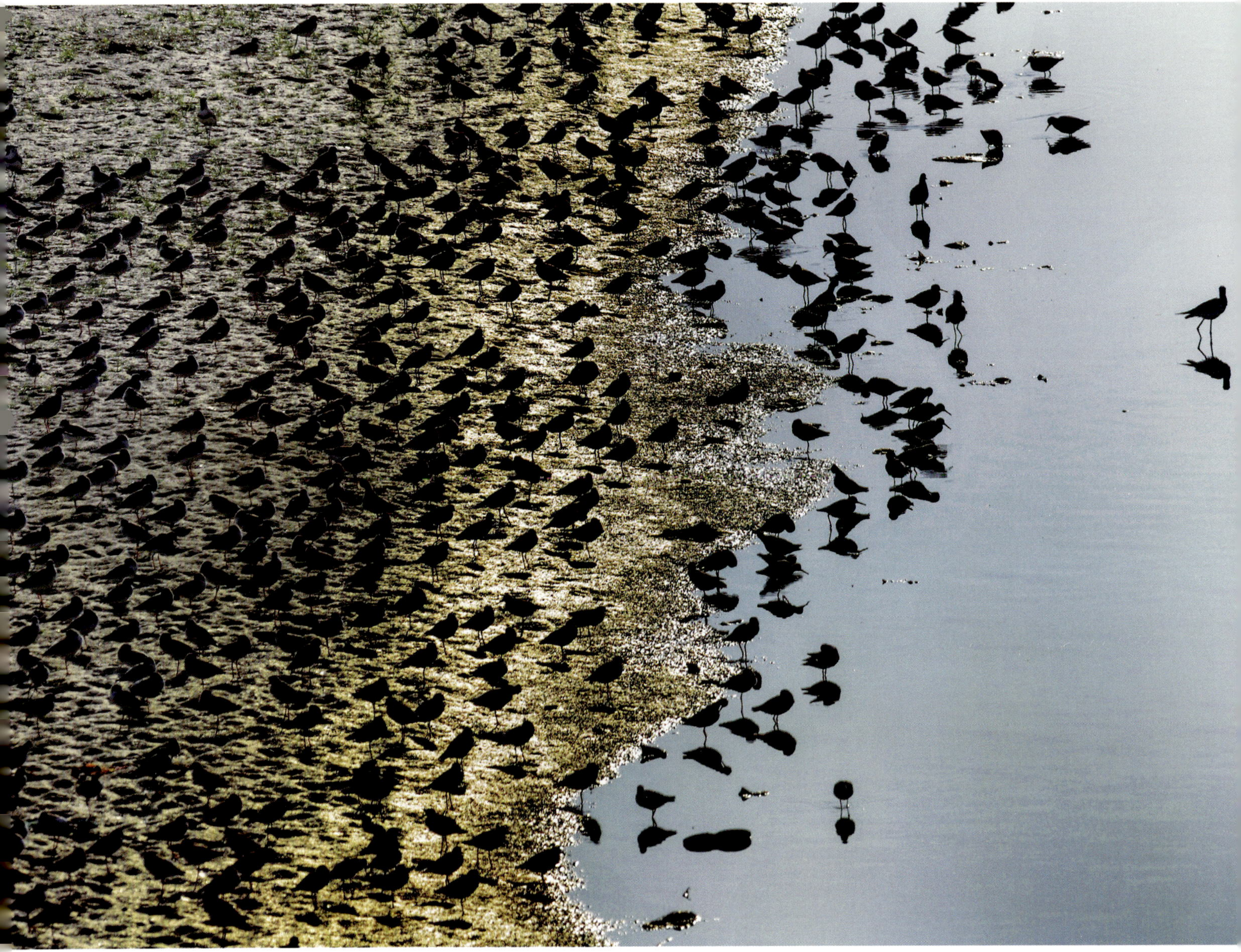

"

One caste, one religion, one God for man; one form and the same blood in all; I cannot find any differences.

~

Whatever be the religion of a man, it is enough if it makes him virtuous.

~

Ask not, say not, think not caste.

~

Acts that one performs for one's own sake should also aim the good of others.

~

Gain freedom through education, gain strength through organisation, gain prosperity through industry.

~

Love of others is my happiness, Love that is mine is happiness for others. And so, truly, deeds that benefit a man must be a cause for others' happiness too.

~

Men may differ in their faiths, their languages and their modes of dressing; but there can be no evil in inter-dining and intermarriage, because all belong to the same kind of creation.

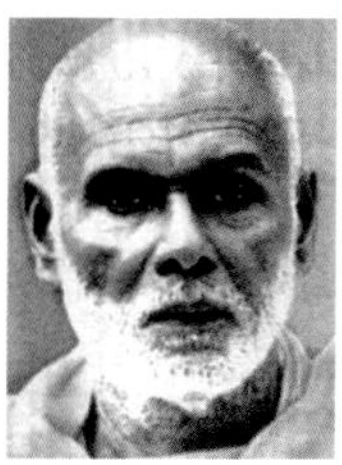

Shree Narayana Guru (1856–1927). He was a saint-reformer and led a quiet but important social revolution. A hero of the downtrodden, he asserted, "One people, One dharma, One God for all." Gurudevan, as he was fondly known to his followers, protested casteism and promoted new values of spirituality and social equality. He embraced all who were tabooed as untouchables and opposed any injustice towards these weakly privileged folks. He taught that all men belong to one and the same caste, all men belong to one and the same religion, and all men belong to one and the same God. He is renowned for his knowledge of the Vedas, openness to other's views, poetic proficiency, non-violent philosophy and persistent resolve to correct social wrongs.

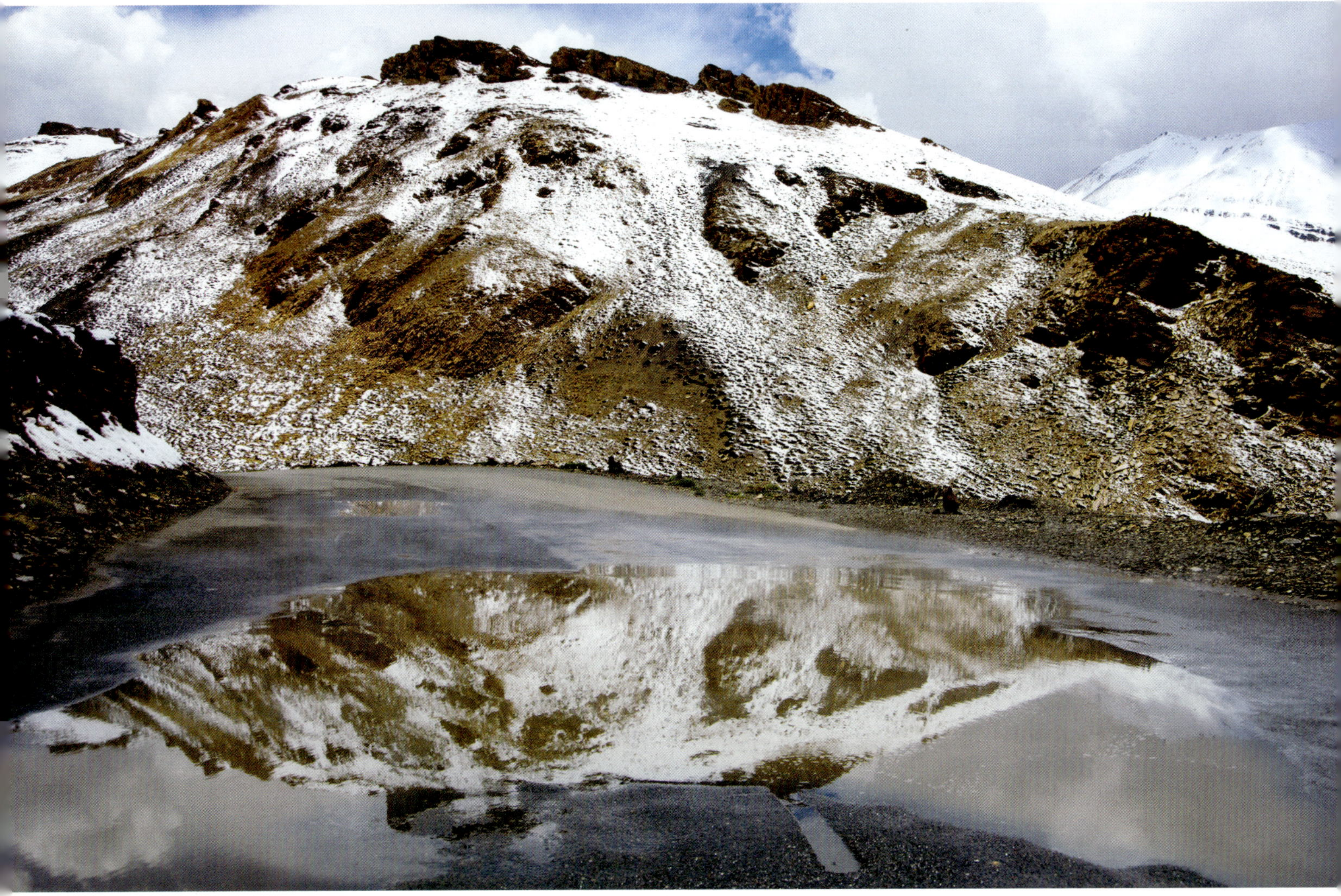

"

Whatever work you undertake, do it seriously, thoroughly and well; never leave it half-done or undone, never feel yourself satisfied unless and until you have given it your very best. Cultivate the habits of discipline and toleration. Surrender not the convictions you hold dear but learn to appreciate the points of view of your opponents.

~

Political and social justice requires not the disintegration of a country and destruction or humiliation of a class which shows initiative, intelligence and drive, but equality of opportunity for all, and genuine freedom for self-fulfilment, in which all men irrespective of caste or creed may share.

~

What we deplore is not that the gate of western knowledge was thrown open to Indians, but that such knowledge was imported to India at the sacrifice of our own cultural heritage. What was needed was a proper synthesis between the two systems and not neglect, far less destruction, of the Indian base.

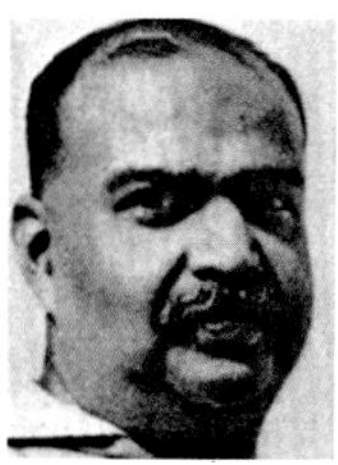

Shyama Prasad Mukherjee (1901–1953). He was born in Calcutta. He was a well-known Indian academician, politician, and barrister, who served as a minister of Industry and Supply in Prime Minister Jawaharlal Nehru's cabinet. After some time he developed differences with the Indian National Congress and with Nehru and quit. He later founded the right-wing nationalist party Bhartiya Jan Sangh, which later evolved into the Bhartiya Janta Party.

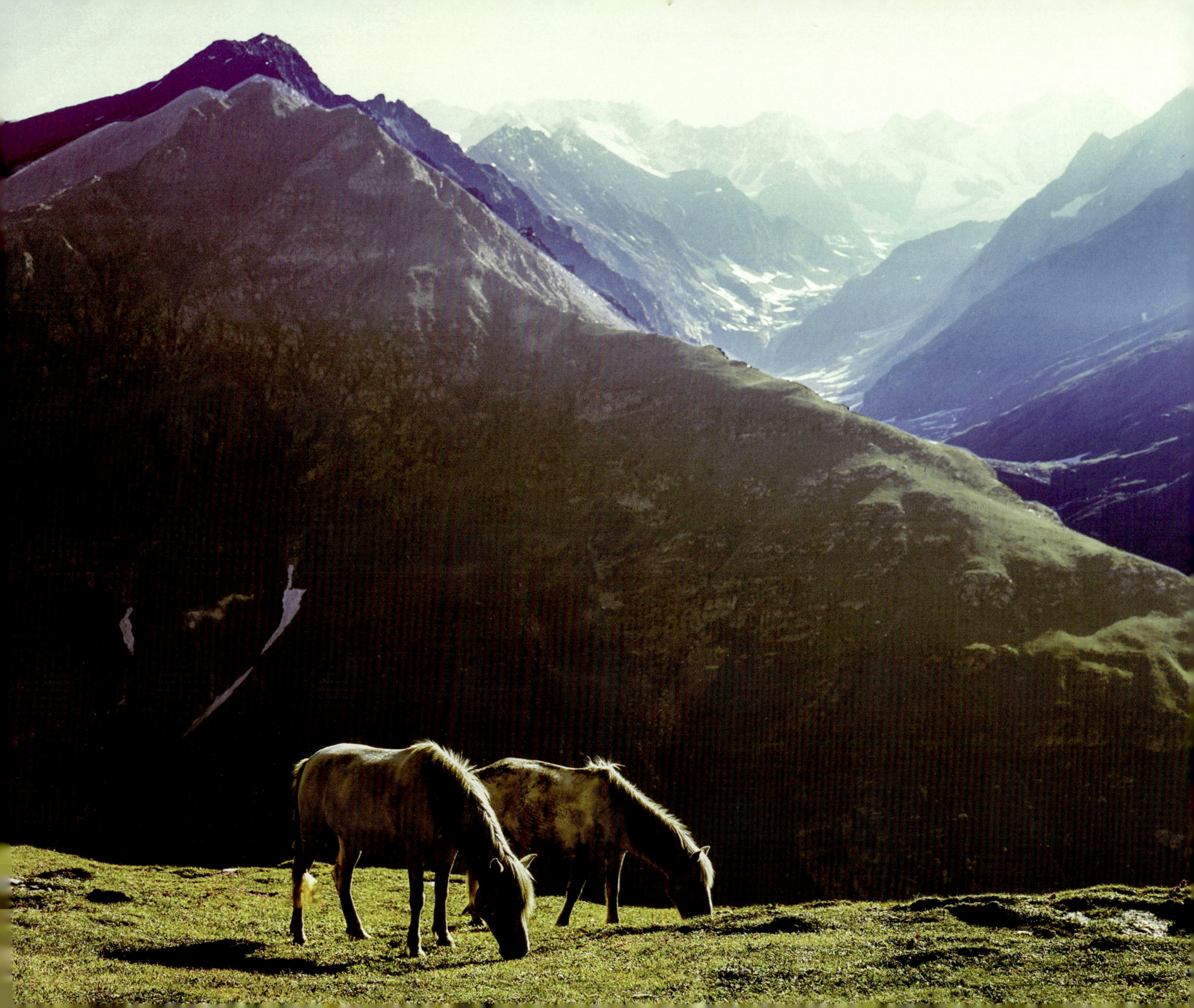

"

I am the master of my failure...If I never fail, how will I ever learn?

~

To an observer situated on the moon or on one of the planets, the most noticeable feature on the surface of our globe would no doubt be the large areas covered by oceanic water. The sunlit face of the earth would appear to shine by the light diffused back into space from the land and water-covered areas. In the history of science, we often find that the study of some natural phenomenon has been the starting point in the development of a new branch of knowledge.

~

A voyage to Europe in the summer of 1921 gave me the first opportunity of observing the wonderful blue opalescence of the Mediterranean Sea. It seemed not unlikely that the phenomenon owed its origin to the scattering of sunlight by the molecules of the water.

~

You can't always choose who comes into your life, but you can learn what lesson they teach you.

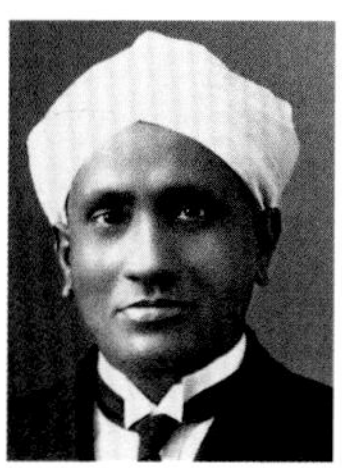

Sir C.V. Raman (1888–1970). Raman was born in Madras and did exemplary work in light scattering, for which in 1930 he received the Nobel Prize for Physics. For his commendable research he was awarded the Bharat Ratna in 1954. C.V. Raman was immersed in a scientific atmosphere from his childhood days as his father was a lecturer in mathematics and physics. Raman has been bestowed with a number of honorary doctorates and memberships of scientific societies. He was elected a Fellow of the Royal Society early in his career and in 1929 was knighted. Raman became the first Indian director of the Indian Institute of Science in Bangalore and in 1947 became independent India's first National Professor. In 1948 he founded the Raman Research Institute in Bangalore, where he worked until the end of his life.

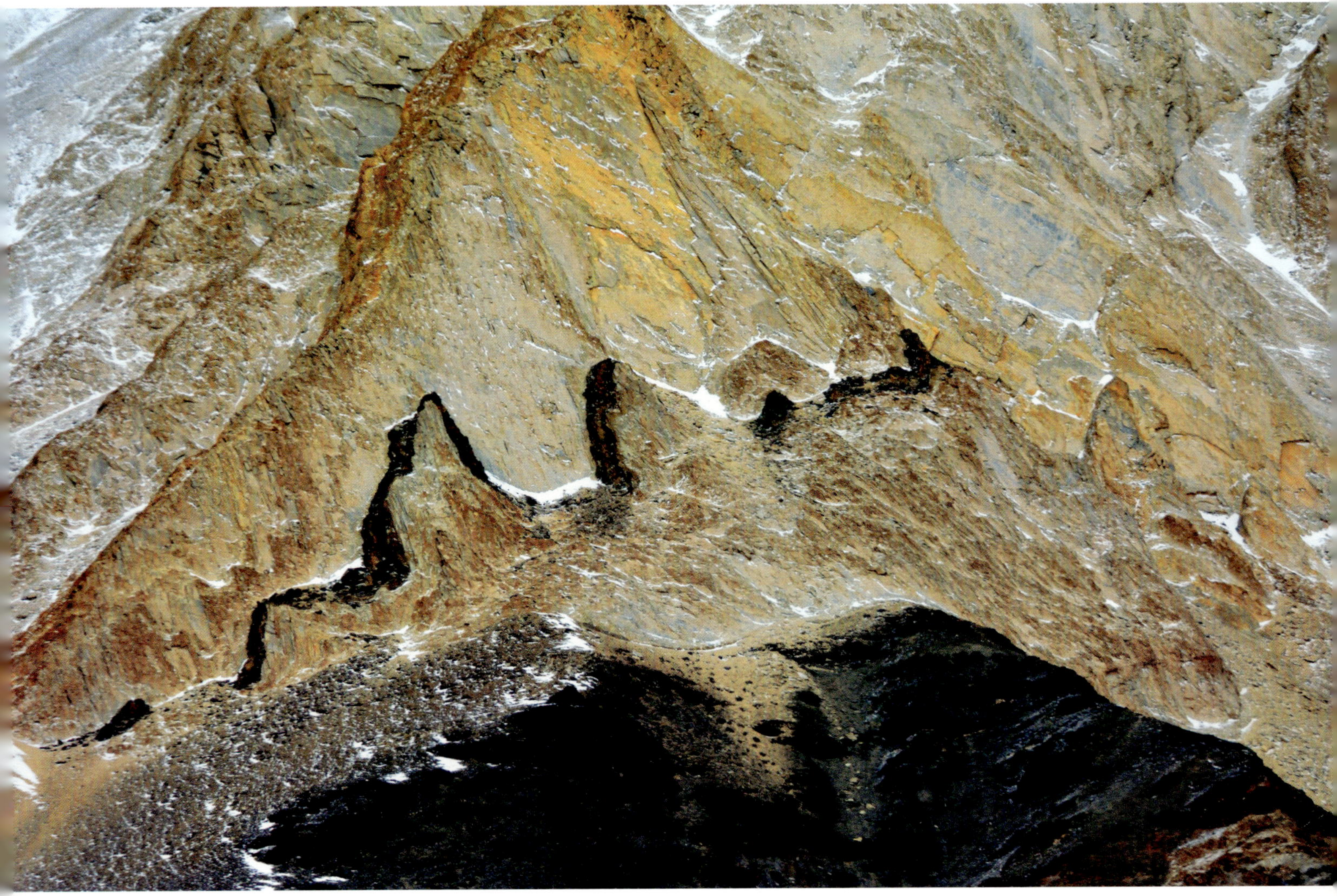

"

I was educated at Cambridge. How admirable is the Western method of submitting all theory to scrupulous experimental verification! That empirical procedure has gone hand in hand with the gift for introspection, which is my Eastern heritage. Together they have enabled me to sunder the silences of natural realms long uncommunicative. The telltale charts of my crescograph 2 are evidence for the most sceptical that plants have a sensitive nervous system and a varied emotional life. Love, hate, joy, fear, pleasure, pain, excitability, stupor, and countless appropriate responses to stimuli are as universal in plants as in animals.

~

I have recently returned from an expedition to scientific societies of the West. Their members exhibited intense interest in delicate instruments of my invention, which demonstrate the indivisible unity of all life. The Bose crescograph has the enormity of ten million magnifications. The microscope enlarges only a few thousand times; yet it brought vital impetus to biological science.

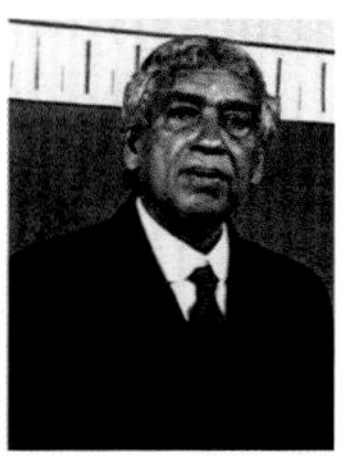

Sir Jagdish Chandra Bose (1858–1937) was a prominent Indian scientist and proved by experimentation that both animals and plants share much in common. He made a sophisticated instrument called the crescograph, which could measure the growth of plants. Later on, the instrument received widespread commendation. Sir J.C. made subtle investigations of plant science and radio and microwave optics. In a way he laid the foundations of experimental science in the Indian subcontinent. In 1904 he became the first Indian to get a US patent. Prior to his death in 1937, he set up the Bose Institute at Calcutta (now Kolkata). He is considered the father of radio science as well as of Bengali science fiction. A crater on the moon has been named after him as an honour.

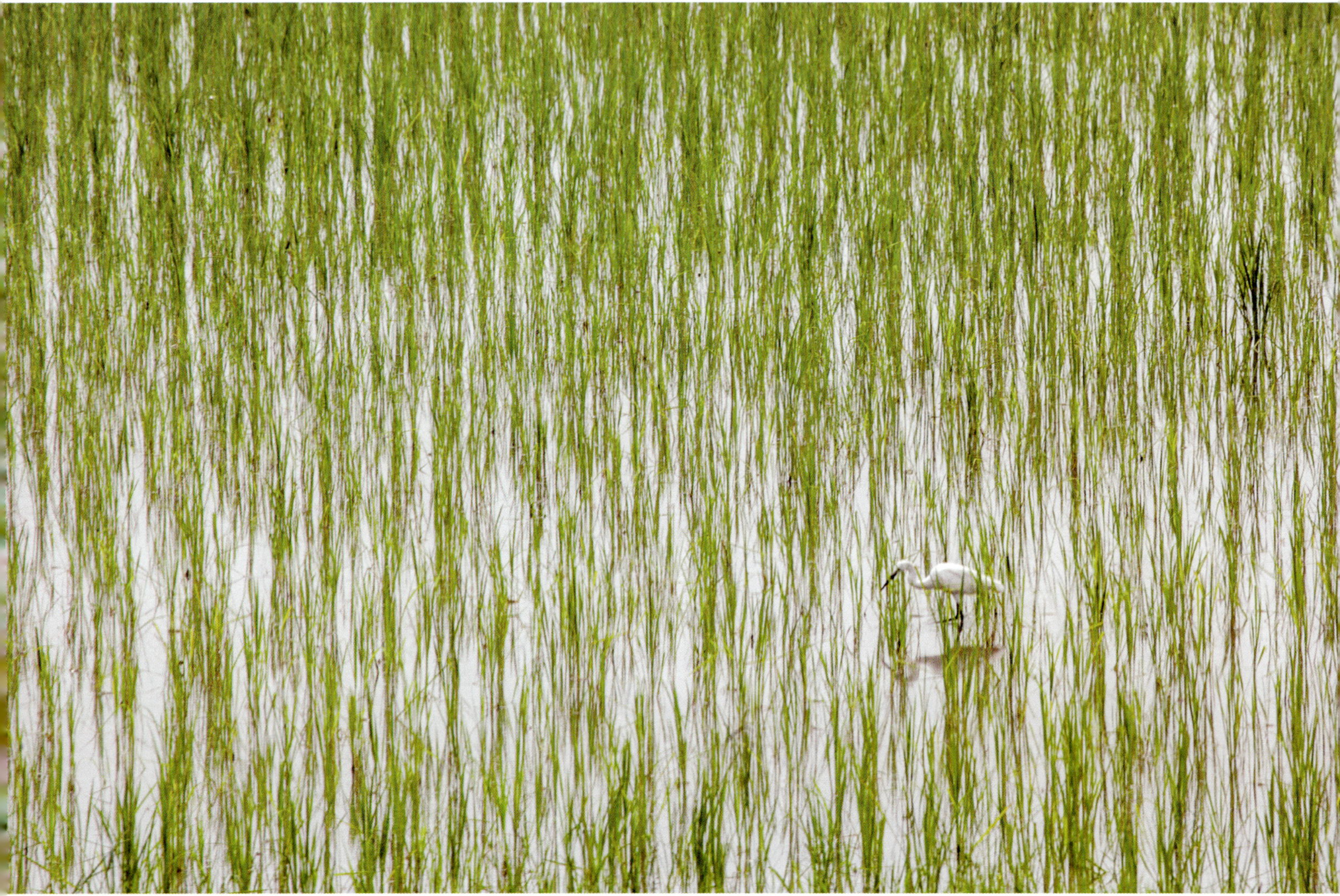

"

Put your heart, mind, and soul into even your smallest acts. This is the secret of success.

~

It is divinity that shapes, not only your ends, but also your acts, your words and thoughts.

~

Do not love leisure. Waste not a minute. Be bold. Realise the Truth, here and now!

~

Humility is not cowardice. Meekness is not weakness.
Humility and meekness are indeed spiritual powers.

~

Life is a pilgrimage. The wise man does not rest by the roadside inns.
He marches direct to the illimitable domain of eternal bliss, his ultimate destination.

~

Always do good to others. Be selfless. Mentally remove everything and be free.
This is divine life. This is the direct way to moksha or salvation.

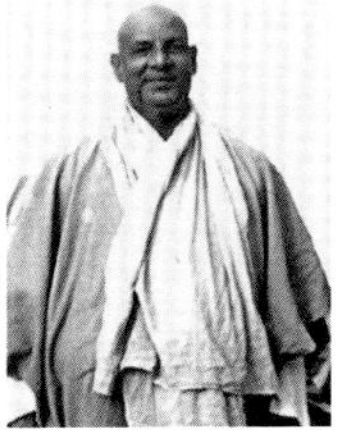

Sivananda Saraswati (1887–1963). Sivananda was born in Tamil Nadu. He was a Hindu spiritual teacher. He studied medicine before assuming a spiritual life. He founded the Yoga-Vedanta Forest Academy and the Divine Life Society, and has authored more than 200 books on yoga, Vedanta and many other subjects. He believed in synthesis in everything, in yoga as well as in the alleviation of human suffering. He desired to serve people genuine Ayurvedic preparations made from Himalayan herbs. His devoted disciples are drawn from all religions, cults and creeds.

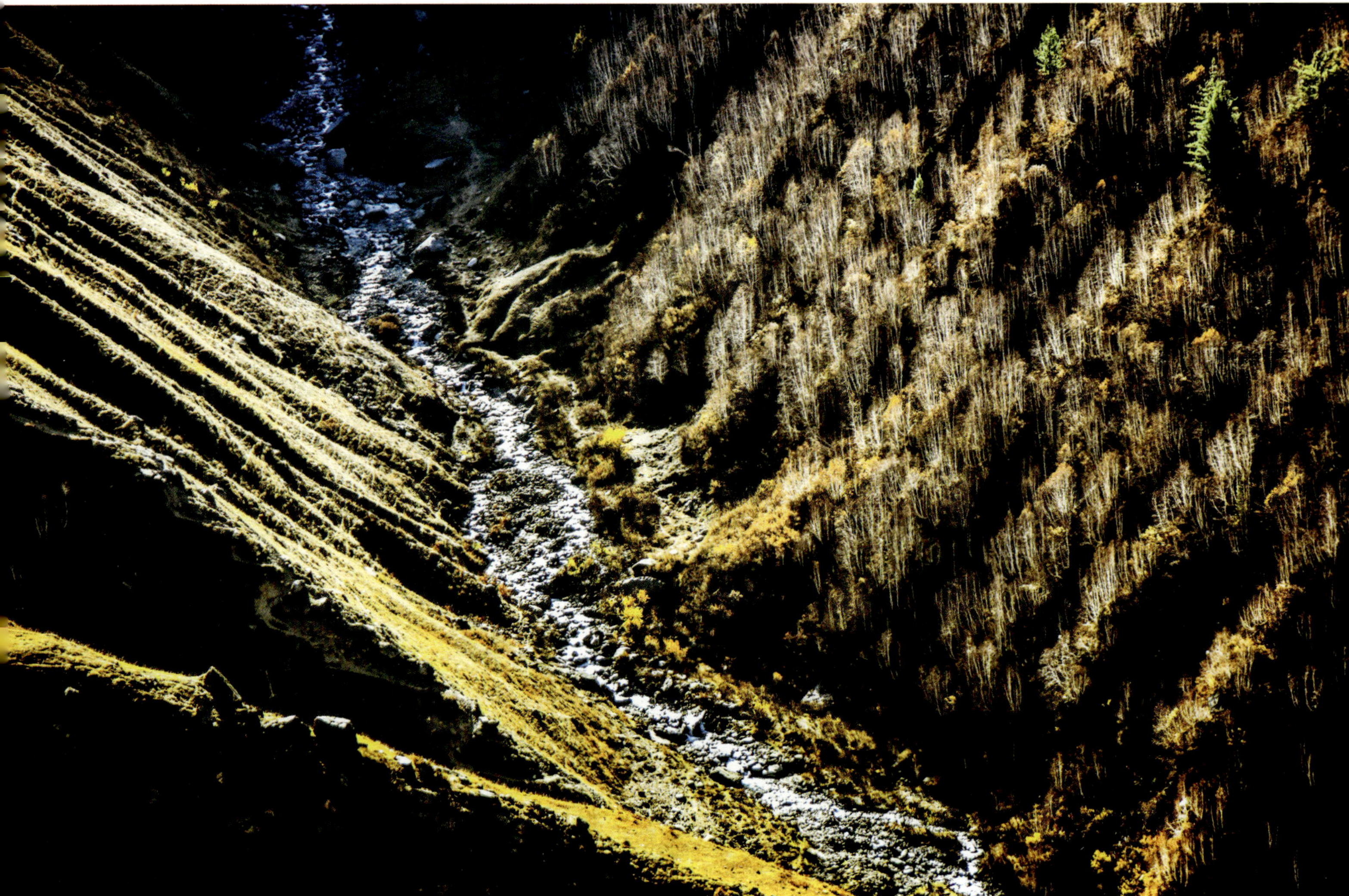

Spirituality is indeed the master key of the Indian mind; the sense of the infinitive is native to it.

~

India is the meeting place of the religions, and among these Hinduism alone is by itself a vast and complex thing, not so much a religion as a great diversified and yet subtly unified mass of spiritual thought, realisation and aspiration.

~

India of the ages is not dead, nor has she spoken her last creative word; she lives and has still something to do for herself and the human peoples.

~

True knowledge is not attained by thinking. It is what you are; it is what you become.

~

But few are those who tread the sunlit path;
Only the pure in soul can walk in light.

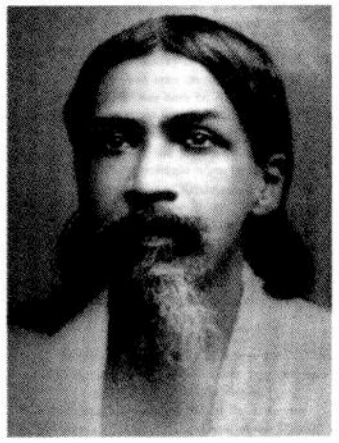

Sri Aurobindo (1872–1950). Aurobindo Ghose, also known as Sri Aurobindo, was a spiritual guru, an exceptional scholar, and a national leader. His participation in the Indian national movement was not long, but it was relevant. He came to prominence due to his robust involvement in the freedom struggle against the British; gradually, however, he became a spiritual and yogic guru. He moved to Pondicherry, where he used spiritual activities to work on human evolution. He was nominated for the Nobel Prize in Literature in 1943 and the Nobel Prize for Peace in 1950. His political and philosophical works were lauded by President Rajendra Prasad and by Prime Minister Jawaharlal Nehru.

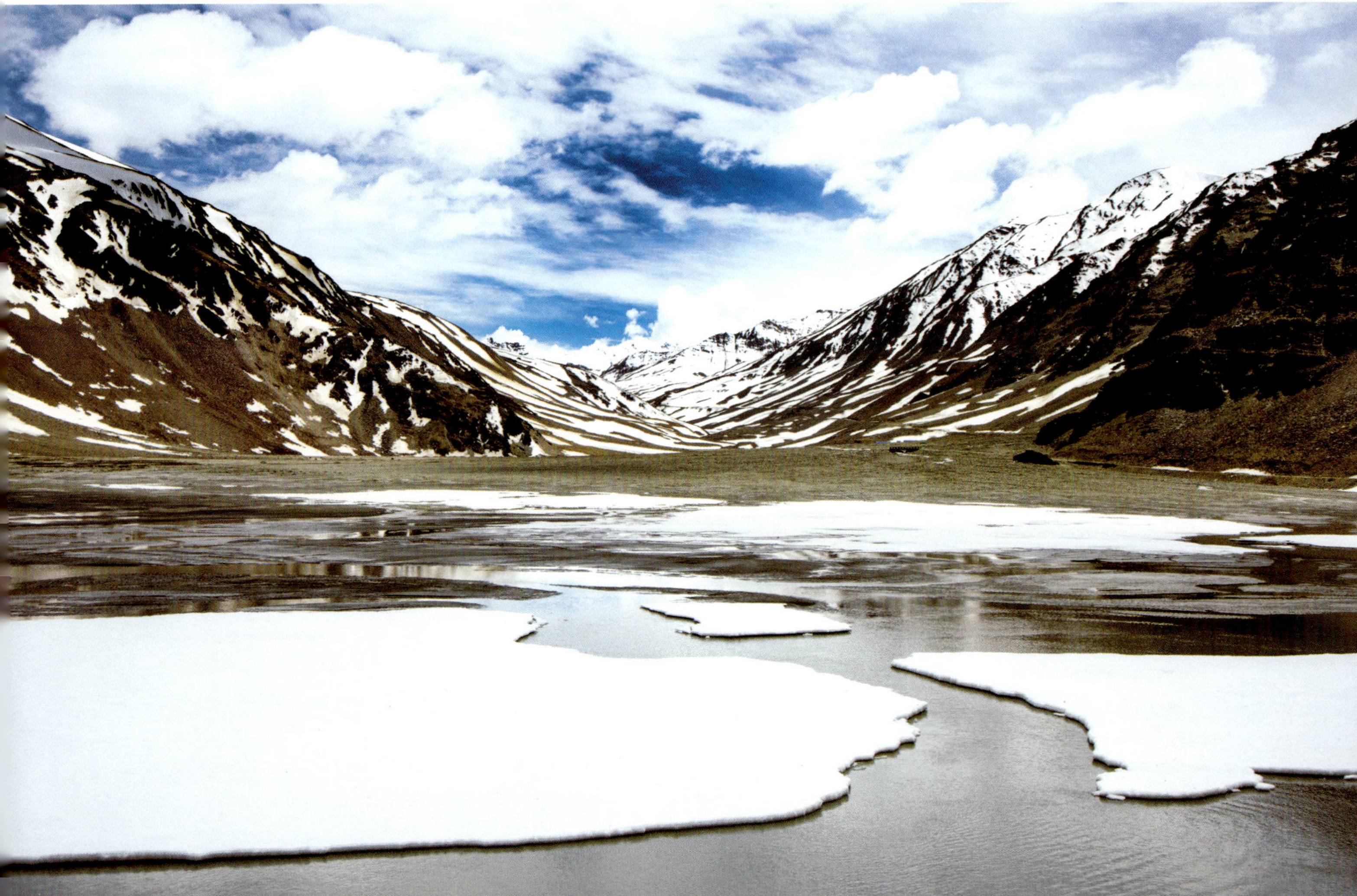

"

One individual may die for an idea, but that idea will, after his death, incarnate itself in a thousand lives.

~

It is our duty to pay for our liberty with our own blood. The freedom that
we shall win through our sacrifice and exertions, we shall be able to preserve with our own strength.

~

No real change in history has ever been achieved by discussions.

~

Freedom is not given—it is taken.

~

Nationalism is inspired by the highest ideals of the human race, *satyam* the true, *shivam* the god,
sundaram the beautiful. Nationalism in India has...
roused the creative faculties which for centuries had been lying dormant in our people.

~

Forget not that the grossest crime is to compromise with injustice and wrong.
Remember the eternal law: you must give, if you want to get.

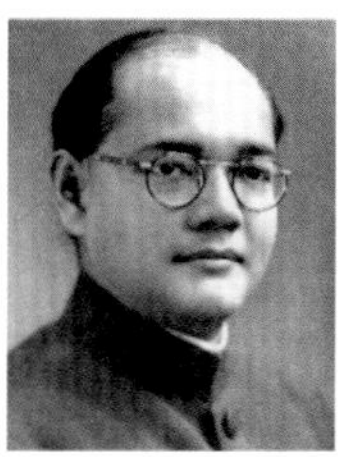

Subhas Chandra Bose (1897–1945). Popularly known as Netaji, he was a rebel, and utterly defiant of the British occupation of India. His goal and ambition was to see a free India. His burning patriotism made him a hero of the masses. He made valiant attempts to forge a unity with Germany and Japan to create an alliance to shake off the foreign yoke. This had a troubled legacy. He formed a small army of volunteers, regardless of cast or religion, who vowed loyalty to him to fight the British violently. He did not believe in non-violence and thus had major differences with Nehru and Gandhi. His disappearance and death is a mystery that has not been solved till date.

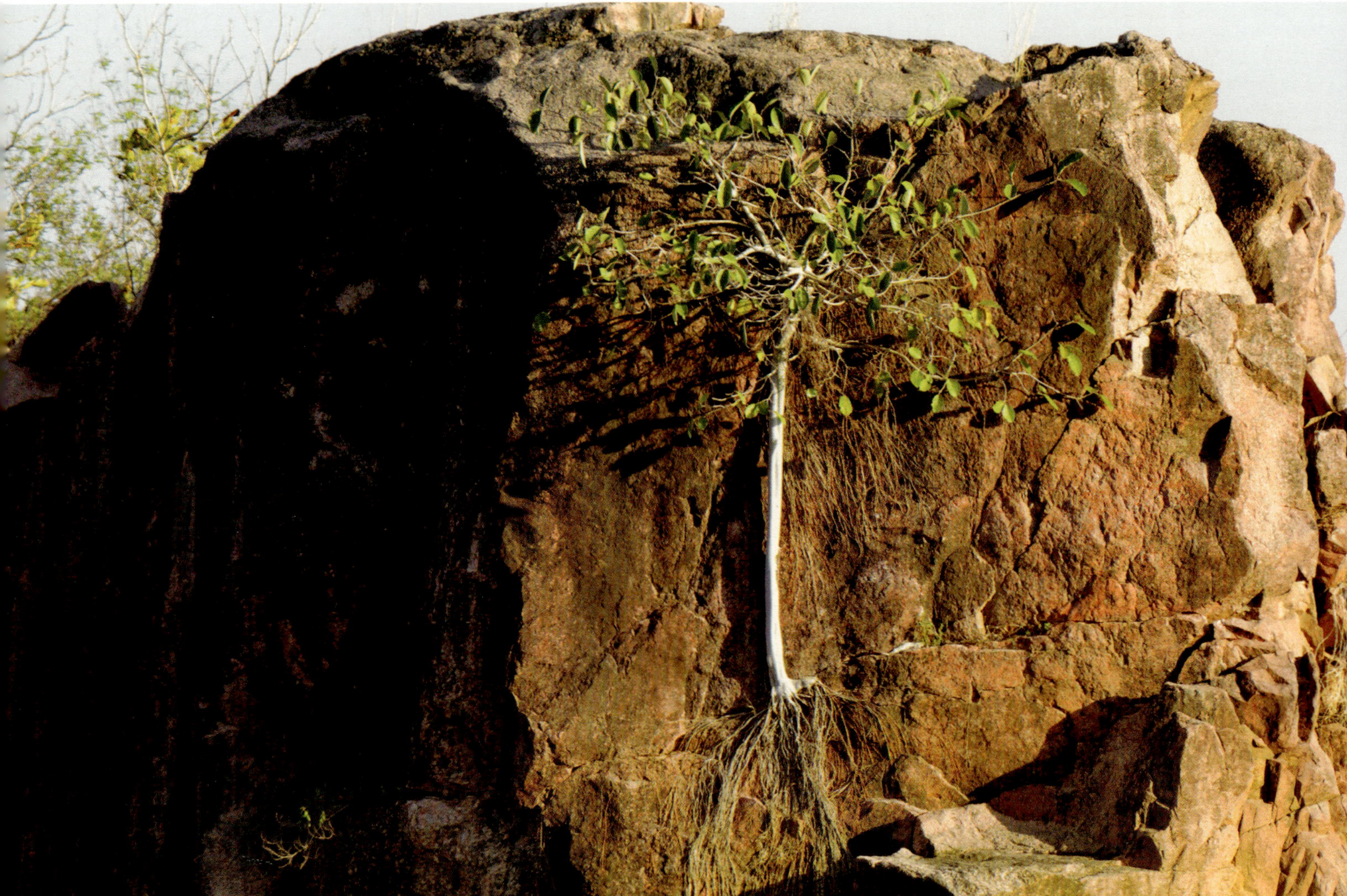

“

Success or achievement is not the final goal. It is the ‘spirit’ in which you act that puts the seal of beauty upon your life.

~

Flood your mind with love. Look into the eyes of the other and embrace the person with whom you have quarreled. Words are not necessary. Both will have their eyes flooded, and the joy of tears will wash away all quarrels.

~

A perfect man’s mind...It reflects everything, rejects nothing...
It receives everything but keeps nothing...Like a mirror.
The suffering of each depends not upon the factual happenings...
but upon the texture of each one’s mind.

~

By telling a lie, you create two personalities...
one weakening the other, with no gain whatsoever.

~

Efficiency is the capacity to bring proficiency into expression.

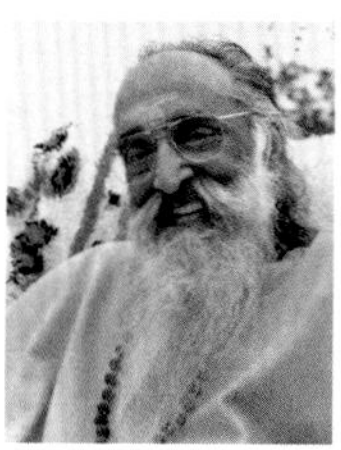

Swami Chinmayananda (1916–1993). Also known as Balakrishnan, he was born to a noble family in Kerala. The rigidity of the daily routine of worship became a part of his mentality. From an early age he had an inquisitive nature and questioned everything. Balakrishnan had doubts regarding conflicting ideologies. He studied *Panchadasi* and other Vedanta texts, as well as the Upanishads. Having mastered these, Balakrishnan started his own Jnana Yajna Mission and travelled around the country holding classes on the scriptures; this earned him a reputation as a great orator and a promoter of India’s culture, literature and scriptures. His centres are both in India and abroad.

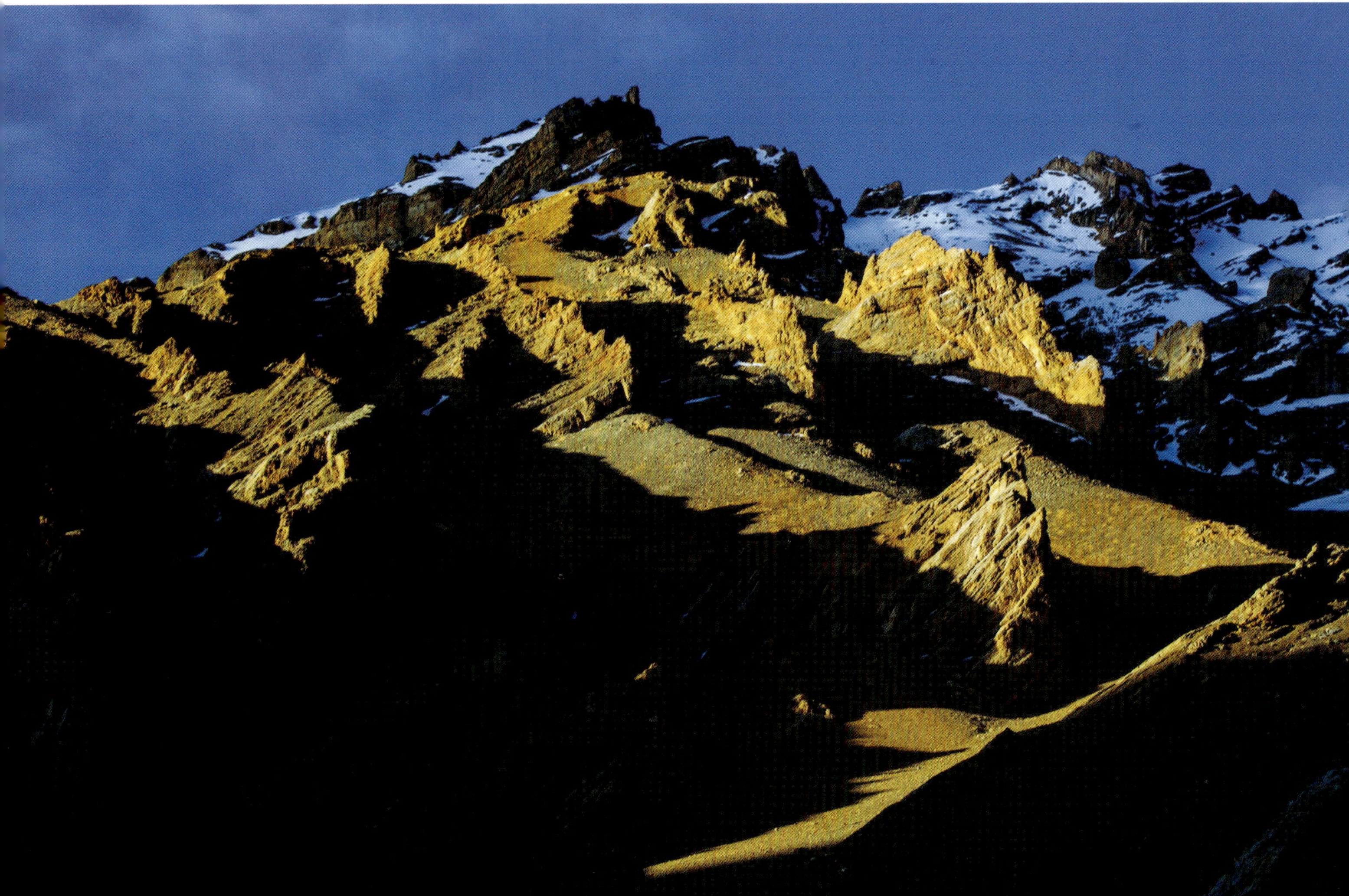

“

Everything in this material world is subject to perish in due course of time.

~

One cannot calculate the amount of loss there is in
wasting valuable time. Either materially or spiritually
one should be very alert in utilising the time which he has at his disposal.

~

Everything is complete—God’s creation, God’s beauty and God’s bodily features. All these are so complete that all one’s desires can become fully satisfied when one sees the beauty of the Lord.

~

Of all sacrifices, the chanting of Hare Krishna, Hare Krishna, Krishna Krishna,
Hare Hare/Hare Rama, Hare Rama, Rama Rama, Hare Hare is the purest representation of Krishna.

~

By chanting Krishna’s names, one will be transferred to
the supreme planet, Krishnaloka, without a doubt.

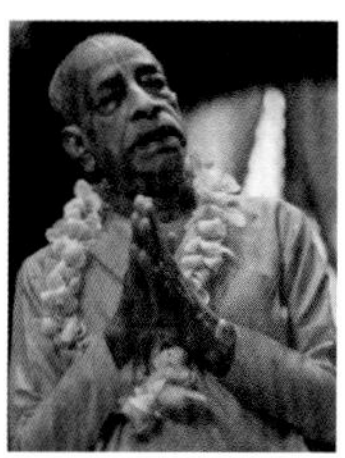

Swami Prabhupada (1896–1977). Srila Prabhupada was an Indian spiritual teacher. He created the International Society for Krishna Consciousness (ISKCON). He is placed among the most important Vedic scholars and translators of modern times. He is also considered one of the world’s most prominent contemporary authorities on bhakti yoga. He realised the purpose of his life at the age of 26, when he met his spiritual master, Srila Bhaktisiddhanta Sarasvati Thakura, who told him to go to the West to spread Krishna Consciousness. ISKON is today a worldwide organisation of over 550 centres.

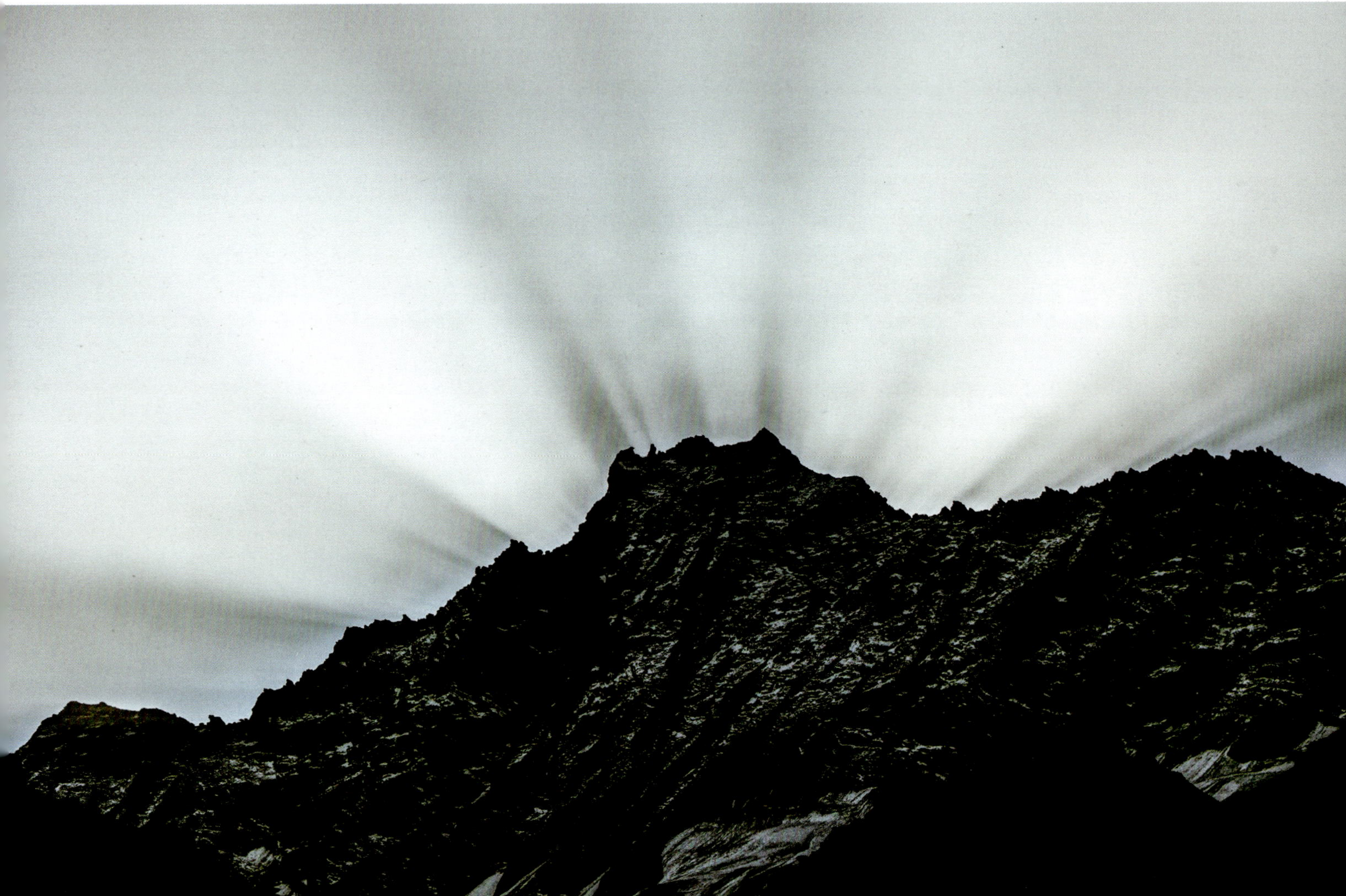

The very best method of spreading the Vedantic philosophy is to live it.

~

Rise above desires, and they are fulfilled.

~

Immortal is the true divinity that you are.

~

Truth, get hold of that, realise that, feel that, live that.

~

Heaven is within you, seek happiness not in the objects of sense; realise that happiness is within yourself.

~

God is not separate from you; that God is not in this heaven or that hell, but in your own self.

~

We cannot possess the whole world, and even if we possess that, what does that amount to?
Gain the whole world and lose your own soul—what does that amount to?
This earth of yours is simply a point in astronomical calculations.

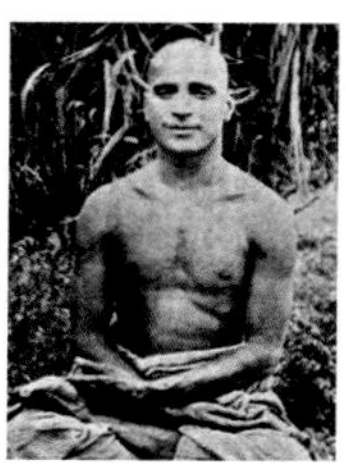

Swami Rama Tirtha (1873–1906). Rama Tirtha started his spiritual journey as a devotee of God and afterwards turned to Vedanta. The effect of his presence was incredible. Swami Rama's ambition to spread the teachings of Vedanta led him to leave India for the shores of Japan. He travelled with his disciple Swami Narayana. After a successful visit to Tokyo, he departed for the US. He spent over a year in San Francisco with Dr Albert Hiller. He gained a large following and founded myriad societies. One of these is the Hermetic Brotherhood, dedicated to the study of Vedanta.

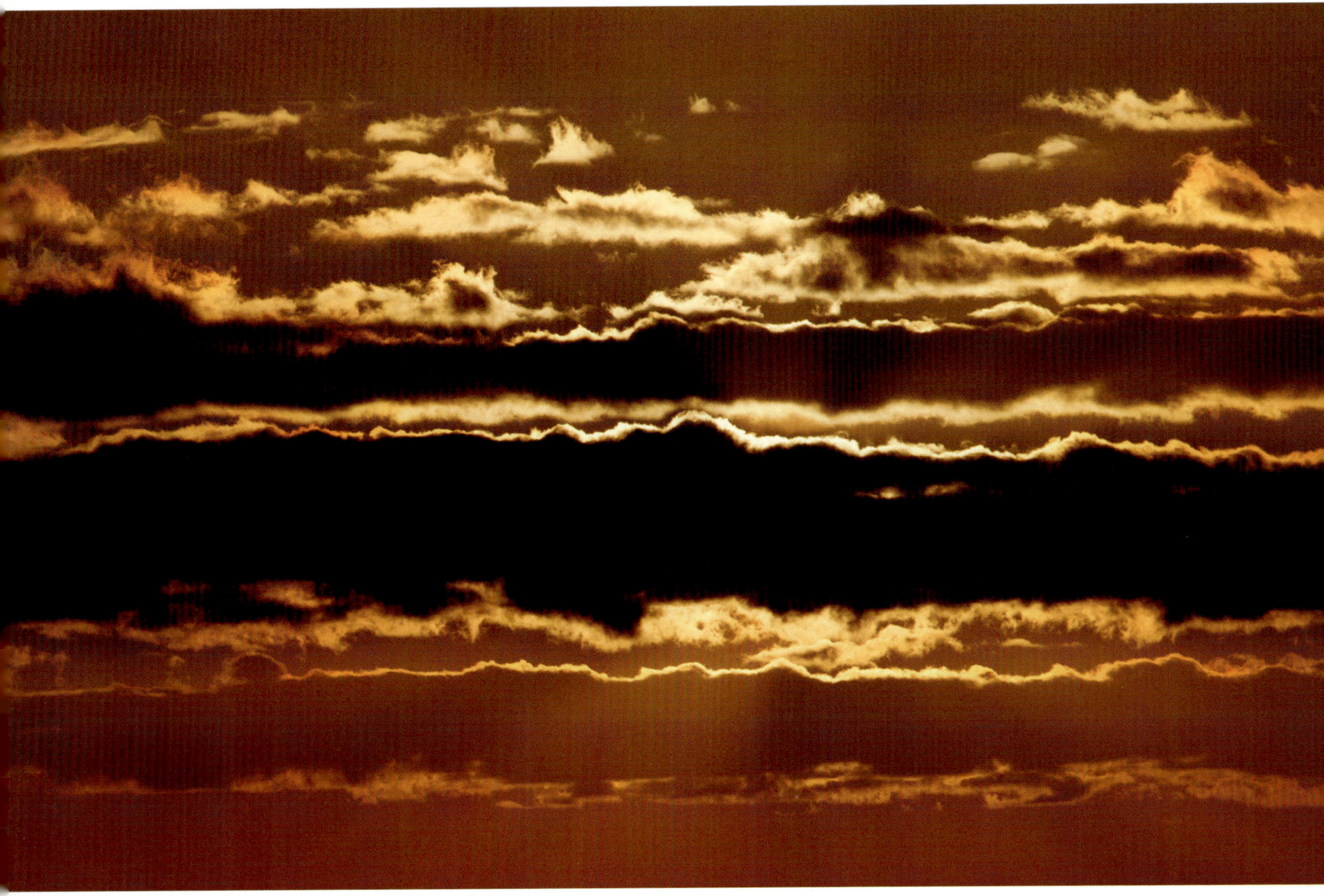

“

You have to grow from the inside out. None can teach you,
none can make you spiritual. There is no other teacher but your own soul.

~

We are what our thoughts have made us; so take care about what you think.
Words are secondary. Thoughts live; they travel far.

~

Arise! Awake! and stop not until the goal is reached.
The more we come out and do good to others,
the more our hearts will be purified, and God will be in them.

~

That man has reached immortality who is disturbed by nothing material.

~

Truth can be stated in a thousand different ways, yet each one can be true.

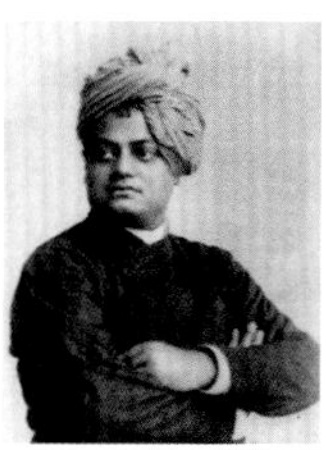

Swami Vivekananda (1863–1902). It was from a young age that he had a spiritual bent of mind. In 1884, by the time he finished his graduation, he had studied Western subjects, and had also closely read Hindu texts. He took the vows of *sannyasi* in 1887, and hence assumed a new name, Swami Vivekananda. He revitalised Hinduism and helped to get it recognised as a major religion. He not only popularised Indian philosophies of Vedanta and yoga among foreign audiences but also was responsible for the positive response of Indian spiritual self-improvement techniques in the West. Vivekananda spent most of his life preaching Vedanta philosophy to people all over the globe. His birthday is celebrated as National Youth Day in India.

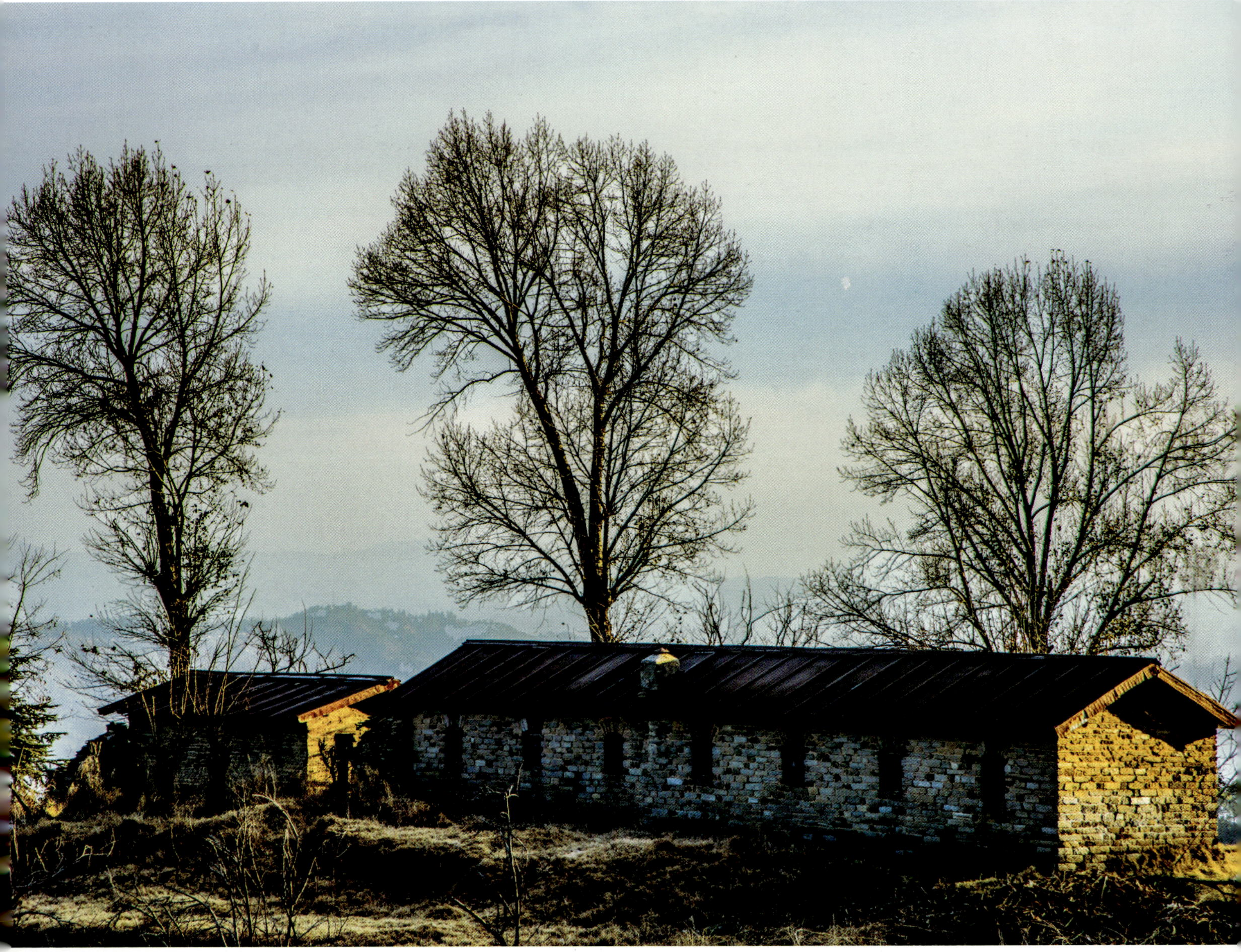

"

Idleness is a word the meaning of which is not rightly comprehended by the people. They think that abstaining from manual work, lack of alertness in doing labor and laziness in routine duties is all that idleness implies. However, they do not realise that the real idleness is the idleness of heart and mind.

~

When a nation becomes devoid of arts and learning, it invites poverty. And when poverty comes, it brings in its wake thousands of crimes.

~

Remember that the words Hindu and Muslim are only meant for religious distinction: otherwise all persons who reside in this country belong to one and the same nation.

~

If we ignore that aspect of ours which we owe to God, both of us, on the basis of being common inhabitants of India, actually constitute one nation: and the progress of this country and that of both of us is possible through mutual cooperation.

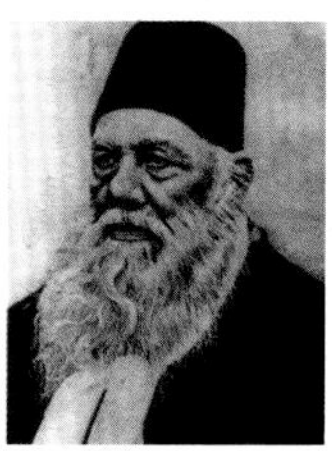

Syed Ahmad Khan (1817–1898). Sir Syed Ahmad Khan was an educator, philosopher, and social activist. He was dedicated to the area of education and asserted that it was the sole way to uplift the common people. Khan supported promoting schooling in the Western manner and aided in setting up many schools for accomplishing this purpose. He established the Anglo-Mohammedan Oriental College. He was a British loyalist and formed the Muslim League to advocate for pro-British activities and beliefs, thus raising suspicion in the minds of Indian politicians. Nonetheless, he commanded great respect from both Hindus and Muslims for his progressive views. He lived the last two decades of his life in Aligarh and died at the age of 80.

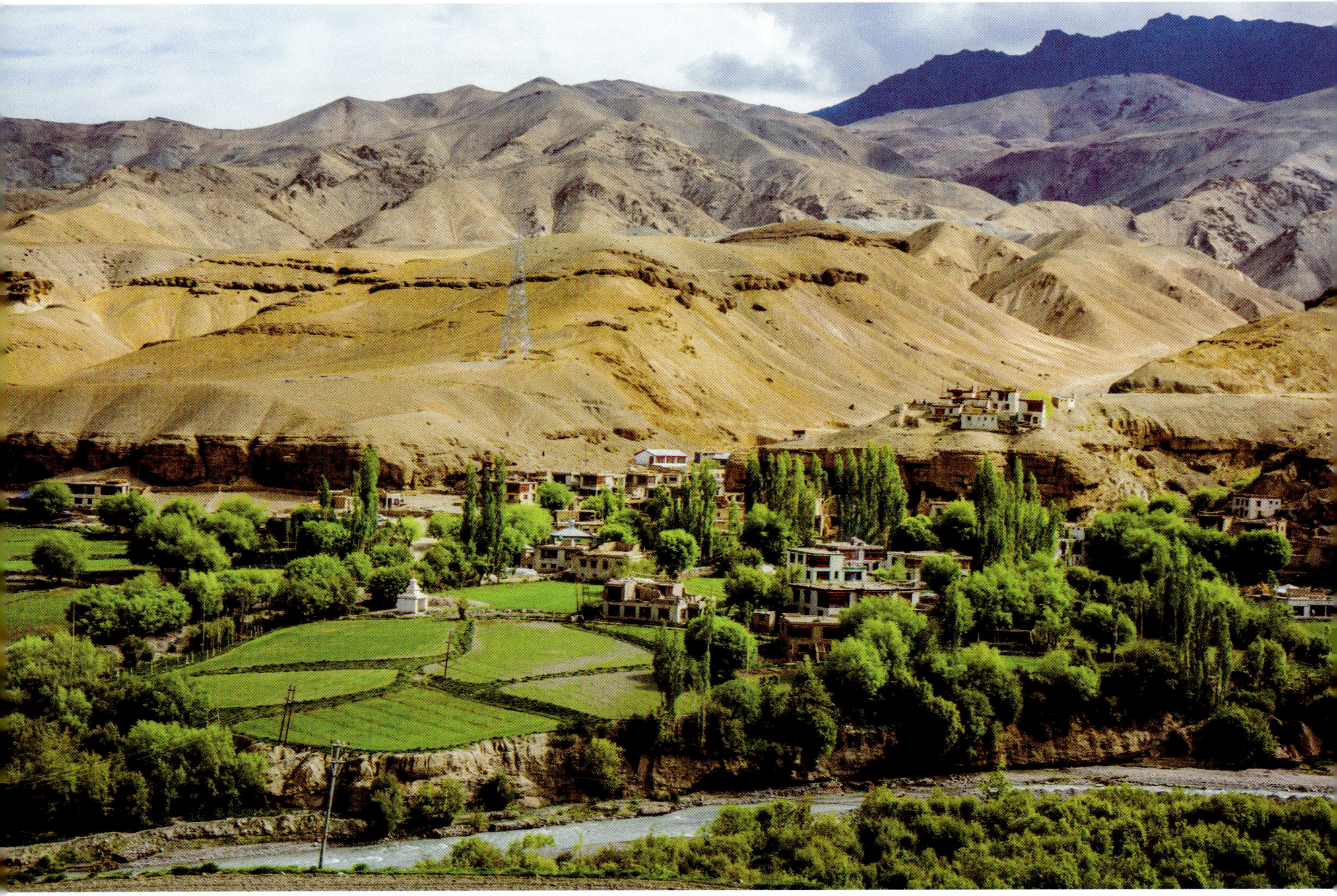

“

Forsake not the friendship of those who have been your staff in adversity,
Forget not be benevolence of the blameless.

~

Those are fools, however learned, who have not learned to walk with the world.

~

Folded hands may conceal a dagger—Likewise a foe’s tears.

~

Although an act of help done timely might be small in nature,
it is truly larger than the world itself.

~

Foolish people inflict pain upon themselves which is worse than what an enemy can bring upon.

~

Consider a man’s good qualities, and consider his faults; and judge his character by that which is more.

~

If people scrutinise their own faults as they do the faults of others,
Mankind will be freed of all evil.

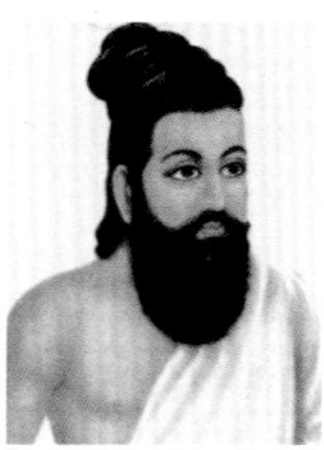

Thiruvalluvar was a famous Tamil philosopher and poet. His great addition to Tamil literature, and indeed literature in general, was *Thirukkural*, a piece mainly on ethics. There is much uncertainty about the exact years of his existence, but it is assumed he was born in Tamil Nadu and lived between the 4th century BC and the 1st century BC. Thiruvalluvar was considered the greatest scholar of the Tamil language, though there is no archaeological evidence of his existence. He is also affectionately called *Deiva Pulavar* (Divine Poet).

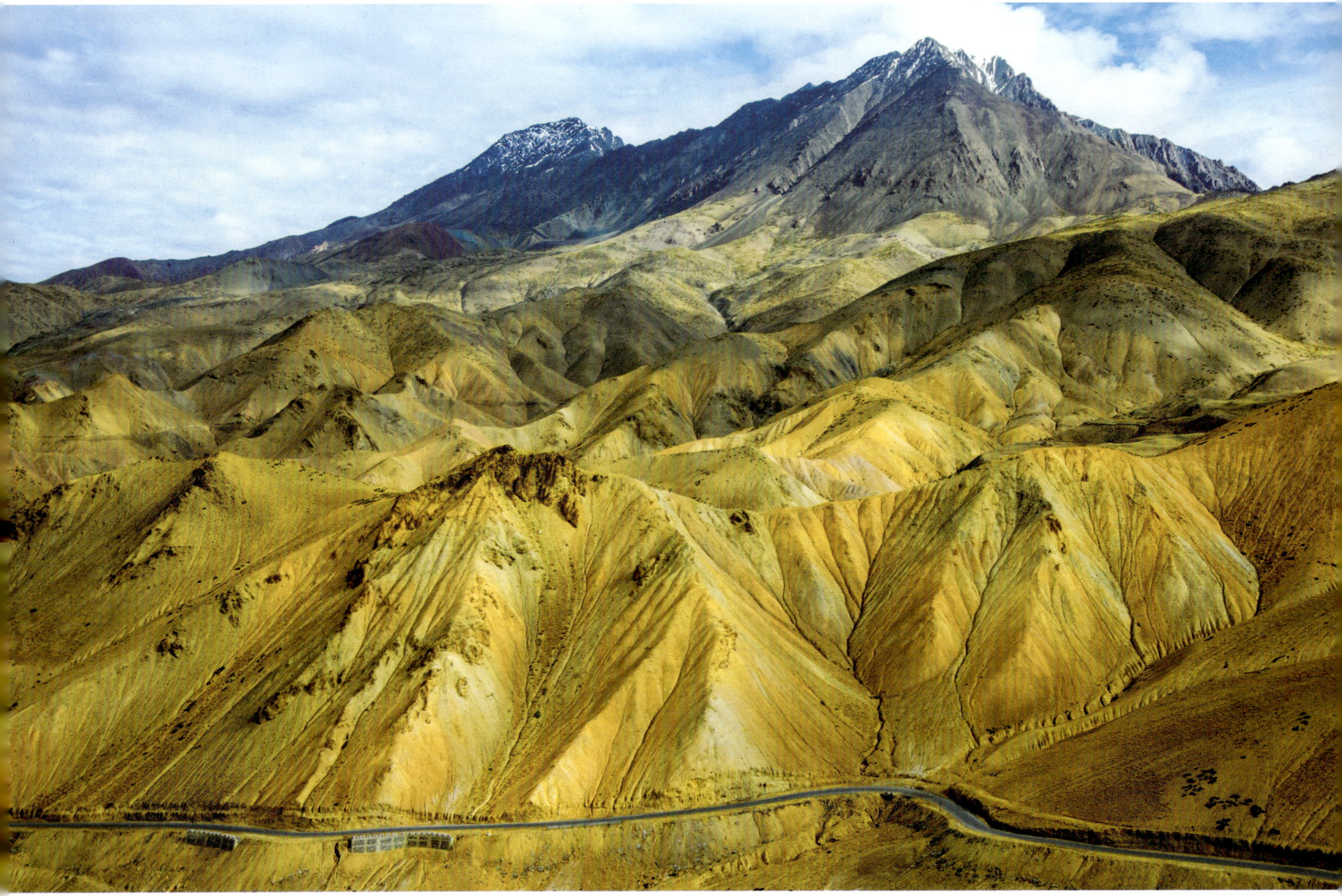

“

I am looking for a poem that says everything so I don't have to write anymore.

~

We must forget bodily consciousness like a deer which is infatuated by music.
We must look up to God as the young ones of a tortoise look up to their mother.
As a fountain rises upwards, even so must one's spirit rise to God.
One should entertain no idea whatsoever except that of God.

~

Words are the only jewels I possess, Words are the only clothes I wear,
Words are only the food that sustain my life,
Words are the only wealth I distribute among people.

~

When one looks into a mirror it seems as if one is looking at a different object,
yet one is looking at oneself. I am the brook that has merged into the river.
My country is now the whole universe.

~

Liberation cannot be purchased in a marketplace,
nor can it be acquired by wandering in the woods or forest.

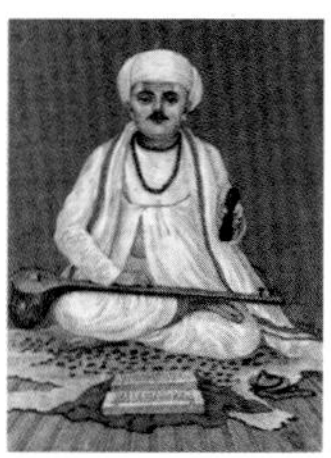

Tukaram was a poet and saint of the Bhakti Movement in Maharashtra in the 17th century. Arguably, he is the most acclaimed poet in the Marathi language. Poetry as a genre is incomplete without Tukaram. He sang spiritual songs at gatherings called kirtans. Tukaram is known for his *abhang* devotional poetry and community-oriented worship. He urged that individuals should make God the centre of their universe. He did not advise people to renounce the world or lead the life of an ascetic. He accepted disciples and devotees without discrimination of gender.

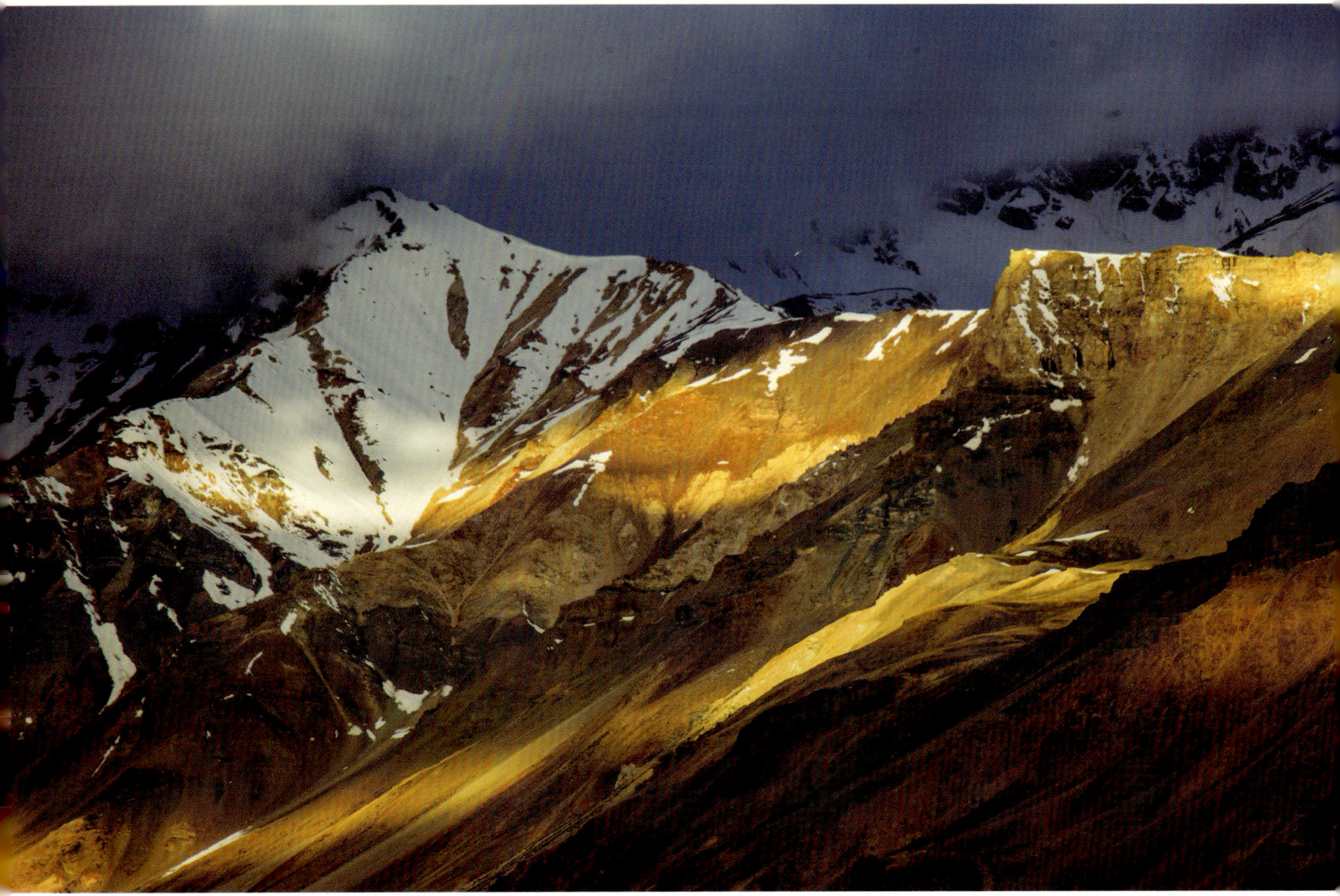

"

O Lord, let anyone accept any sadhana, he is free to follow its pursuit.
But to me Your name is the granter of all boons.

~

Karma, upasana, jnana—the various paths outlined in the Vedas
for the emancipation of the soul—all are good.
But I seek only one shelter and that is Your name; I seek nothing besides.

~

I have enjoyed the sweetness of Your name.
It is the fulfiller of my wishes here and in the world to come.

~

A man may have his affection riveted anywhere as also his faith,
but I recognise my relationship with the name Rama; it is my father and mother.

~

I swear by Shankara and state the truth without hiding it,
that Tulsidas sees all good accruing to him only by repeating Your name.

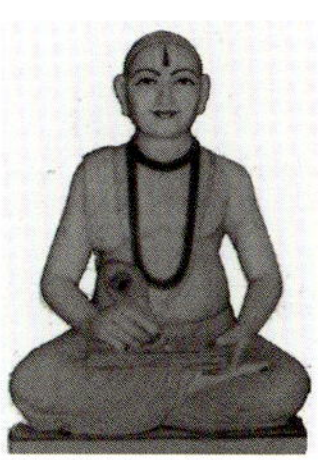

Tulsidas, also known as Goswami Tulsidas, was a 16th century saint-poet and a devotee of Lord Rama. His most famous work is *Ramcharitmanas*, which is a translation of a Sanskrit version into Awadhi. He also wrote *Hanuman Chalisa*, a well-known hymn dedicated to Lord Hanuman. Tulsidas lived his entire life in Varanasi, where Tulsi Ghat is named after this famous resident. *Ram Lila*, the folk theatre adaptation of *Ramayana*, is also believed to be Tulsidas's creation. He was a Brahmin and is believed to be an incarnation of Valmiki, the author of *Ramayana*. His wife rebuked him for his intense love for her and said that he would be immortal if he directed all that love towards Lord Rama. These words pierced his heart like an arrow and he left home immediately to become an ascetic. He wrote 12 books in all.

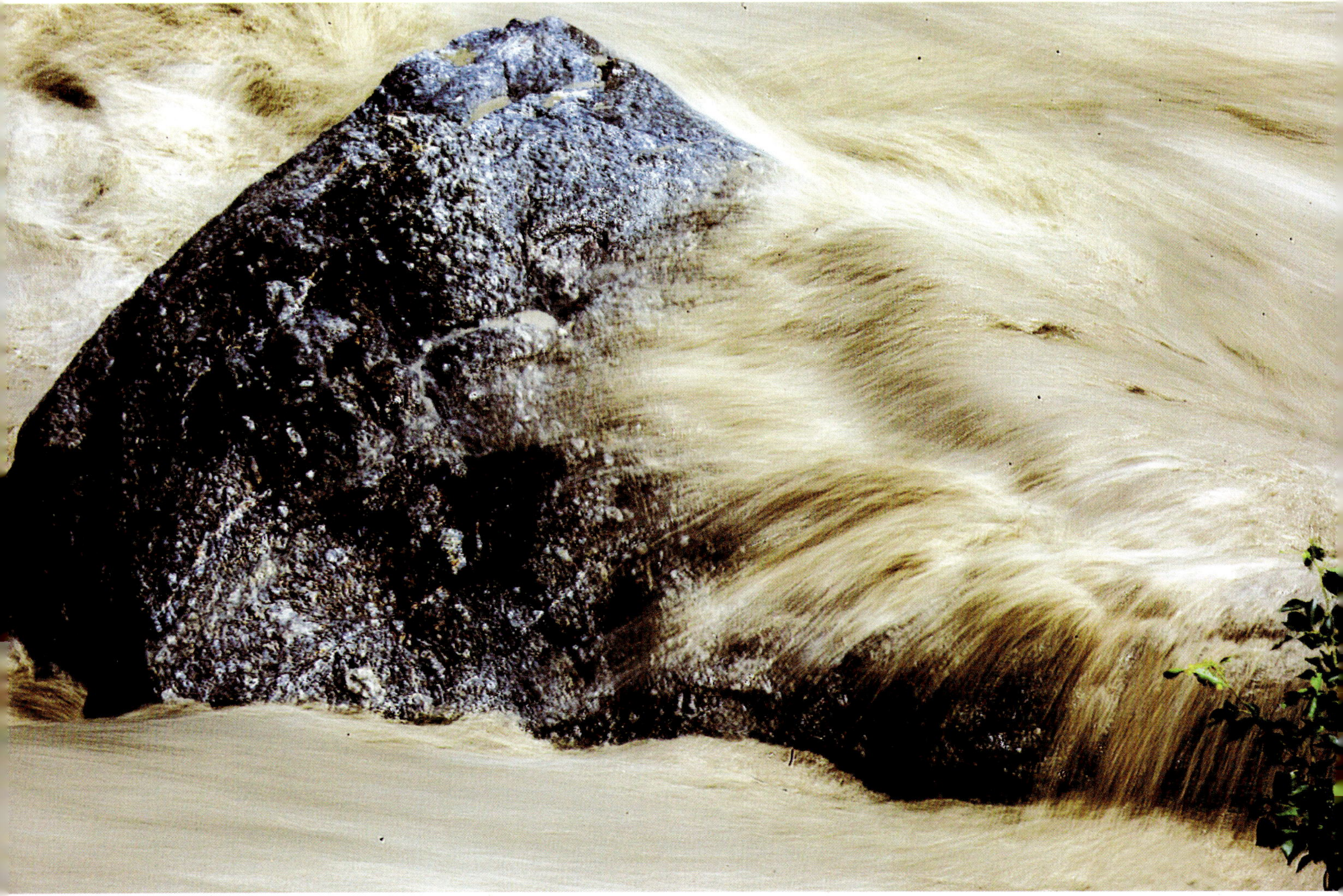

"

If a man achieves victory over this body, who in the world can exercise power over him?
He who rules himself rules over the whole world.

~

We have seen from experience that, if we are in the habit of walking regularly on the same road, we are able to think about other things while walking, without paying attention to our steps.

~

In the Bhagavad Gita, there is no long discussion, nothing elaborate.
The main reason for this is that everything stated in the Gita is meant to be tested in the life of every man; it is intended to be verified in practice.

~

Do not allow yourself to imagine that revolutionary
thinking can be propagated by governmental power.
Innumerable actions are going on through us all the time.
If we started counting them, we should never come to an end.

~

It is a curious phenomenon that God has made the hearts of the poor rich and those of the rich poor.

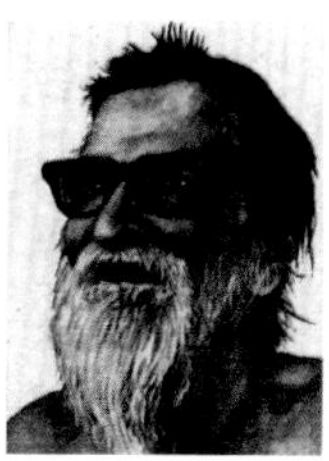

Vinoba Bhave (1895–1982) was born on 11 September 1895 as Vinayaka Rao Bhave in Maharashtra. Throughout his life he promoted non-violence. He diligently battled against corruption through non-violent means and encouraged people to have a religious and spiritual outlook on life. He introduced many programmes for the welfare of the people, including the well-known Bhoodan-Gramdan movement, through which he collected more than 1,000 acres of land. For his involvement in the independence movement, he was jailed several times. Bhave used his imprisonment time for reading and writing. Many of his highly praised works were written when he was in jail.

IMAGE CREDIT

P. 9. A.P.J. Abdul Kalam, sourced from the Niyogi Books database.

P. 11. Adi Shankara: Hvadga, CC BY-SA 3.0, *https://commons.wikimedia.org/wiki/File:Shri_Shankaracharya.jpg*

P. 17. Baba Amte, *https://en.wikipedia.org/wiki/File:Baba_Amte_(1914-2008).jpg*

P. 25. Bulleh Shah: Tahirakram, CC BY-SA 3.0, *https://commons.wikimedia.org/wiki/Category:Bulleh_Shah#/media/File:BullehShah.jpg*

P. 39. Gautam Buddha: Krishna Kumar Shrestha, CC BY-SA 4.0, *https://commons.wikimedia.org/wiki/File:Gautam_buddha_in_meditation.gif*

P. 47. Harivansh Rai Bachchan: Pradeep Chandra.

P. 65. Lal Bahadur Shastri: Viksb, CC BY-SA 3.0, *https://commons.wikimedia.org/wiki/File:Lal_Bahadur_Shastri_(cropped).jpg*

P. 69. Mahavira: Dayodaya, CC BY-SA 3.0, *https://commons.wikimedia.org/wiki/File:Mahavir.jpg*

P. 73. Meerabai: Onef9day, CC BY-SA 3.0, *https://upload.wikimedia.org/wikipedia/commons/8/89/Meerabai_painting.jpg*

P. 85. Nizamuddin Auliya: Amy W., sourced from *https://www.pinterest.com/pin/120471358757489964/*

P. 99. Rahul Sankrityayan, *http://bharatdiscovery.org/bharatkosh/w/images/0/0f/Rahul_Sankrityayan.JPG*

P. 111. Ram Manohar Lohia, *http://en.bharatdiscovery.org/w/images/b/b3/Ram-Manohar-Lohia.jpg*

P. 115. Ranade: Boy14youdude, CC BY-SA 4.0, *https://en.wikipedia.org/wiki/Ramachandra_Dattatrya_Ranade#/media/File:Downloadrdranade.jpg*

P. 121. Sant Eknath, *http://en.bharatdiscovery.org/india/%E0%A4%8F%E0%A4%95%E0%A4%A8%E0%A4%BE%E0%A4%A5*

P. 129. Sheikh Farid, *https://alchetron.com/Fariduddin-Ganjshakar-943006-W*

P. 153. Syed Ahmad Khan: Commonlingua, CC BY-SA 3.0, *https://en.wikipedia.org/wiki/File:Sir_Syed1.jpg*

P. 155. Thiruvalluvar, *https://alchetron.com/Thiruvalluvar-953397-W*

P. 159. Tulsidas: Nmisra, CC BY-SA 3.0, *https://en.wikipedia.org/wiki/Tulsidas#/media/File:Gosvami_Tulsidas.jpg (CC)*

All other images are public domain images from Wikimedia Commons.